THE CAPTAIN CLASS FRIGATES IN THE SECOND WORLD WAR

THE CAPTAIN CLASS FRIGATES IN THE SECOND WORLD WAR

An operational history of the American-built
Destroyer Escorts serving under the White
Ensign from 1943–46

DONALD COLLINGWOOD

LEO COOPER

First published in Great Britain in 1998 by
LEO COOPER
an imprint of
Pen & Sword Books Ltd
47 Church Street
Barnsley S70 2AS

ISBN 085052 615 9

A CIP record for this book is available
from the British Library

Typeset by SetSystems Ltd, Saffron Walden, Essex
Printed in England by Redwood Books, Trowbridge, Wiltshire

CONTENTS

PREFACE

The seventy-eight American built Destroyer Escorts which were allocated to the Royal Navy under Lease Lend agreement and were classified as the Captain class Frigates when commissioned in 1943–44 were part of the massive contribution to the Allied maritime war effort made by Kaiser and the United States Navy shipyards.

The story of their design, construction, working up and eventual operational achievements is a unique and little known facet of the Royal Navy's history. Many thousands of British sailors served in them and those who survive frequently bewail the fact that their achievements are not more widely appreciated.

I have attempted to remedy this in the chapters which follow. I have covered their whole story as far as my researches and permitted space allow. Life in one escort vessel was very similar to that in sister ships and the exploits of one escort group were very similar to those of others. It is therefore inevitable that there is some similarity between chapters. This was unavoidable if the full story of all the Captains was to be covered and their overall contribution to final victory recorded.

The Destroyer Escorts (or DE's, as those serving in them persisted in calling them) were essentially escort vessels. Much of their existence in groups assigned purely as Close Escorts was boring and extremely uncomfortable, with the 'Cruel Sea' as the main enemy. The German historian Cajus Becker complained that only ten per cent of all Allied convoys were ever contacted by U-boats, a situation confirmed by one of our famous convoy Commodores (Rear Admiral Creighton) who wrote that many convoy commodores, merchant seamen and escort ship crews ploughed the Atlantic routes for four or five years without seeing a ship sunk or hearing a shot fired. The convoy system was nevertheless essential for the protection of our vital supply lines and it was due to the seamanship skills, vigilance and fortitude of the escort ships' crews that so many of our merchant ships and major naval vessels survived. U-boat actions did not take place every day but when a U-boat pack did strike the battle would often be horrifying and bloody.

It is generally accepted that the worst of the battles in the Atlantic were over by 1943, so the Captains were not in commission during the peak period of the U-boat pack actions. Nevertheless, the Captains which served in the roving Support Groups were very successful and sank a commendable number (thirty-six) of U-boats during the last two years of the war. As a matter of fact, a statistical analysis of U-boat sinkings I made some time ago revealed that of the ten major classes of RN escort vessels (comprising some 389 ships), the Captains were the fourth most successful class in locating and destroying U-boats. Their prowess in this respect was only exceeded by the Loch class frigates, the Black Swan class sloops and the converted 'V and W' destroyers.

It must be emphasized, however, that battle honours for the North Atlantic were not awarded only to those ships which notched up U-boat 'kills'. Submarine hunting was strictly a team pursuit and those which spent much time in the 'outfield' were often as deserving of praise as those which actually scored the runs.

I was privileged to serve as the Ordinance Artificer in *Cubitt* from November, 1943, to March, 1946, and had first hand knowledge of the Captains in Nore Command but in order to write the individual histories which follow, I used information from a number of secondary sources as well as the primary sources in the Admiralty files in the Public Record Office. These are, as Captain Roskill once said, the bare bones of naval history. They have to be fleshed out by those who actually lived that history. This present work would not be as complete as it is without the 'flesh' enthusiastically provided by so many men who served in these gallant ships. Some were friends and shipmates, some became friends during the research period and some I have never met in person, but I hope that I have done justice to their memories of the ships, for which we share a common nostalgia. Some of their names are mentioned hereunder but I am sincerely grateful to all who rendered me any assistance however small.

ACKNOWLEDGEMENTS

I owe my thanks to Arsen Charles, one time Curator of the Museum in Charlestown Navy Yard at Boston for giving me copies of so many photographs and documents relating to the building of the Destroyer Escorts and giving permission for publication. I am also grateful to the present Curator for confirming that permission.

My thanks are also due to the Director of the Imperial War Museum (London) for allowing me to include pictures from the extensive collection of ship photos in the Museum archives and to the photographic staff who so willingly assisted me to locate particular photographs.

My warmest thanks to Mrs Wood, widow of the late Lieutenant W. Wood RAN, First Lieutenant of HMS *Holmes*, for so kindly allowing me to use the reproduction of his painting of that ship.

I am also indebted to the author Peter Elliot, who loaned me copies of a set of wartime signals referring to Royal Naval ship movements in the Western Atlantic in 1943–44 which pinpointed early movements of the Captains after commissioning.

During the research period in the early 1980's, I was also in correspondence with a vast number of men who had served in the Captains and many were able to provide me with valuable information not recorded elsewhere. The list of names is too long for full inclusion here but those who provided the most valued information are mentioned below. It is unfortunate that since my researches began so long ago and publication has taken so long to achieve, some of those mentioned have since 'Passed the Bar' and so, sadly, my acknowledgement is posthumous in these cases:

ERA Ashenden; Ron Ayers; Sub-Lieutenant J. Baggs; Fred Barr; Roy Bentham; John Brady; Alf Brown; W. Burke; Frank Chapman; Les Cheeseman; Commander E. Chavasse; Ron Collision; Captain Featherstone-Dilke; Geoff Finn; Rear Admiral Dudley-Davenport; Frank Dawson; George Dyer; P. R. Elvin; Lieutenant M. Forte; Bill Garland; Geoff Goodchild; S. Grayson; Dennis Grinnell; Lieutenant-Commander A. L. Hammond; B. Harrop; Alan Hope; Vic Jackman; George Lester; S. A. Lewis; Sub-Lieutenant P. Mallett (South Africa) Ken Maltby; William McCoy; N. McElroy; A. McGregor; T. W. McPhail; L. Morton; Dave Murray; Arthur Newton; Frank Owen; A. Penwarden; Frank Phelps; Lieutenant I. Pilditch; Mervyn Price; Bill Read; 'Robbie' Robins; Ted Rowson; P. Seaborn; Geo. Seymour; Lieutenant A. Shepherd; Harry Smith; J. Smith; A. Storey; Jim Watts; Phil Webb; R. Willis; Lieutenant W. A. Wood (Australia); Frank Woodley; D. Yeomans; Geo. Young.

To those not mentioned by name, I also extend my most grateful thanks.

Wantage   D.J.C.
1998

GLOSSARY OF TERMS AND ABBREVIATIONS

AA	Anti-Aircraft
A and A	Alterations and Additions (to a ship's original design)
AB	Able Seaman
AB S/D	Able Seaman submarine detector rating
AB S/T	Able Seaman Torpedoman
AD	Air defence
AP	Armour piercing (ammunition)
A/S	Anti-submarine
Asdic	The British name for the Sonar submarine detector
BRLO	British Resident Liaison Officer
Captain (D)	Commander of a destroyer flotilla
CERA	Chief Engine Room Artificer
CFCF	Coastal Forces Control Frigate
CO	Commanding Officer (ie. ship's Captain)
CPO	Chief Petty Officer
CPO 'Buffer'	Chief Bosun's Mate (the 'buffer' between the First Lieutenant and the crew)
CTL	Constructive Total Loss
CW candidates	Lower deck ratings who were potential officers and undergoing sea experience
DC	Depth-Charge
D-Day	The day upon which a major operation is to begin. D-Day for the Normandy Invasion was 6 June, 1944.
DE	Destroyer Escort
DF	Destroyer Flotilla (eg. 1st DF)
DSC	Distinguished Service Cross
DSM	Distinguished Service Medal
DSO	Distinguished Service Order

EA	Electrical Artificer
E-boat	German high speed Motor Torpedo-boat
EG	Escort Group
ERA	Engine Room Artificer
First Lieutenant	Executive Officer and Second-in-Command of a small ship
FOBAA	Flag Officer British Assault Area (in Normandy)
FOXER	A noise-making device towed as a decoy to deflect acoustic torpedoes
G7E	The standard German electrical torpedo
HE	High explosive (ammunition)
Hedgehog	Ahead throwing A/S mortar
HFDF	High Frequency Direction Finder. A device, known to all as 'Huff Duff', for locating submarines by intercepting their radio transmissions.
HMCS	His Majesty's Canadian Ship
HMNZS	His Majesty's New Zealand Ship
HSD	Higher Submarine Detector rating (a PO)
Jolly Roger	The black and white flag, carrying the skull and crossbones emblem, flown by ships entering harbour from an operation in which they have sunk an enemy submarine
KFK	A German barge armed with air defence guns for harbour and canal defence
LCF	Landing craft fitted with flame throwers
LCG	Landing craft mounting two 4.7″ naval guns and five Oerlikons
LCS	LCG converted to fire banks of rockets
LTO	Leading Torpedo Operator
LENTIL	A German explosive motorboat
MGB	Motor Gunboat
MO	Medical Officer
MTB	Motor Torpedo-boat
Mulberry Harbour	Artificial harbour, constructed chiefly out of huge concrete caissons which were towed across the Channel on D-Day, 1944, and sunk off Arromanches
NEGER	German manned torpedo
NOIC	Naval Officer in Charge
Nore Command	The Royal Naval Home Command which had Chatham as its Home Port
OA	Ordnance Artificer
Oerlikon	A 20mm heavy machine gun (or cannon) firing explosive ammunition for use in the AD role but also used against such targets as surfaced U-boats or E-boats.

OOW	Officer of the Watch
Ord.Mech	Ordnance Mechanic
OS	Ordinary Seaman
OYSTER	A German pressure mine
Pink List	An Admiralty list issued every four days giving the location of every ship in the Royal Navy in harbour.
PO	Petty Officer
Pom-Pom	A heavy machine gun firing 2pdr HE shells. Sited right in the bow of a DE for use against E-boats or in the AD role.
PT-boat	A USN patrol boat equivalent to the Royal Navy's MTB
RAN	Royal Australian Navy
RCN	Royal Canadian Navy
RNCVR	Royal Canadian Naval Volunteer Reserve
RN	Royal Navy
RNR	Royal Naval Reserve
RNVR	Royal Naval Volunteer Reserve (wartime commissioned officers held RNVR commissions)
SBA	Sick Berth Attendant
SO	Senior Officer (Escort Group Leader)
SPO	Stoker Petty Officer
TBS	Talk Between Ships (radio telephone)
T5 'GNAT'	German *ZAUNKÖNIG* homing torpedo
Trout Line	A defensive line of minesweepers and other small craft moored close together to form an extended barrier protecting the Normandy Assault Area
U-boat	German submarine (*Unterseeboot*)
USN	United States Navy
V & W destroyers	British destroyers of 1918–20 vintage – all with names beginning with V or W
WA	Western Approaches
W/T	Wireless telegraphy

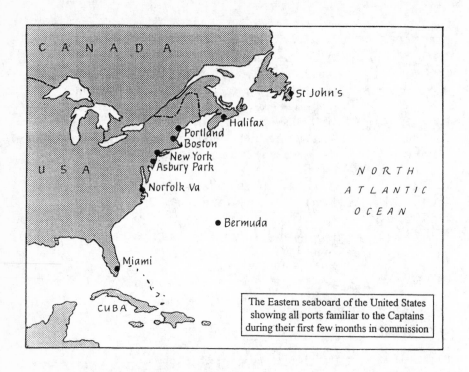

The Eastern seaboard of the United States
showing all ports familiar to the Captains
during their first few months in commission

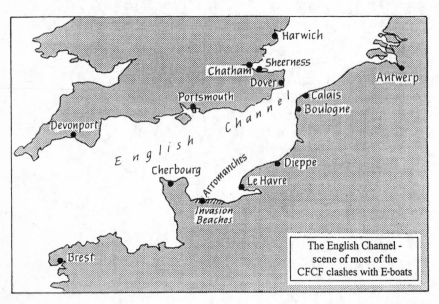

The English Channel -
scene of most of the
CFCF clashes with E-boats

LIST OF ILLUSTRATIONS

THE GENESIS OF THE
CAPTAIN CLASS FRIGATES

Before dealing with the histories of the individual ships in the Captain class, it is of some interest to examine the circumstances, almost unique in the history of the Royal Navy, which made it necessary to obtain a large number of warships from a foreign power, albeit an ally. It has long been a matter of tradition that captured ships are legitimately absorbed into the victor's fleet. Our most recent example being the U-boat which surrendered and was commissioned as HMS *Graph* during the Second World War. Until 1943, this had been the only way that foreign built ships ever appeared in service with the Navy, apart from a small number of coastal submarines (the H Class) bought from the United States in the First World War.

THE INTER WAR YEARS

What, then, were the reasons for the unprecedented need for us to obtain the seventy-eight US built Captain Class in 1943?

The generation which fought in that war know the answer only too well. A combination of factors such as disarmament programmes, treaties limiting the size of fleets and the curtailment of public expenditure for drastic economic reasons all contributed to the situation in 1939 in which our armed forces were so inadequately equipped to face a major war. Numerically the Royal Navy was more than a match for the combined fleets of Italy and Germany but apart from the battleships *Nelson* and *Rodney*, of 1925, all our capital ships, most of our light cruisers and a substantial number of Fleet destroyers dated from the First World War.

Ironically, one of the most stringent of the economic restraints imposed upon defence spending had been invoked by the very man who, in 1940, would find himself driven to go cap in hand to President Roosevelt for urgent assistance over the immediate provision of escort vessels with which to fight the raging U-boat menace in the Atlantic – Winston Churchill. In 1925, Churchill, as Chancellor of the Exchequer, had defended the economies he had imposed upon the Naval Estimates by invoking the Ten Year Rule introduced by the Government in 1919. This 'rule' assumed that there would be no major war in Europe for ten years and rolled forward year by year, although Churchill did concede that it should now be the subject of annual review. Nevertheless, it was 1932 before the Committee of Imperial Defence recommended its abandonment and even then they failed to call for any plan to remedy the manifest deficiencies of the armed forces. Not until the late 1930's was the reality of the German threat recognized and some urgent, but inadequate, measure of rearmament begun – far too late.

In addition to age, our fleet also suffered many other shortcomings. Despite the experiences of the First World War, which had seen the advent of two new major threats to surface vessels (the submarine and aircraft), naval policies between the wars still revolved about set battles reminiscent of Trafalgar and Jutland. Few 'experts' in the Admiralty thought that aeroplanes had any credible capacity for sinking surface ships. As for submarines, Admiralty and government attitudes seem to have stultified at the stage of considering them to be 'piratical' and 'damned un-British'. A surprising number of senior officers and many Members of Parliament actually subscribed to the idea that the only sensible solution was for submarines to be internationally outlawed. There were also widely held naive beliefs that never again would any major power wage all out submarine warfare against merchant ships.

The consequence of these archaic attitudes was that our naval ships, particularly destroyers, had pitifully inadequate air defence (AD) armament and that the Navy had only a handful of vessels which had been specifically designed as convoy escorts. Some concern about the latter shortcoming does seem to have been awakened in the late 1930's when the Hunt class escort destroyers were designed – but by then our time was running out. Construction of these ships began in 1938 but their capabilities did not quite fit their description. They had, in the new twin 4" MK XIX guns, excellent AD defences. Coupled with the MK IV HACS directors and fire control systems these weapons constituted the first up to date defence against air attack and were a considerable advance on previous destroyer 4.7" guns. Although of heavier calibre these had had an elevation restriction of 40 degrees and were useless against the dive bombing attacks. The Hunts also had a respectable turn of speed but had short range endurance and carried minimal depth-charge (DC) outfits (twenty charges). They also carried torpedo tubes, a clear indication that the Admiralty really intended them for fleet duties first and foremost. The Hunts' specifications certainly did not meet the requirements of ocean escort work. However, they would do sterling work in the Mediterranean and North Sea, which were theatres of conflict in which air attack was the main hazard. Few Hunts served in the Battle of the Atlantic.

At about the same time, a panic programme for building substantial numbers of the Flower class corvettes was also started. This was the only type of escort vessel which our shipyards had the capacity to build quickly and in large numbers. If, as some Admiralty experts believed, any German U-boat offensive would be confined to our coastal waters, these sturdy little craft would have been quite adequate but their limited capacity for carrying depth-charges severely restricted their usefulness in prolonged actions far out into the Atlantic. Most of all, their top speed was less than that of a surfaced U-boat and the enemy could thus easily outrun them.

Thus, despite these belated efforts, the outbreak of war found the Royal Navy very poorly equipped for convoy protection and in a very short time, we were to find that the short sighted policies of the inter-war period would result in a state of near disaster at sea. Contrary to the beliefs of the 'old school' in the Admiralty, by mid-1940 the Luftwaffe had demonstrated, in no uncertain terms, that aeroplanes *could* sink ships. Twenty-two destroyers had been sunk during the first nine months and at least half of these had succumbed to air attack. They represented some twenty per cent of our pre-war destroyer strength and new construction could not even keep up with this rate of attrition.

CRISIS IN THE ATLANTIC

Meanwhile a comparative handful of U-boats were ranging further into the Atlantic than had been anticipated and were destroying colossal tonnages of merchant shipping almost without opposition. This situation would persist until well into 1943. During those first four years of war, no less than 2,385 merchantmen would be sunk by U-boats. Most convoys in 1940 were fortunate if they had an escort consisting of more than a couple of corvettes and a few anti-submarine (A/S) trawlers to protect them. The only really effective A/S vessels, apart from the handful of pre-war sloops, were the Fleet destroyers. However with their numbers already depleted, it became increasingly difficult to spare enough of them for convoy duties. With the threat of increased U-boat production, it was feared that the Battle of the Atlantic had scarcely begun.

This desperate period must surely mock the nadir of Britain's maritime history. The Fleet, in which the nation had always put such blind trust, was proving powerless to fulfil its primary purpose to protect the shipping on our vital supply routes. Understandably, there was great bitterness and resentment amongst our merchant seamen that short sighted policies were resulting in their virtual slaughter. There was also fury and frustration among the crews of the pitifully few escort vessels, who could often do little more than rescue the heroic survivors from the stricken merchant ships. Churchill and the War Cabinet were horrified by the realisation that if the situation got much worse, Britain faced the possibility of defeat at the hands of the U-boats in the Atlantic and that such a defeat would render our survival impossible.

* * *

The only solution was to obtain escort vessels in large numbers and to obtain them quickly. With our shipyards already working at full capacity, there was no hope of salvation through the efforts of home production and the only answer seemed to be to obtain escort ships 'ready made'. The only source of such ships was, of course, the United States; Churchill pleaded earnestly with President Roosevelt for the immediate loan of ships from the United States Navy (USN) but, although many in the US administration were sympathetic, the strong isolationist lobby in American politics rigidly opposed the provision of such support to a belligerent country. It is perhaps not appreciated by the present generation, but it is a fact, that apart from isolationist policy, there were also factions within the United States which displayed active anti-British attitudes. Many of their influential politicians hated the privileged trade cartels within the British Empire even more than they feared a Europe dominated by Hitler. Sad to relate, many of those holding such views practically gloated at the prospect of Britain's defeat and subsequent demise as a colonial power.

Eventually these isolationist attitudes softened to the extent that loopholes were found in the Neutrality Laws which enabled Roosevelt to authorize limited assistance to the United Kingdom – but it must be pointed out that this change of heart was not entirely motivated by an altruistic desire to preserve democracy in Europe. Japan was 'sabre rattling' in the Pacific and, despite the national desire for peace, most Americans were aware that war with Japan was a distinct possibility – and that if Japan *did* attack, the whole might of the United States Navy would be needed in the Pacific theatre. Should Germany have then

4

taken over Europe however, they were daunted at the prospect of their whole eastern seaboard being open to German attack. Even the diehard isolationists were prepared to relax their principles and allow aid to Britain, if only to the extent of helping us win the Battle of the Atlantic and keep the Germans from getting mastery of that ocean.

It thus became politic for the United States to give us enough aid to survive, if not to conquer. Legal experts suddenly discovered that neutrality laws did not forbid the supply of *surplus* war materials to belligerent nations and Roosevelt quickly authorized the transfer of fifty of their oldest destroyers to the Royal Navy. These were all First World War vintage and had been laid up in reserve for many years without proper maintenance but their acquisition would increase our destroyer fleet by some fifty per cent. There were problems about payment for them however. We still owed America vast sums in war debts from the First World War and they were not ready to let us extend our credit. Churchill eventually solved the problem by his famous horse-trading deal, offering ninety-nine year leases of Crown Territory, such as Bermuda and Placentia Bay, to the Americans. Such bases were of little consequence to the USA in peacetime but they appreciated their potential value should they be attacked by Germany.

The acquisition of the fifty old 'Four stackers' as they were at once dubbed by the Navy, was the first time that the RN had taken delivery of large numbers of foreign built ships. Churchill felt that they would be a significant factor in the battle with the U-boats. Not everyone shared his optimism, least of all the unfortunate men who had to live in their primitive mess decks and operate their ancient machinery. Our own old V and W destroyers were of similar vintage but we had nurtured them and they were in much better operational shape. Many of these old US destroyers required extensive work to make them seaworthy and some never achieved that status. Quite a few of them were in and out of dockyard hands repeatedly with engine and boiler defects or leaking hulls, some being under repair for as much as fifty per cent of the time. Primitive steering gear continually failed and caused scores of collisions with convoy ships. All in all, our seamen were convinced that Churchill had got the worst of a bad bargain. To be fair, however, the few 'Four stackers' which did remain in service for respectable periods did do sterling work in the Atlantic and they certainly relieved some of our valuable Fleet Destroyers from humble escort duty. P. Goodheart has written of them euphemistically as 'Fifty ships that saved the world' but few would now agree with that evaluation.

THE BIRTH OF THE CAPTAINS

The 'Four stackers' were by no means the last American ships to sail under the White Ensign but later types, of which the Captains were only one example, were of modern design and construction. The provision of such modern vessels only became possible after the Lease Lend agreements had been made. The Atlantic battle was still our major concern and almost before the ink was dry on the agreement documents, Churchill was lobbying for large numbers of purpose designed escort vessels to be built for us in the United States. USN ship designers had been working for some time on plans for small destroyers which would be cheaper to produce than conventional ships. Six designs had been produced but the peacetime USN was, however, not very interested and the designs were shelved until experts studying the Admiralty specifications for the escorts we needed realized that one of the six shelved designs seemed to foot the bill fairly well. This was for the 'Evarts' class of destroyer escort with diesel/electric propulsion units and the Royal Navy eagerly approved and placed initial orders for fifty of these vessels. That was in 1941. However, since new construction lines had to be set up, it was estimated that first deliveries would not be until 1943. Shortly after this initial order was placed, the Admiralty managed to negotiate further orders for another 100 vessels. However, by this time America was also at war and the United States Navy had become an eager customer for the Evarts and later agreements (between the USA, Britain and Canada) about the allocation of new construction escorts eventually reduced the British share to seventy-eight.

Once the vast US war effort got into top gear and Kaiser and the USN had fully mastered the art of mass producing ships, the DE building programme was increased to produce staggering numbers of the destroyer escorts. With the USN as an eager customer, an incredible total of over 500 of them had been built before the war ended in 1945. A number of US Navy yards began to turn out DE's but, in addition, there were some new shipyards, such as that of Bethlehem Steel at Hingham Massachussetts, which came into being solely in order to build these vessels.

These vast production lines did not come into existence without some early teething troubles. American industry was eventually to achieve miracles in the production of war materials but in the first stages there were inevitable bottlenecks. One of the first problems was that there were not enough firms to turn out so many identical sets of propulsion units. This holdup was overcome by diversifying the design and eventually no less than six variations on the original Evarts design were in production, ringing the changes between a number of propulsion units including diesel, diesel/electric and turbo/electric. All the DE's transferred to the Royal Navy were either diesel/electric Evarts or the turbo/electric Buckleys and, with one exception, they were all built at Boston – the Evarts in the Charlestown Navy Yard and the Buckleys in the Bethlehem-Steel shipyard, newly constructed at nearby Hingham.

In general terms, these American DE's were the equivalent of our Hunt class destroyers. The Buckleys had a speed of just over 24 knots. The diesel Evarts were some 4 knots slower (but had greater endurance at sea between the refuelling requirements). The DE's main armament was greatly inferior to that of the Hunts however, consisting as it did of three single 3″ dual purpose guns. On the other hand, close range air defence was good. They mounted seven or eight 20mm Oerikon cannons and, in some cases, twin 40mm Bofors guns mounted aft. Main radar sets were the extremely efficient US Type SL and although not fitted initially, all the British DE's were eventually given standard Type 144 series Asdic (submarine tracking) gear. A/S weapons consisted of four 'K' gun DC throwers together with stern dropping rails. Behind 'A' gun there was also a Mark 10 'Hedgehog' ahead throwing mortar.

The basic American design had called for quad 1.1″ anti-aircraft mountings in a position in front of 'Y' gun, controlled by a simple black box tachometric director sight on a high tower but none of the British contingent had these weapons. In some cases, when they could be spared, twin Bofors were fitted as an alternative but the ships mostly arrived in the UK with these gun positions empty. The spaces were later utilized to mount two or three extra Oerlikons. The US ships also had triple torpedo tubes mounted on the superstructure deck. Since the Royal Navy only needed the ships for convoy work, these were omitted from its share of the destroyer escorts. Another addition to the armament in the case of ships to be used in waters where E-boats operated, was a single 2pdr Pom Pom mounted right in the eyes of the ship as a bow chaser but none of these were fitted until the ships reached Britain. To British eyes, accustomed to traditional Admiralty ship designs, the appearance of the DE's was unusual. There was no break of the foc'sle as in British destroyers and sloops. The deckline flowed in a graceful sheer from foc'sle to midships. This was a feature which DE men came to look upon as 'very handsome'. The funnels were also unusual. In the case of the Evarts, they were topped by daringly raked cowls which gave them the modern appearance much favoured by most navies apart from our own. The Buckley funnels were also unique but not so greatly admired. With two boiler rooms a fair distance apart, it was customary to provide two funnels but the US designers had made do with only one and the flues from each boiler were led into it by two very

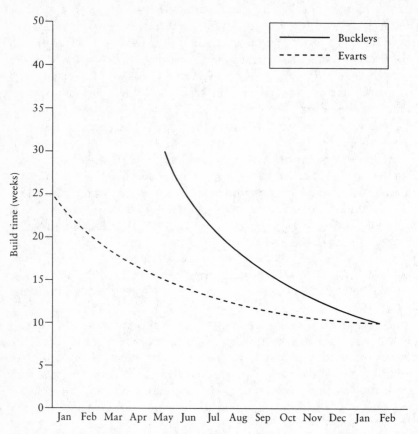

Fig. 1. Chart to show the construction programme of the British DE's from January, 1943 – February, 1944

conspicuous sloping ducts – a system unknown in RN ships, apart from the Neptune class cruisers.

MANNING AND INITIAL TRAINING

In peace and war, British tars have been accustomed to undertaking uncomfortable journeys to join ships to which they have been drafted but it is probably true to say that never have so many travelled so far as the men detailed to join the Captain class ships!

With manpower resources stretched to the limit to meet the requirements of the many new construction ships coming into commission, it must have been a daunting task for the Drafting Commanders in the three home ports to find crews for the DE's as well. The complement of

8

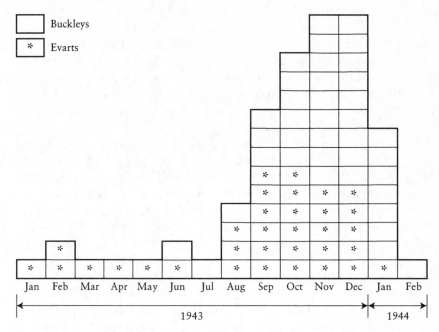

Buckleys

* Evarts

| | Jan | Feb | Mar | Apr | May | Jun | Jul | Aug | Sep | Oct | Nov | Dec | Jan | Feb |

1943   1944

Fig. 2. Average build time for DE's by types between January, 1943, and February, 1944.

the Captains was about 180 and this number had to be found seventy-eight times over in the short space of a year, during which the ships were to be transferred to the Royal Navy. They then had to be transported several thousands of miles to Boston in batches synchronised with the dates of completion of each ship. The amount of work necessary to keep the manpower supply line constantly on the move must have been colossal. The first of the ships were handed over in early 1943 and Figure 1 shows that in these early days it was relatively easy to keep on schedule. At this time USN policy, was to hand over every third DE completed to the Royal Navy and we received only nine ships in the first six months. As the Boston production lines really got into the swing of things, the production rate accelerated remarkably and eventually whole consecutive batches of DE's were allocated to the RN.

The drafting authorities were able to keep the pipeline flowing smoothly in the early stages but there were problems later when production times at the Boston yards decreased, and completion dates were sometimes in advance of predictions. By November, 1943, there was near chaos at Boston. Several of the completed ships had no crews available to commission them. They could not be left to occupy berths in the Charlestown Navy Yard and the Naval Officer in Charge (NOIC) at Boston had to muster scratch crews from ships already commissioned. With whatever officers were available, these men were then marched down to perform pseudo commissioning ceremonies. No less than four ships had these dummy handovers and were declared in commission but had no crews. In order to clear them from the yard, it was then necessary to scrape together steaming crews who took the ships to Halifax where they were laid up in Care and Custody until their crews eventually arrived.

Fortunately, the Royal Canadian Navy (RCN) came to the rescue and prevented further manpower problems. A number of River class frigates were building in the UK for the Canadians and their authorities agreed that, instead of men being sent across in troopships to commission them, they could be used to ferry some of the DE's to Lissahally in Northern Ireland for handover to the RN crews. Thus after a temporary setback, the smooth transfer of DE's to the Royal Navy proceeded apace. Most of the men who were drafted to the DE's during 1943 had little idea what type of ship they were to join. Draft chits normally bore ships names but not so where the Captains were concerned. Owing to the uncertainties over the rate of handover of ships by the USN, it was never known in advance which ship an allocated crew would eventually commission and the draft chits thus had cryptic notations such as DE(C)14. Some mentioned HMS *Saker* but this really didn't mean very much as *Saker* was merely the RN transit accommodation outside New York. Many men designated for this latter establishment actually believed that they were bound for some quiet shore billet in the USA or for long periods of standing by British ships which were being refitted in American shipyards.

More than 12,000 men wended their way from the three depots to join the Captains. Their trek began by entraining either to Liverpool or the Clyde. From there they embarked in troopships for the passage to New York or Halifax. Large fast liners such as the *Queen Mary* and *Andes* were used on these routes and although trooping passages were notoriously uncomfortable, due to overcrowding, they only had to be endured for a few days. Moreover, since most of the drafts consisted of young 'Hostilities Only' ratings, the novelty of being at sea for the first time was in most cases an enjoyable experience.

Those who landed at New York will remember the excitement and wonder of gazing at the famous skyline previously only familiar in Hollywood films – they may also recall their revulsion at the sight of thousands of condoms and vast streams of untreated excrement floating down the river from the sewage outfalls. However, such unpleasantness was forgotten when they disembarked and several pleasant surprises awaited them. The first was the discovery that, unlike in Britain, while sailors on draft had to manhandle all their heavy baggage when changing from one means of transport to another, here in America they were exempt from this chore. Stevedores unloaded all their kitbags, hammocks, toolboxes and suitcases onto trolleys and that kit was not seen again until they reached their final destination at Asbury Park or Boston. This was luxury travel indeed but morale was boosted even further when the drafts were mustered in a dockside shed for a parade at which a USN paymaster handed out ten dollars to each man. This generous custom was extended as a welcome to all Allied servicemen who visited America during the war. Some unkind critics have suggested that the motives were not entirely altruistic and claimed that the cash handouts were only made to protect American civilians from begging activities by penniless foreign troops. Our men had no scruples about accepting this welcome gift. The exchange rate at the time was four dollars to the pound and $10 was thus a small fortune to our poorly paid men who were greatly disadvantaged by the high cost of living in the United States. Todays readers may well be unaware that in 1943 there was no such thing as 'Local Overseas Allowance' to compensate servicemen for high costs in foreign countries. Wherever in the world they served, our soldiers, sailors and airmen received just their normal rate of pay. If the cost of living was high, that was just hard luck.

Further progress on the journey depended upon the state of completion of the ships the men were destined to join. In the first months of the programme many weeks would pass before the crews were needed at Boston. Their first destination was HMS *Saker*, which consisted of two hotels, Berkeley Carteret and Monterey at Asbury Park, New Jersey, which had been requisitioned by the USN as transit accommodation. At this time the hotels were still administered by USN personnel and *Saker* was looked upon as a matelot's paradise with unlimited delicious food and real beds to sleep in. Living here was an altogether better prospect than the ridiculously overcrowded messes and the wartime standard victuals that men had been accustomed to in the barracks in their home ports in Britain. In addition, it was discovered that, with British sailors being still a novelty in New Jersey, the hospitality lavished upon them by the civilian population was second only to the fabulous reception that naval ratings received in South Africa during the early stages of the war. New York was also within easy reach of *Saker* and our lads were welcome in all the USO clubs, the Stage Door Canteen and so on and were given the same facilities for free tickets to dances and stage shows as US servicemen. By and large Asbury Park was a most popular haven away from the vicissitudes of war. Men allocated to the early DE's spent up to two months enjoying this good life and many had seen a great deal more of the

United States before passing on to the ships at Boston. Training facilities were offered by various branches of the United States Navy and many of our men were sent to take advantage of them. The Engine Room and Electrical staff were accepted as having particular problems arising from their unfamiliarity with American equipment. The turbo/electric and diesel/electric propulsion units fitted in the DE's were utterly unlike anything our men had worked on before. Some of the Hostilities Only Engine Room Artificers (ERA's) and Motor Mechanics had previous diesel experience in merchant ships but few of the regular service engineers had worked on large diesel installations before. Even fewer had the electrical knowledge they would need in order to drive and maintain the DE's power plants.

At the beginning of the programme, the USN had similar problems and in order to overcome them, the General Electric Co. had been persuaded to build full-sized working versions of both diesel and turbo engine rooms at their factories at Cleveland and Syracuse. These were, of course, primarily intended to train USN personnel but in the first months of 1943, many of our engineers, ERA's and Electrical Artificiers (EA's) were offered places on the excellent training courses run there, ending up with impressive certificates. Some of these men, on returning to *Saker*, were then used as instructors to give theoretical courses to Stokers awaiting onward draft to their various ships.

Those courses at what became known as the 'Land Ship Knox' were by no means all work and no play. The good people of Cleveland and Syracuse had never seen British naval uniforms before the advent of the DE's and vied with one another to offer hospitality to our men. No accommodation was provided on the courses but the men were paid a subsistence allowance of $24 per week and this enabled them to afford reasonable lodgings with American families. They found that the telephone in these lodgings rang frequently every evening as they received calls from local citizens inviting them out to their homes or for riotous nights on the town. This hectic night life made it hard for them to concentrate during the daytime lectures and demonstrations at the GEC mock ups but somehow they managed to assimilate enough of the lessons to give an adequate grounding in the strange complexities of the DE engine and motor rooms. Some months later, the situation had changed. The novelty of having British uniforms around had begun to wear off and entertainment was not being offered so freely. There was also a tendency for the men to lodge in the YMCA rather than in private lodgings. By staying at a hostel there was, no doubt, a substantial part of the $24 allowance left over to subsidize their runs ashore, now that there was a need to finance their own entertainment more often.

When production of the ships began to accelerate in August, 1943, the demands for these valuable courses exceeeded the capacity to provide them. USN personnel were, of course, given priority and few of our men were sent on them in the later days. By November, the only training given to Engine Room (ER) ratings was at sea during the trials running period at Boston. USN Engine Room Chief Petty Officers (CPO's) came aboard during trials and gave practical advice and instruction literally 'on the job'. This was certainly learning the hard way but the sound engineering knowledge of our ERA's enabled them to master the strange complicated machinery fairly quickly and by the end of the trials period they were quite competent to take the ships to sea. Later on, training was given in the United Kingdom to those who did not get to the United States and joined their ships at Lissahally. This was achieved by reducing the complement of one Buckley and one Evarts when they arrived at Belfast and using them to run from Liverpool to give two weeks training at sea to ER staff before joining their ships.

Ratings from other branches were also given training by the USN during their stand-by period. Telegraphists, radar operators, submarine detector ratings and so on were given places for instruction at a number of USN bases around the United States. Some Asdic operators were given courses with their USN counterparts at a training base at Key West in sunny Florida. Communications ratings also received training at a base in Miami but there is some doubt as to its value since radio procedures in the two navies differed considerably. These miscellaneous courses also petered out during the later months. In consequence the length of stay at Saker was also considerably reduced – but few complained about this. By that time the two hotels were under RN administration and the standard of food and accommodation had deteriorated until conditions there were little better than in Naval barracks in the three home ports. Under such circumstances, no one minded moving on to Boston where the accommodation was reputed to be still administered by the USN.

The onward passage to Massachusetts took the men one stage nearer to the ships they were destined to commission but after reaching Boston it was still several weeks before most of them even caught sight of a DE. Their first accommodation was in the USN Induction Centre known as Fargo Barracks. This was a vast building in the centre of the city that had begun life as a wool warehouse but had been commandeered by the United States Navy and transformed into a typically luxurious Induction Center for the USN new entries and others awaiting draft. Some of the dormitories were allocated exclusively to RN personnel but the British contingent lived closely with their American counterparts and shared domestic fatigues with them. Relationships between the two nationalities were fairly amicable; most of the Americans were new entries, still half civilian, half sailor and had not as yet adopted the vicious attitude towards 'Limeys' that seemed common among more seasoned USN sailors. Lulled into a sense of false security by the friendly atmosphere inside Fargo Barracks, many of our youngsters were shocked to find themselves the victims of some pretty brutal fights when they ventured into the night spots in the city. Charlestown Navy Yard is one of the main naval centres in America and sailors from the many USN vessels berthed there considered that the bars and other places in certain areas were their particular stamping grounds. Any British tars who ventured into such areas as Scollay Square, for instance, were almost certain to be involved in fights and, as they were usually outnumbered, many suffered some terrible beatings. Even in peace time, there had been fierce rivalry and conflict between American and British sailors wherever they met around the world. Now that they were allies fighting for a common cause, they seemed to hate one another almost as much as they hated the enemy!

Life in Boston had its better side however. There was the usual free issue of tickets to shows and other forms of entertainment, which was fortunate for our men, since otherwise they would have had a pretty dull time on their meagre rates of pay! Recreation facilities in Fargo itself were also first rate. The one most abiding memory for most of the thousands who passed through there was, however, the *food*. After years of austerity and rationing in Britain few of the men could believe their eyes when unheard of luxuries such as steak, chicken, ice cream and fruit pies were served up in the cafeteria so regularly and in such abundance that the American sailors were actually complaining of a boring diet! Some idea of the lavishness of USN victuals in Fargo can be gleaned from the Xmas Day menu for 1943 which is reproduced here (Figure 3). Many of our lads had never dreamed of such a feast much less had it set before them. They had indeed come to the land of plenty and they found it difficult to reconcile the different attitude to victualling in the two navies. Petty Officer (PO) Mc Gregor, on his way to join *Bentinck* recalls that his large draft of 1500 men arrived at Fargo two hours later than scheduled. Apart from men joining DE's the draft included others to recommission *Queen Elizabeth* and *Phoebe*, both of which had been refitting at Boston. They had disembarked at Halifax from the troopship *Mariposa* and were onward routed in two trains which caused hold-ups on the line. The galley at Fargo had prepared 1500 meals to be ready on their arrival but when the two hour delay was reported to the USN victualling officer he immediately ordered them to be thrown out as garbage and arrangements made to prepare 1500 more. This incident became legendary among successive

U. S. NAVY RECEIVING STATION
BOSTON

FARGO BARRACKS . . . . . . South Boston

DRY DOCK BARRACKS . . . . . South Boston

FRAZIER BARRACKS . Charlestown Navy Yard

Christmas Dinner

DECEMBER 25, 1943

Menu

FARGO COCKTAIL

SWEET MIXED PICKLES   HEARTS OF CELERY

RIPE OLIVES   STUFFED GREEN OLIVES   QUEEN OLIVES

CREAM OF CELERY SOUP

TOASTED SALTINES

ROAST STUFFED VERMONT TURKEY

OYSTER DRESSING   CRANBERRY SAUCE   GIBLET GRAVY

CANDIED SWEET POTATOES   SNOWFLAKE POTATOES

FRESH HUBBARD SQUASH   FRESH FROZEN PEAS

HAWAIIAN SALAD

SWEET DRESSING

HOT MINCE PIE   FRUIT CAKE

CHOCOLATE MALTED ICE CREAM

MacINTOSH APPLES   VALENCIA ORANGES

TOKAY GRAPES

MIXED NUTS   ASSORTED HARD CANDY

CREAMERY BUTTER   PARKER HOUSE ROLLS

COFFEE   CIGARETTES

Fig. 3. Christmas Dinner at Fargo Barracks, 1943.

15

drafts arriving at Boston. The men were well aware that such considerate action would never have taken place in a British barracks, even in peacetime with no rationing problems, and the story greatly enhanced the reputation of the USN as excellent hosts to the RN.

As each ship neared completion, its crew moved one last stage closer. Leaving Fargo, they were accommodated in buildings in the shipyards themselves. The Evarts men were put into the Frazier Barracks built in the Charlestown Navy Yard where all our Evarts were constructed and those assigned to Buckley's moved out to three blocks inside the Bethlehem Steel shipyard at nearby Hingham.

There were full messing arrangements in the Frazier Barracks but at Hingham the blocks had accommodation only. Men billeted there were given a special Victualling Allowance of 1$ 50c per day and were expected to use this to feed themselves in the vast canteen used by the shipyard workers. This may not seem over generous but meals in that establishment were subsidised and, in all fairness, the allowance was enough to provide three very substantial meals each day. It was inevitable, however, that not all of the allowance was used for this purpose. Since the barracks consisted of dormitories only, the men had to go out into the town for all their spare time entertainment. A few of them did become friendly with some of the shipyard workers and were invited into their homes in a nearby shanty town of caravans and temporary bungalows but most had to finance their own entertainment. The high cost of living soon emptied their pockets, so there was an understandable tendency to live frugally and save some of the allowance as extra pocket money. Fortunately, the sojourn at the shipyard did not last long enough for an economical diet of coffee and doughnuts to cause malnutrition. Even with pay augmented in this manner, social life at Hingham was not on the same level as it had been at Asbury Park or Boston.

The shipyard, which, as we know, had been newly constructed for the sole purpose of building the DEs, was a considerable distance from the city. There was a small barely furnished bar a short distance from the main gate where beer was 10c per bottle. This was cheap by US standards but had to be drunk straight off the ice to numb the taste buds against its vile flavour. There was a more sophisticated establishment known as 'The Red Barn' further down the road; this had more comfort but the beer was more expensive, and just as unpalatable. Perhaps the most popular place was the 'Popeye Roadhouse' which boasted a floor show. However, only the most affluent of the RN contingent could afford to patronize this place. Not only was there a cover charge but beer was 30c per small bottle. This was equivalent to 1s 6d in our money which was astronomical to men accustomed to paying 4½d for the same sized bottle, or 4d for a whole pint of mild beer at Home.

Needless to say, there was little drunkenness at Hingham. Typically it was not until about the final week before completion that any of the men, apart from the officers, had their first glimpse of the ships they had come so far to collect and first impressions were deceptive. Wiseacres with some previous experience of standing by ships in British yards frequently took one look at the state of the ship they were due to commission and confidently predicted another couple of months standby at the very least. Such wiseacres were literally dumbfounded to find themselves carrying their kitbag and hammock on board just a week later.

COMMISSIONING

There were, and still are, some fantastic stories about the construction times of the Destroyer Escorts. Many still believe that they came into being in a matter of about three weeks after the keel was laid! In truth, the prototypes took as long to build as conventional ships – nine to twelve months being typical – but as production techniques were developed and the construction teams got into the swing of things, these times were cut down to about 5 months for the ships being completed in November, 1943, and to as little as three months for the last batch delivered to the RN. There were exceptions to this however. For the sake of publicity certain ships were chosen for specially orchestrated 'record construction' bids. During one of these *Fitzroy* was completed in just over seven weeks but this was indeed an exception.

Turning out ships at so high a rate was still a fantastic achievement, even in the land in which mass production originated. Not everyone was convinced that these methods produced sound ships. British sailors still had more faith in rivets than welds and the fact that most of the work force was semi-skilled and that many were women, gave rise to the belief that the ships would not survive a heavy tempest, let alone action damage. There *were* some shoddy welds and skimped workmanship, as will be described in later chapters but let there be no doubt about it, the vast majority of the DE's were *very* sturdy vessels and many stood up very well, even after receiving mine or torpedo damage.

Once the ships were handed over to the Royal Navy and commissioned, they came under the command of the C-in-C Western Atlantic and there was a senior British Naval Officer at Boston to deal with local problems but until the handover they were still very much

13 March 1943

COMMANDANT'S CIRCULAR NO. 25–43

Subject: H.M.S. BERRY (BDE – 3) – Christening and Commissioning

1. H.M.S. BERRY (BDE – 3) will be christened at 1630 on 15 March 1943. The ceremony will take place at the bow of the vessel in her present berth at Pier 8 East, inboard.

2. The Comandant has designated Mrs. Gladys Mary Seal as sponsor of the vessel.

3. Immediately after the vessel has been christened, she will be placed in commission in the British Navy by her commanding officer.Lieut.Comdr. Legassick, R.N.V.R.

Fig. 4. A copy of the commissioning announcement for HMS *Berry*

the property of Rear Admiral R. Theobald USN who was Commandant of the Boston Yard. His staff provided USN officers to assist the RN CO's and advise them on USN protocol and procedure. They also handled the administrative aspects of the handover and commissioning ceremonies. A copy of a typical announcement is appended by courtesy of Arsen Charles, Curator of the Museum in Charlestown Naval Yard where copies of all such documents are held (Figure 4). A lady of some social standing was appointed to act as sponsor to each ship and it was this lady who actually wielded the champagne bottle at the RN christening. Some of these good ladies maintained contact with the ships' companies long after they left Boston and often sent comforts, as did the women of the WVS back at home. During the earlier months, when DE's were not being commissioned in large numbers, some of the crews spent some weeks at Boston and many of the lads established lasting friendships among local families who had opened their homes to the sons of their British Allies. On some occasions it was possible to repay this kindness by entertaining all these new friends at a Commissioning Dance. A memento of one of these, held by *Bickerton*, is at Figure 5. Later on, when the construction programme was in full swing, few spent very long at Boston and not many enjoyed this social fraternization.

The photographs of the barracks and the Hingham shipyard will no

The ship's company of

H. M. S. Bickerton

request, by kind permission of the Captain,

the pleasure of the company of

at their Ship's Commissioning Dance

to be held at the Union Jack Club

118 Milk Street, Boston

on Monday, the first of November at 8 p. m.

R. S. V. P.

the Secretary, Dance Committee
H. M. S. Bickerton,
c-o British Fleet Mail Officer,
Fargo Barracks, South Boston

Fig. 5. Invitation to HMS Bickerton's Commissioning Dance.

doubt evoke many memories among ex-DE men and bring to mind instances of how strange they all felt in this affluent land which they had only previously seen through the medium of Hollywood films. The aerial view of the Bethlehem Steel shipyard clearly shows extensive car parks and it was difficult for the men to grasp that these rows of large shiny cars actually belonged to the shipyard workers. It must be remembered that car ownership in UK during the '30s and '40s was almost entirely confined to the professional classes and Britishers found it very difficult to accept that welders, fitters and even unskilled labourers could afford to drive to work in Cadillacs and Chevrolets. Such examples highlighted the huge difference in living standards between the two countries. There can be no doubt that experiences like this, which demonstrated Britain's position as the poor relation, did much to awaken doubts about our political system among the naive youngsters and kindled resolve to make revolutionary changes in post-war Britain. But that is another story.

Few of the men had any opportunity to go on board the DE's before commissioning day but when that came opinions about the ships' strange external appearance were forgotten as the messdecks and machinery spaces were curiously explored. Those men who had never been to sea before, accepted everything without much comment but the rest, particularly those who had served in small ships, could hardly believe the various luxuries they discovered. The good living enjoyed by American civilians was obviously reflected in the equally high standards provided for their servicemen. Without any exaggeration, it must be said that, as far as living space and comfort are concerned, USN ships of 1943 were at least twenty years in advance of contemporary British ships. To begin with, every man had his own bunk and the chore of lashing up and stowing hammocks was a thing of the past in the Destroyer Escorts. Some lower deck men were not entirely convinced that this was such a good thing. Apart from the inconvenience, hammocks *were* comfortable to sleep in but even the sceptics came around to accepting bunks as preferable in the end. Another major innovation was that the DE's, in line with all the USN ships, were built with a cafeteria style messing system. Meals were taken from the galley into a servery complete with dish-washing machines, ice cream makers and coffee percolators, where dutymen serviced the meals on to compartmentalized trays for, individual collection by the men. One of the most astounding discoveries was that the ships even had small but efficient laundries. Many years were to pass after the war before British destroyers had any other facility than galvanized buckets in primitive bathrooms in which lower deck men could do their laundry. Other strange luxuries were iced water drinking fountains in the messdecks and reasonably sized steel lockers in place of the ridiculously small and inaccessible seat locker found in British destroyers.

The senior rates fared even better. The only separate enclosed mess in the Buckleys was the one provided for USN CPO's. This had accommodation for sixteen men and was in excess of the number of Chiefs in the RN complement. In the absence of a PO's mess, it was decided, in most ships, that this CPO's accommodation would become a combined Chiefs' and PO's' mess. Billeted in it there were typically the Chief ERA, four ERA's with CPO rate, the CPO Cox'n, CPO 'Buffer', the Chief Stoker, the Ordnance Artificer, an Electrical Artificer, two gunnery PO's., a PO Torpedoman, PO Telegraphist, PO Yeoman of Signals and the PO officers' steward.

In fact, the mess was in two parts; one situated under 'A' gun was the sleeping quarters and contained nothing but the tall kit lockers and the three-tier bunks. Aft of this, on the starboard side there were the living quarters which, apart from the usual mess table and seats, were furnished with an armchair and a settee, a sideboard, complete with pop-up toaster and a coffee percolator and, wonder of wonders, a large domestic type refrigerator, the like of which was unknown outside wardrooms in British ships! On the port side, beyond a passage way, was the bathroom. This contained wash basins and shower stalls and the most primitive toilet facility ever seen. This consisted of a simple two-seater trough, without even a canvas screen in front to conceal its user from their shipmates using the basins or showers. Everyone had been highly delighted and impressed to find messing arrangements so superior to any in contemporary British ships, but were utterly bemused by the fact that the Americans should have so much luxury and then spoil it with this primitive 'thunder trough'! Fortunately, more civilised arrangements were provided in due course. During the subsequent mini-refit at Belfast, the trough was removed and a properly enclosed WC was fitted.

Many found it puzzling that the Americans could provide such spacious mess decks compared with British ships of similar size and could only surmise that it was due to the length-to-breadth ratio of the DE's being a generous 8.3 to 1, whereas RN destroyers were tradition-ally long and narrow, with a length-to-breadth of 10 to 1. This difference in ratio does not seem much but in fact it would provide about ten per cent extra internal space for a ship of the same length but of 10:1 ratio. Another difference was in the wardroom accommodation. In British destroyers, officers still had cabins under the quarterdecks but all officers accommodation in the DE's was in the superstructure, leaving more space below for messdecks.

WORKING-UP

Having marched on board and attended the commissioning ceremony the crews only had a few days during which stores and ammunition were embarked before their period away from the war came to an end and they returned once more to the reality of life at sea. For about a week, the ships made daily trips to sea from Charlestown Navy Yard during which the acceptance trials were carried out. One aspect of the DE's which very soon impressed their new owners was their remarkable handling qualities. They had twin rudders which enabled them to make very tight turns and it is on record that during one of the Buckley trials the ship made a 180 degree turn, at 24 knots, in the amazingly short distance of 410 yards and took only 70 seconds to do so. This is a performance which experienced destroyer men will agree is pretty impressive!

It did not take very long before one of their less admired features became evident. None of the daily trips took them very far out to sea but they often went far enough to find choppy water and the crews soon learned that the ships were very lively in anything but calm seas. The British DE's lacked a considerable amount of designed topweight since none of them had the triple torpedo tubes up on the superstructure deck and very few had any gun mountings in the positions intended to carry heavy multi-barrel close range weapons. This must have had a significant effect on the metacentric height which determines a ship's stability. Many vicious rolls of up to 60 degrees were recorded but this is not exceptional among small ships. It was the *speed* of the roll which gave the DE's a bad name. It is probable that being bottom heavy is as bad as being top heavy as far as speed of motion is concerned but one thing is certain, even hardened mariners took a long time to find their sealegs in the DE's and many of them even suffered from sea sickness for the first time in years.

In most cases there were few teething troubles during the trials period and they were generally completed in about a week. It was with mixed feelings that the crews then faced the prospect of serious working-up exercises. Having been in the wonderland of the USA for months on end, living in conditions which made the war at sea seem very remote and even unreal, it was difficult to come to terms with the fact that the good times were over and that they would soon be in the thick of things again. There was one thing that helped sweeten this bitter pill though; none of the crews knew to which theatre of war their ships would be taking them to but it *was* known that they were first bound for Belfast and a minor refit when they left US waters. This knowledge and the prospect of home leave was enough to raise the men's spirits high whatever the prospect to follow.

* * *

Before following on with the stories of the ships as they worked-up to fighting efficiency at Casco Bay and Bermuda, it is perhaps fitting to relate some of the legendary incidents that took place during the trials periods at Boston. Considering that almost half the crews and many of the officers were newcomers to life at sea and that the ships they had commissioned had many alien aspects, even for experienced men, it is not surprising that there were a number of mishaps as they struggled to become efficient crews. Many were trivial and caused only mild amusement among the American onlookers but some were potentially dangerous and caused considerable concern to Admiral Theobald's staff.

The most legendary of these serious incidents was the occasion which gave rise to banner headlines in the local Boston press:

'BRITISH SHIP FIRES ON US SOIL FOR THE FIRST TIME SINCE THE WAR OF INDEPENDENCE'

It happened, of course, during the gunnery acceptance trials of one of the ships. I have never been able to establish for certain which one it was. The incident became so well known to all the DE crews who subsequently passed through Boston, that truth has become mixed with fiction. The mists of time have clouded memories and there are witnesses from four different ships who claim that it was their particular ship which was involved! The most probable culprit was *Bayntun*, the very first of the DE's handed over. The actual cause of the incident is shrouded in as much mystery as the name of the ship concerned. The bare facts were that during gun trials, a 3″ practice shell (solid shot) was inadvertently fired towards land and ended up in a cemetery on the outskirts of Boston. It was perhaps a fortunate place for it to land, since had it landed in a populated area, even a solid shot could have caused considerable damage and casualties. There must certainly have been a Court of Inquiry but it is unlikely that anyone in *Bayntun* was to blame. The gun trials were not practice shoots. The purpose was to fire each gun in turn to establish that its mechanism worked and that it was properly secured to the deck. They were conducted by a USN base staff gunnery officer who supervised the pointing of the guns. They were accompanied by others of the base staff, sometimes USN gunners mates and sometimes British OA's serving ashore for a time before being allocated to a DE. The onus of ensuring that the guns were fired on a safe bearing must have been squarely upon the gun trials officers, who were well acquainted with the local geography and I find it difficult to believe that such a man could have been careless enough to allow a gun pointing towards Boston to be fired. A more plausible scenario is that the gun fired prematurely by accident before the control officer had checked its bearing. As will be explained later, the US 3″/50 cal guns *did* have an inherent fault in their firing mechanism which made them prone to go off immediately the breech had closed, regardless of whether or not the gunlayer had pressed his trigger and it is fairly certain that this was the cause of *Bayntun*'s accident. In spite of the incident not being their fault, it probably resulted in the gunnery staff in *Bayntun* enduring unmerciful ribbing during the rest of their time at Boston. They must have all kept copies of the local papers as souvenirs of their notoriety but unfortunately the author has not been able to find any of them. Arsen Charles, the curator of the present day museum in Charlestown Navy Yard, tried hard to find out more details but although he found a former Parks Department employee who was an eye witness to the shell's landing, he was unable to get more information from the local press.

Another incident which could have soured relationships between the two Navies involved *Byard*. She was returning into Charlestown Yard after a day at sea during the trials period and was directed to a berth astern of the *Constitution*, a preserved American wooden ship revered by them as much as we revere the *Victory*. There was some delay in communications via the engine room telegraph. Instead of slowing down as the ship approached the jetty, she continued with unabated speed and her bows proceeded to wreak havoc as they tore into the wooden jetty and scraped along, tearing up pipework and cables along its edge amidst a shower of sparks and clouds of steam. Even more hair raising to her CO was the fact that her bows were moving inexorably towards the *Constitution* and he realized that if she was to be damaged, he would not only be chased by a USN lynch mob, but that his Naval career would be at a sticky end. Fortunately for everyone concerned, the worst did not happen. Somehow, in the last moments of blind panic, the ERA on watch in the motor room finally reversed the screws and calamity was averted by seconds. Happily, there were no official repercussions from the Admiral's staff about the damage done. Possibly they were so relieved that *Constitution* had come to no harm that they were persuaded to take a lenient view. One of her chroniclers in the group paying-off book records that they almost congratulated her CO for the damage he'd caused on the grounds that they considering the jetty to be much out of date and they had long been considering its refurbishment. Despite this polite official attitude, one may well imagine the catcalls and witty comments they had to face every time they approached a jetty in Boston after that.

The final example of a classic accident again involves weaponry. This time it was the Hedgehog ahead throwing A/S mortar in *Riou*. Captain Featherstone-Dilke, who was then her First Lieutenant, remembers that whilst the ship was berthed in the Navy Yard during the trials period one of the ship's company managed to obtain persmission to bring in his girl friend and show her round the ship. When they reached the Hedgehog she naively asked how it worked. He began a literal demonstration by turning the firing handles and to his utter dismay a full pattern of 24 projectiles sailed into the air, passing over the dockyard wall and falling on the parade ground of a US Army barracks outside. The Officer of the Watch (OOW) sent a working party to retrieve them and the amusing aftermath of the mishap was that the soldiers in the barracks were heard to remark very favourably about the 'brave Limeys' who calmly picked up the bombs and nonchalantly carried them back to their ship. Little did they know that they were only practice missiles and were full of sand!

Once again there was probably a court of inquiry set up to investigate this happening but its findings are long since forgotten. What had obviously happened was that the practice bombs had been loaded in preparation for trial firings the next day but that the PO TI had sadly neglected to lock the firing circuits to 'SAFE' and no doubt he, at least, lost one of his Good Conduct (GC) badges for his negligence.

This *faux pas* took place in the early part of January, 1944, and was, as far as can be established, the last time that the Americans had to marvel at the inexperienced antics of their British allies, because few of the British DE's remained to be commissioned after that.

Having said farewell to the bright lights of Boston, the first part of the serious working up programme took place at Casco Bay, Portland, Maine.

The DE's which passed through during the summer probably had a reasonable time there but by the time most began to arrive, after November, it was a very frigid and inhospitable place. The most vivid memories that men have of it are of endless hours spent chipping ice away from the guns and the upperworks.

Apart from getting the men shaken down into ships routine after the easy life at Boston, the chief purpose of the stay at Casco was to carry out preliminary A/S exercises. The main work-up was to be done at Bermuda but, before letting the newly commissioned ships loose in Atlantic waters where U-boats lurked it, it was prudent to give the A/S crews at least some training. The week there also revealed some of the many problems which had to be faced in subsequent months before the inexperienced youngsters who comprised up to fifty per cent of the ships companies could somehow be transformed into an efficient fighting force. The RN had been engaged in continuous action around the world for four years. During that time, an average of one ship per week had been lost. Each sinking represented the loss of a few more of our experienced mariners and the problem of finding action-seasoned men to form the nucleus around whom to build and train efficient crews was becoming more and more difficult. The ranks of the pre-war regulars and the reservists who formed the backbone of the 1939 Navy had been decimated during the earlier part of the war. Most of the few who still survived were now Chiefs, PO's or Leading hands, invaluable as leaders of the newly called up recruits but sadly ever decreasing in numbers. There were also, by this time, quite a number of 'Hostilities Only' ratings who had served long enough to become senior rates. By dint of hard experience in battle, they had become the new professionals and, with the remaining regulars, these staid hands were carefully shared out to ensure that every ship had a hard core of experienced leaders. Some of the men they led had also had some sea experience but the complement lists of DE's which still exist reveal that up to half the Seaman branch had never been in ships before. There was a similar state of affairs in other branches but for some reason the Engine Rooms did not fare so badly and had only some twenty-five per cent of inexperienced Stokers.

The basic training for conscripts after call-up was a bare six weeks, which was hopelessly inadequate for specialist branches. Heads of such specialist departments were soon to discover this at Casco Bay. There was, for example, a great demand upon the shore base staff for the loan of signal generators which were essential to give audio lessons to Asdic operators. The new entries had received basic training after being called up but during the first exercises with live submarines at Casco it became evident that their expertise was frighteningly below standard. The purpose of the work-up should have been simply to give them practice at detecting submarines but PO Higher Submarine Detector (HSD) F. Woodley in *Louis* found that, in the event, many of them needed to be given basic instruction about how to operate their instruments. ERA A. J. Brown of *Deane* found similar problems and discovered that many of the new entry second class stokers were incapable of performing even such basic tasks as the manual control of boiler feed water. The hours spent at sea during the exercises had to be utilized as intensive instruction sessions in the boiler rooms. Many of the junior officers were just as inexperienced. Some had been CW candidates and had at least been to sea before but, apart from a sprinkling of long service Gunners and Bosuns, the remainder were brand new Royal Naval Volunteer Reserve (RNVR) Sub-Lieutenants straight out of training and were not even in possession of watchkeeping certificates. The Commanding Officers, First Lieutenants and Engineers were, of course, men of considerable sea experience (either RN, Royal Naval Reserve (RNR) or RNVR) but life was hard for them until their juniors had been licked into shape. With so many inexperienced officers, the task of turning raw recruits into efficient crew members fell mostly upon the senior ratings. All were experts in their specializations and most had the patience and understanding to lead rather than drive the men towards efficiency. Some of the raw material they had to work with were awkward characters, unwilling pressed men who were determined not to knuckle down to service discipline, but these were a minority. A large number had been volunteers to join the RN when call-up time came. Some even falsified their age in order to get to sea and many were little more than seventeen years old. Such lads had an earnest desire to follow in the finest traditions of the RN, had genuine admiration and respect for their senior rates and were keen to learn. These factors played no small part in the task of getting the ships to operational efficiency in remarkably short times.

The week of rough shake down at Casco Bay was followed by a more extensive programme of exercises, evolutions and even shore training sessions at Bermuda. The routine was by no means as harsh and nerve-racking as that which the notorious 'Monkey' Stephenson presided over at Tobermory, but it was a thorough course of training which put everyone through their paces. In view of their future roles as escort ships, the training was heavily biased towards A/S work. Nevertheless, during the three week period all the other branches were put through the hoop with communication exercises, surface and AD target firings and seamanship evolutions until everyone became familiar with the American equipment and, in some cases, its shortcomings.

The warm equable weather was a welcome change after the 'blue nose' conditions at Casco Bay but it was not always pleasant. The Bermuda area is notorious for sudden hurricane force storms and few of the DE's escaped at least one battering from these awesome tempests which often wreaked havoc with the upper deck fittings as well as causing even experienced mariners to suffer from the vile miseries of '*mal de mer*'. These storm conditions revealed one of the idiosyncrasies of the DE's; the Arma gyro compasses were found to be prone to failure during violent ship motions. Mercury would spill out into places it was not intended to be and the mechanisms would transmit false compass bearings causing inexperienced navigators to become lost if the malfunctioning was not immediately noticed. Another annoying DE habit which also caused some consternation was that sudden shock, such as the firing of shallow set depth-charges tended to cause the main breaker switches in the motor rooms to fall open. In ships where the final propulsion units were electric motors, the unexpected loss of power literally stopped the ship in its tracks. This fault became known as 'breakeritis' and was, of course, soon remedied but it was the source of some puzzlement and minor panic the first time it happened in one of the ships.

As the ships companies became more experienced and conversant with their equipment, the number of untoward incidents diminished. However, until this began to happen, there were a number of embarrassing happenings similar to those which had taken place in the earlier days at Boston. Some of these were not without an element of farce. Consider, for example, an incident which befell *Blackwood*. She had just completed a towing exercise and, as all seamen will know, this entails disconnecting the chain from one anchor so that it (the chain) can be used for the purpose of being towed by another ship. During this exercise, the disconnected port anchor was secured from falling overboard by shackling it to a short length of cable, which was in turn secured to a deck fitting. In this case, after the exercise was completed, the anchor should have been reconnected to its cable in the normal manner but the inexperienced foc'sle party had neglected to do so, probably being caught up in some other sudden evolution. At the end of the day's work, when *Blackwood* turned back towards Bermuda for the night, the young Sub-Lieutenant in charge of the foc'sle realized how things were just as the ship reached its allocated mooring position and the First Lieutenant had bellowed out the order to 'Slip the port anchor.' Diplomatically, the young officer pretended not to have heard, fully expecting that the First Lieutenant would immediately become aware of the situation and belay the last order. Sad to tell, he did *not* notice the situation and his only reaction was almost to leap over the front of the bridge and give vent to some very nautical language. Shrugging resignedly, the young Sub-Lieutenant did give the necessary order and the whole cable party looked on in horrified disbelief as the anchor and its short length of chain disppeared inexorably into the depths of the harbour! It must have been a judgement of Solomon for the CO when he later had to decide how to apportion the blame for the loss of the anchor but at least the Sub-Lieutenant had a sound defence in that he had obeyed the last order!

Another incident which could have had dangerous consequences was when *Bazeley* sent a 3" shell whistling over the town of Hamilton during a night exercise shoot. As with *Bayntun* at Boston, it is unlikely that the cause was carelessness on the part of whoever was detailed to ensure that the guns were fired on a safe bearing. It was more probable that it was another case of premature firing due to a faulty breech mechanism, so perhaps it is time to explain these failures.

To put matters bluntly, the 3"/50 calibre guns were pretty useless apart from their ability to produce loud bangs. No gun of such small calibre had ever been installed as main armament in RN escort ships before. The DE's should have been equipped with the standard 5" USN destroyer guns. One class of their own DE's *did* have such weapons but, in all fairness, it must be admitted that production of large numbers of these turret mountings was beyond the capacity of an overstrained US armament industry. Contracts for the DE guns had to be put out to a number of firms with no previous armament experience. These firms were diverse indeed; *Cubitt*'s breech mechanisms had been turned out by the Continental Canning Co. and the fuze-setting machines came from Singers of sewing machine fame. The design of the 3" gun mountings was extremely basic, so that practically any factory with machine tool capacity could build them but, even so, some of the manufacturing tolerances were beyond the level of skill of some of their inexperienced machinists.

The unusual 'walking worm' training gear was prone to seize up solid in rough weather and could only be freed by brute force. The vertical sliding breech blocks often failed to close properly and had to be knocked home with heavy lead hammers kept in readiness for this purpose. There was also a defect which caused premature firing on many occasions. The breech-block housed firing mechanism, which included a spring loaded plunger which released the striker when retracted. Many of these plungers were too tightly fitting in their housings and, despite the spring loading, would often stick in the retracted position. This meant that the striker would be released immediately the breech closed, regardless of whether or not the gunlayer had pressed his trigger. USN maintenance literature recognized this fault and recommended that these plungers should not be greased but merely lubricated with light machine oil. This did not always completely solve the problem. Ordnance artificers or base staff eventually had to machine off a few thousandths of an inch from the plungers but the fault persisted to the very end in some DE's. Having eulogized about so many aspects of the DE's, this criticism of their armament is made reluctantly but, in all truth, the first practice firings convinced most CO's and Gunnery Officers that the 3″ guns were really quite inadequate as main armament. The 13lb projectiles were useless against anything larger than an E-boat and later chapters will describe many instances of them bouncing harmlessly off U-boat casings and even off the thin plating of merchant vessels. As for AD fire; whereas a 35lb 4″ shell bursting within 40 feet of an aircraft would cause serious or fatal damage, on seeing the tiny bursts of the 3″ rounds, the gunners surmised that they would virtually have to explode in the pilot's cockpit in order to produce any damage.

The most significant defect in the DE's was the lack of a fire control director or gunnery computer. The Naval Historian, Peter Elliot, mentions that the DE's had 'an optical fire control system' but this was certainly not the case in British Destroyer Escorts. Many of the USN DE's had rangefinders and Mk 51 directors on the bridge but no British DE's were so fitted. There *was* a curious instrument on the gunnery control platform which contained primitive clockwork mechanism which was a cross between a Vickers Range Clock and a Dumaresque. By setting initial range and bearing, this contraption produced gun ranges and deflections which had to be verbally transmitted to the sight setters at the guns. This was about as antiquated as the gunnery instruments in use during the First World War. It did occasionally result in getting shell splashes reasonably close to a surface target but it was totally incapable of dealing with the three dimensional problems of AD fire. With practice, the gun crews eventually became quite proficient at AD fire under local control, using standard cartwheel-type open sights but the tiny air-bursts of the HE shells didn't give much confidence that the DE's could hold their own in a heavy air attack.

The concentrated training programme at Bermuda did not allow much time for runs ashore there but, in any case, there were few attractions for lower deck personnel, apart from sight-seeing and swimming. The officers were welcomed into the homes and clubs of the wealthy colonial types but lower deck ratings were *persona non grata* in such social circles. They were merely tolerated and there were few amenities for their lower class taste. There was a USO Club built for the benefit of the American leaseholders of the island but this wasn't too popular as beer was rationed to two bottles per man, presumably to avoid exposing the colonials to drunken brawls between American and British sailors. Most of the men found that the dockyard canteen was one of the most popular places to spend an evening. It lacked the glamour of the bright lights of Boston but at least the beer was more to their taste and the prices much kinder to their pockets!

THE WESTERN APPROACHES COMMAND

There were few regrets when the working up periods came to an end. The ships passed through the course in twos or threes and on completion they became operational units. After brief returns to various US ports, they usually became additional escorts for convoys from Halifax or Argentia Bay for passage back to UK.

On reaching home, all the DE's became members of the Western Approaches Command and, with a few exceptions, their first port of call was Belfast. There they were taken in hand for a modification refit lasting some weeks in Pollock Dock. In messdeck parlance, the purpose of these refits was 'to tear the ships apart and rebuild them more on Admiralty lines' but they were not as drastic as that! Since we had been fighting the Atlantic battle for fours years, the Royal Navy naturally had a more comprehensive knowledge of what equipment was essential for effective A/S warfare than the Americans and the purpose of the Pollock Dock work was to bring the ships more in line with the latest standards of RN escort vessels. Some of the modifications were not too popular on the lower deck because they were seen to be reducing some of the luxuries inherent in the American design. The cafeteria messing systems were discontinued and the dishwashers, ice cream machines and ice water fountains were all removed. The major changes were, however, all concerned with fighting efficiency. The USN outfit of depth-charges, for instance, was inadequate for protracted attacks and more stowage was provided in upper deck racks until the total capacity was for 200 charges. Depth-charge handling facilities in the magazines were also unsuitable and had to be modified. Much of the steelwork around the binnacle had to be replaced by non-ferrous materials and communications between the bridge and the radar office had to be installed. Similar arrangements also had to be added between the bridge and radio office and the High Frequency Direction Finding (HFDF) office. The unreliable Arma gyro compasses were replaced by Admiralty pattern Sperry units and the Type 128D/DV Asdic sets were modified to Type 144 and 147B sets were added. Domestic changes included 'Messing arrangements to be brought to RN standards' (the end of the unpopular cafeteria system), 'Heads to be brought to RN standards' (the end of the embarrassing troughs),' Living accommodation and bathrooms to be covered with latest Admiralty insulating materials' (cork granules). Other changes included the re-siting of the pitometer log and the fitting of battens to improve stowage in provision rooms. Splinter shields were to be fitted around the 3″ guns and the Mk4 elevating column Oerlikon mountings, almost impossible to maintain at sea, were to be replaced by simple Mk VIA mountings. Some of these modifications had to be deferred; *Cubitt*, for example did not get 3″ gunshields until February, 1945, and she never did lose the accursed Mk 4 Oerlikon mounts. All in all, there were 109 items in the A and A lists for the Evarts and 94 for the Buckleys. These kept the dockyard workmen busy in Pollock Dock for several weeks.

Whilst on the subject of these changes, it is of interest to note that not all the modifications were looked upon kindly by the USN when the surviving DE's were returning to the States. All ships so returned were surveyed for fitness for further service (even though most of them were due to be sold as scrap) and some of the surveyors made acid comments about some of the changes wrought whilst in RN hands. One of the commonest complaints was that we had destroyed the fireproof integrity of the ships. Originally, all internal doors and cabin furniture had been made of steel; all furnishings such as curtains, upholstery and bedding covers on the bunks were made of fireproof fibre glass cloth and all paintwork in the ships was fire resistant. During their commission with the Royal Navy much of the wardroom and office furniture had been removed and replaced by wooden items; curtains and upholstery had been replaced by pretty chintz material. All paintwork had been liberally plastered with standard Admiralty grey paint which may have been durable but was certainly not fire resistant.

The ships' companies were given welcome home leave whilst the Pollock Dock refits were progressed and, sadly, this was the last time that many of the men ever saw their loved ones before being killed in action, as several of the ships had extremely short lives. When all the work was complete, the DE's were handed over to the Western Approaches Command for allocation to active groups. Many worked with existing groups as 'supernumeraries' until their time came for permanent group allocation but when sufficient numbers had accumulated, they were formed into new Groups each consisting of three Buckleys and three Evarts. The 1st, 3rd, 4th and 5th Belfast groups were formed in this manner. Later, the 15th Group, which had all Evarts was formed and the 21st Group, which had all Buckleys. Others ended up in mixed groups with old destroyers and corvettes. When the Belfast groups were complete, a number of Buckleys were transferred to local flotillas in the Nore, Portsmouth and Devonport Commands. There they were employed on North Sea and Channel convoy work and vital E-boat patrols during and after the Normany landings.

Despite the fact that the DE's arrived too late to take part in most of the serious actions against U-boat packs in the Battle of the Atlantic (the worst of which were over by May 1943), the British contingent aquitted themselves with much honour during the final stages of the war against Germany. Between them they sank thirty-six U-boats. During this same period, all other types of British escort vessels (numbering well over 200) sank only fifty between them. The Captains also sank or damaged a large number of E-boats in the Channel and North Sea. During all these operations, seventeen of them were lost or became so badly damaged that they were written off as constructive total losses (CTL). These resulted in the deaths of about 700 men and the wounding of perhaps twice this number. With such a record, the service of these ships deserves to be recorded for posterity and it was with this purpose in mind that the author produced this work.

Initially, it had been intended to put the individual ships' records in alphabetical order but this encyclopaedic approach resulted in much repetition and the present format of treating each Escort Group in a separate chapter was adopted. Even this layout has certain untidy aspects; whilst most of the DE's served with the same group throughout their RN careers, others had a nomadic existence and served in two or sometimes three different groups. To trace some of their careers it is therefore necessary to thumb through more than one chapter and there are also anomalies in that some of the very first to commission are not mentioned until the last chapter. The groups have been treated in chronological order as far as possible, starting with the 4th EG, which was the first to be formed. Hopefully, the indexing will facilitate the tracing of individual ships exploits in cases where they served in more than one Group.

As final comments in this Introduction it is perhaps of interest to point out that although it was the original intention of the Admiralty Ships Names Committee to name all the DE's after famous captains of the Nelson era, it was not possible to adhere to this resolve when the numbers escalated to seventy-eight! Some of the ships thus bear names of captains (and admirals) of much earlier times. *Cubitt*, for example, was named after the captain of the second *Mary Rose* in 1666.

It may also be questioned why these ships, known to the USN as Destroyer Escorts, were given 'K' pendant numbers and classified as 'frigates' once they sailed under the White Ensign. The simple explanation for this is that Admiralty requirements for any sort of destroyer is that they *must* have torpedo tubes. All the British DE's were 'fitted for, but not with' torpedo tubes and thus could only be categorized as frigates.

From force of habit the crews of the Captains persisted in using the American designation Destroyer Escort throughout their time in the ships.

– 2 –

THE 4TH ESCORT GROUP

Bazeley, Bentinck, (Blackwood), (Burges).
Byard, Calder, Drury, Pasley.

T he 4th was the very first of the Western Approaches Escort
Groups to be made up entirely of Captain class frigates and,
with the exception of *Pasley*, which did not join until a year
after its formation, all its members were among the first of the DE's to
be allocated to the RN.

The first was *Bazeley* (DE 2), the second of the Evarts class to be
completed. She had been laid down in April, 1942, but as a prototype
she was not mass produced and it was not until 18 February, 1943,
that she was ready for commissioning at Boston. She was christened by
Mrs Brock, wife of a Captain in the Royal Canadian Navy (RCN) and
mother of *Bazeley*'s first CO, Lieutenant-Commander J. V. Brock,
Royal Canadian Navy Volunteer Reserve (RCNVR).

Trials at Boston occupied about four weeks and seem to have passed
without any untoward incident and in due course she departed for a
visit to Brooklyn Navy Yard via the Cape Cod Canal and Long Island
Sound on 20 March. She was then scheduled for a three week work-up
period at Bermuda but, much to the delight of her crew, who were keen
to get back to Britain, a signal was received which curtailed her sojourn
at Bermuda and promised an earlier passage home than had been
expected. A fast ship was required to deliver some urgent cargo to the
UK and *Bazeley* had been chosen for this task. The nature of this cargo
was confidential; one rumour had it that it consisted of secret bomb
sights needed by the RAF. Whatever its nature may have been, it was
contained in crates which had to be stowed below decks. This posed
quite a problem as there was no available space in a DE large enough
for the purpose. Her CO eventually came up with a compromise
solution; he suggested that the bulkhead between the wardroom and

one of the officer's cabins be taken out. The enlarged wardroom would then accommodate the important crates and, with an eye to future comfort, he pointed out to his officers that if the alteration could be made permanent, they would be compensated for temporary inconvenience by having a more spacious wardroom for the remainder of the commission. The dockyard authorities agreed to the alteration and, on completion, the ship duly proceeded to Yorktown. The mysterious crates were taken on board and *Bazeley* set out for her fast voyage home on 10 April. But fate and the Admiralty unkindly stepped in to thwart their early homecoming.

The cruiser *Argonaut* happened to be on her way to undergo repairs in America after being damaged in action and *Bazeley* was signalled to rendezvous with her and escort her during the final state of her voyage. This diversion was not intended to delay *Bazeley* for very long but, as it turned out, the results were disastrous. Wishing to meet the cruiser as soon as possible, Lieutenant-Commander Brock rang down to the engine room to increase speed to 500 revolutions but this proved to be more than the diesels could maintain for very long. A piston shattered, causing the shut down of one engine and reduced speed to 16 knots. The outcome was that they not only failed to rendezvous with *Argonaut* but also suffered the indignity of being ordered back to Boston for repairs. With much chagrin, the crew watched their precious cargo being off-loaded and transferred to another frigate (*Berry*) and settled down to accept a period at Charlestown Navy Yard for repairs. The staff experts at Boston came on board for a survey and first estimates were that the repairs could be done quickly. However, they did not quite live up to their usual reputation for getting things done. It was six weeks before *Bazeley* was ready for sea again. As some consolation for missing an early return home, her crew did enjoy a period at the West Townsend Rest Camp at Fitchburg. This was greatly enjoyed by the single men, but those with wives and families would have much preferred to have been at home! The officers were naturally concerned about what the reaction of the Navy Yard staff would be to the modified wardroom. However, after some initial resistance, the authorities agreed to make the change permanent. Thereafter *Bazeley* boasted the most commodious wardroom in the Captain class. It was June before repairs were completed and this time there was no escape from the full working up period at Bermuda. She sailed from there with three other future 4th EG members on 30 June, 1943.

The next of the future group to commission was *Blackwood* (DE 4). Laid down in September, 1942, she had benefited from an acceleration in production times and was ready for handover on 27 March, only a month after *Bazeley*, which had been laid down five months earlier.

She suffered some delay in getting away from Boston by virtue of having been used as a test bed to solve one of the design problems which had plagued the Evarts class. The designers had chosen to fit sophisticated taper roller bearings in place of the conventional thrust blocks on the propeller shafts and although these had performed well during shore trials, it was found that they had a tendency to run hot at sea. American design engineers were ordered to investigate the reason and *Blackwood* was chosen as the subject of their tests.

A large team of technicians came aboard and set up a great deal of test apparatus and were soon ready to start work. However there was then some delay, for the overheating only occurred in heavy weather conditions and so the team had to wait patiently until the weather produced the right sea state. Luckily, when the right conditions came along, it did not take the experts long to identify the trouble. The problem was that the considerable hull flexure which occurred in the frigates in rough seas had not been taken into account. This movement was enough to impose stresses on the roller bearings which they had not been designed to suffer. The remedy was quite simple. Some suitable shims were inserted in strategic positions and no further problems ensued. *Blackwood* was then released from her overlong stay at Boston and caught up with the delayed *Bazeley* for the Bermuda workup. She sailed from there as one of the four DE's which left on 30 June on escort duty.

The next of the 4th EG members was *Drury*. She was unique among the Captains in two respects. Not only was she the only one of the British contingent not to be built at Boston but she was also the first of them to suffer a name change. She was laid down at Philadelphia in July, 1941, but many changes in priorities had slowed down work on her until it was almost at a standstill. Then, in January, 1943, her fitting out was resumed and she was ready for commissioning on 12 April. The Admiralty Ships Names Committee had designated her as *Cockburn* after Rear Admiral Cockburn of the 74 gun *Albion*. However, a historian in the Admiralty discovered that this officer had commanded a naval battalion under General Ross in 1813 and had taken part in the assault upon Washington. During this operation he had successfully destroyed many installations in the dockyard. Worse than this, he had also burned down the revered White House! Diplomatic circles were aghast. Not wishing to offend by naming one of the US gift horses after a *persona non grata* in their history books, hasty instructions for a name change were issued. She was given the next available name in alphabetical order, which was *Drury*.

Her trials seem to have been completed without any problems but her work up at Bermuda was protracted by what seemed to be an interminable number of engine room and propeller defects which kept her shuttling back and forth between Bermuda and Boston for some weeks. Superstitious crew members even suggested that she was haunted. Perhaps old Admiral Cockburn was to blame and his ghost was getting its own back for not having his name revived? The repair staff at Boston finally overcame her many problems and, by the end of June, she was ready for her first Atlantic crossing.

Bentinck (which was to be the eventual Group Leader of the 4th EG) was completed on 19 May, 1943, closely followed by *Byard* 18 June and *Calder* on 5 July. None of these had any delays during their early days. *Bentinck* in fact passed through trials and work up so rapidly that she caught up with the diesel division and joined them in escorting the cruiser *Phoebe* and battleship *Queen Elizabeth* to the UK on 30 June. The DE's parted company with the big ships at Plymouth on 9 July and all four (*Bazeley, Blackwood, Drury* and *Bentinck*) then proceeded to their future base at Belfast. *Byard* reached the UK some time later. The complement of the 4th EG was complete when *Calder* arrived at the end of September.

*   *   *

The formation of the Group had begun long before this. Commander E. Chavasse, who described himself as a neutral from Southern Ireland, had been appointed as Group Leader and told to get his command operational by 30 July. As we have seen, *Calder* was still in US waters, furthermore *Bentinck* was being delayed by extensive first of class trials in the Clyde, so the Commander did not even have his Leader ship available. Western Approaches (WA) Command had tried to persuade him to take one of the Evarts class but he was only prepared to do this on a temporary basis. Having already had a distinguished career in the Battle of the Atlantic in the ex-USN Destroyer *Broadway* which was Leader of the Canadian C2 Group, he well knew the importance of having a fast ship under him and he waited patiently until *Bentinck* was available.

For his first operation, he chose *Blackwood* as Leader and to make up the full group of six he had *Byard, Bazeley* and *Drury* all rightful members of 4EG and co-opted *Burges*, which was awaiting allocation to the 3rd EG. A Free Dutch sloop, *Jan Marits*, completed the number. The orders for this first operation were quite straightforward. They were to escort a combined convoy (KMS23 and OS53) as far as Gibraltar. Other ships would join them and the combined convoy would then sail south to a point off Casablanca where 38EG would relieve 4EG, allowing them to refuel and join a homebound convoy for the return trip. Fate was to complicate this simple plan, however.

The convoys set out in early August and the first six days of the trip were quite uneventful. They knew that this state of affairs was unlikely to continue as their route was to take them well within range of German bombers based in France and most convoys were being attacked by aircraft in this area. They were no exception. When they had reached a point some 150 miles NW of Lisbon, they were attacked by seventeen Focke-Wulfs, each carrying two very heavy bombs. Since these air attacks were a regular feature in these waters, the Admiralty had arranged for extra AD cover to be on hand and on this occasion the 4th EG were very relieved to have the eight 4.5" guns of the cruiser, *Scylla* and the 4" guns of the sloops *Fal, Trent, Test* and *Stork* to produce a healthy protective barrage through these dangerous waters. This kept the German planes at very high altitude, making bomb aiming difficult. In his autobiography, Commander Chavasse also records that the Captains joined in the gunfire. He freely admitted that their 3" shells contributed very little to the defensive umbrella that the heavier guns of the other ships were putting up. He wrote that their participation in the barrage was little more effective than throwing up tennis balls. Being close to base and having large reserves of fuel, the Germans were in no hurry and kept up their leisurely attacks for about two hours. The barrage kept them high and their aim was poor, so most of their bombs missed. The gunnery officers in the other DE's were just as disappointed with the ineffectiveness of the 3" guns as their Leader was. Long afterwards, one of them admitted in the group paying off book that the inexperience of his gun crews in *Drury* added to the general waste of ammunition. His after gun had fired seventy rounds but none had exploded because all the fuzes had been wrongly set. The excuse given was that his range tables had not yet come to light. Commander Chavasse, perhaps generously, does not mention this but such gross inefficiency must have warranted a severe reprimand at the very least. *Drury* had taken part in practice AD fire on a number of occasions, so the excuse of mising range tables doesn't hold water. It is more likely that the inexperienced gun crew loaded the rounds without setting the fuzes at all.

The merchant ships were the primary targets, of course, but the escorts were occasionally singled out for attack. Fast ships expertly handled are well nigh impossible targets for high level bombers though, and the nearest bomb recorded by *Blackwood* was at least 200 yards away. Only two of the thirty-four bombs found their mark; one hit and damaged the mercantile *Elizabeth Massey* but she did not sink. Another ship, *Warfield* was not so fortunate. She caught fire and, as she carried ammunition, her crew quickly abandoned. They were picked up by the rescue ship *Rathlin*. *Bazeley* closed in to give aid if necessary and to sink the crippled ship by gunfire. The subsequent attempts to do so were embarrassing. Eighteen rounds were fired at point blank range and every one hit the stricken merchant ship but failed to do any damage. Some merely made little round holes and some were even seen to ricochet off the ship's hull, doing no more than scraping off paint. Trying different tactics, Lieutenant-Commander Brock steamed his ship past *Warfield* at close range and fired shallow set depth charges to explode close to her. It was hoped that these would spring her plates open but that ploy too was a failure. Realizing that *Bazeley* was at great risk if the ammunition ship blew up, Commander Chavasse ordered Brock to abandon these foolhardy attempts and leave *Warfield* to her fate.

By this time, the German planes had dropped all their bombs and returned to base. After recovering from this baptism of fire, the convoy continued on its way. When the burning *Warfield* had been left some five miles astern she exploded spectacularly, making *Bazeley*'s crew only too well aware that they had been dicing with death. She was then allocated to escort the damaged *Elizabeth Massey* which was in great difficulty and could not keep up with the convoy. Sadly, her engine room problems increased and she never did reach Gibraltar but limped into the neutral port of Lisbon, whereupon *Bazeley* left her and rejoined the convoy.

Two other convoys now joined them as planned. Just as the escorts began the usual thankless task of coaxing the new arrivals into their allotted convoy positions, disaster struck in the form of a dense blanket of fog. Confident of *Blackwood*'s efficient radar eye, Commander Chavasse led her into the milling throng of ships to try to control the situation before absolute chaos resulted in multiple collisions. He soon had cause to regret this bold action. All *Blackwood*'s electric power suddenly failed and she drifted to a halt as helpless as any of the blind merchant ships. First thoughts were that it was merely a case of 'breakeritis' and that it would be remedied instantly but many minutes passed and there was still no sign of *Blackwood* coming back to life. The situation was even more frightening than the air attack had been. All on the bridge fervently prayed that no merchant ship would blunder into them as they wallowed helplessly without radar protection. It was quickly realized that the problem was something more serious than the falling off of a main breaker switch but everyone found it extremely difficult to wait in patience as the technicians down below went through all their check routines to diagnose the fault. There were huge sighs of relief when all power was eventually restored. Commander Chavasse, who came from a religious family, records in his memoirs that it really was a miracle of Providence that none of the ships had rammed them, or each other.

Some time after the convoy had eventually been sorted out and sailed into clearer weather, a further emergency began to loom up. They had passed the position where the 38th EG should have met and relieved them and taken charge of the convoys but there was no sign of them. At first there was no great concern; the 4th EG had no choice but to remain with the convoy. But surely it would not be long before the other group turned up to allow them into Casablanca to refuel?

Arrangements had been made for fuel to be waiting at this North African port but they were soon well south of it and sailing on down the West African coast. There were still no signs of the 38th EG. Signals were made to the Admiralty requesting guidance but the latter seemed to be maintaining radio silence as far as the 4th EG was concerned. Resignedly, they continued southwards with the engineers making continuous anxious checks on emptying fuel tanks and navigators desperately plotting to ascertain which port of call they could reach before they finally came to a standstill.

It was not until the seventeenth day of the voyage that the 38th EG fianlly caught up with them, just as they were at the very limit of their endurance. By this time the only possible place they could reach was Dakar, some 1,500 miles beyond their original refuelling port. Whether or not there would be the right kinds of fuel available in this Free French port was conjectural. The Admiralty still maintained a non-committal silence so they had no choice but to stay with the convoy. They had fuel enough to reach Dakar and, at the very worst, they would only be stranded there until a tanker could be sent to their rescue, possibly from Freetown. When their destination was announced to the lower deck, one or two of the older hands, who recalled lecherous runs ashore in such places before the war, spun tot time yarns to the youngsters which made their eyes pop out. No one believed them, of course, but they added spice to the prospect of exploring Dakar.

In the event there was fuel available at Dakar and the crews spent three days there whilst the ships were made ready for the return trip. There is an account of this visit which has an almost comic opera ring in Commander Chavasse's unpublished memoirs.

We spent three days there and found some Free French ships berthed there commanded by an Admiral. I went across to pay my official call upon him and was received with very stiff correctness but no cameraderie. I am sure it was natural that he still resented the bombardment in 1940 of French ships by Admiral Somerville with Force H to keep them out of

German hands at the fall of France. He told me that he would return my call the next day. After leaving him, I had a word with the French Officer of the Watch and borrowed a bugle. I knew that there was a man in *Blackwood* who could in fact blow a bugle and I was determined to soften the old geezer up and receive him in full ceremonial style. When, at the appointed time, he hobbled across with a gouty foot, he wasn't just piped over the side in the manner of small ships, but got the surprise of his life by being received by a full guard of honour with fixed bayonets and the blast of an Admiral's salute on the bugle. He finally went ashore in great good humour, slightly tipsy.

And WE went ashore and had a riotious evening around the town. I believe our chaps had great fun in an establishment called Madame Lilly's; but whether it was due to the good relations with the said Madame or with the gouty French Admiral, I find these words in the post war unofficial record of 4th EG (which I did NOT write) 'As a goodwill mission to the Dakar French this visit was an undoubted success' We may not have received the angel's call for peace on earth but we did perhaps make a small advance in good will towards man – and woman.

Madame Lilly's was, as may be guessed, the local bordello-type estaminet, common in so many foreign ports in those days. The estabishment had been well patronized and, grudgingly, the youngsters had to admit that the tot time tales had been right after all. Many had left childish innocence behind after sharing in the exhibitions and lewd capers with Madam Lilly's girls.

The 4th EG bade sad farewells to Dakar on 26 August, just three weeks after leaving Belfast. During the return voyage, they met and escorted two ships off the African coast. One was the French *Canada* which was taking 800 women and children back to mainland France. She was left at Casablanca and the group continued with *Aorangi* to the UK. Commander Chavasse found nothing worthy of note during this return trip, but those whose interest revolved around shoreside entertainment commented very favourably upon their short visit to Casablanca.

It had been hoped that by the time the group returned to Belfast, *Bentinck* would be ready to assume her role as Group Leader but she was still being held up by her First of Class trials. When, therefore, Commander Chavasse was given details of the Group's next operations in September, he embarked in *Byard* to command as Support Group for two westbound convoys. Apart from the weather being atrocious for this time of year, this trip was quite peaceful. The U-boats were still keeping a low profile and not a single attack was made against either convoy. Commander Chavasse's report mentions that his ships suffered an unacceptable number of gyro failures during the heavy weather, indicating that not all of them had yet had the Arma gyros replaced by Pollock Dock at this time. The crews had a welcome rest period at Argentia whilst waiting for allocation to a return convoy. The USN had set up a large base there, complete with all their usual luxuries and home comforts and they enjoyed American food and amenities in the Post Exchange (PX) and the USO club which awakened memories of halcyon days in Boston. It was only a brief interlude though and they were soon back at the mercy of the elements for an equally rough passage back to Belfast.

Bentinck had finished her trials by the time the Group reached Ulster and, thankfully, Commander Chavasse crossed to the Clyde to take over command. He had two American passengers on the return trip. These were USN Secretary Knox and Admiral Stark, who was C-in-C of all USN forces in Europe. Chavasse relates that during this trip he had heated discussions with Knox about the shortcomings of the old four-stacker US destroyers, speaking with authority having served in one of them and knowing their many defects only too well. Commander Chavasse was well known for speaking his mind, even to senior officers but his forceful comments do not seem to have caused an international rift! Admiral Stark even congratulated him for having taken some of the wind out of Knox's sails.

The 4th EG was now up to full strength; *Bentinck, Bazeley, Byard, Blackwood, Calder* and *Drury*. They also retained *Burges* as a super-numerary until her final group allocation was decided. Their next operation was to take them right into the thick of the renewed U-boat pack offensive. The Germans had withdrawn from the Atlantic after suffering disastrous losses in the earlier months of 1943 but Doenitz was thrusting them back into the fray with new weapons which he hoped would enable them to strike back effectively against the increased number of escorts now ranged against them. These were the T5 'GNAT' torpedoes, equipped with hydrophone devices which enabled them to home in on ships' propeller noises, and were to prove a fairly successful defence against attacking escort vessels.

This next operation began on 10 October, 1943, when they set out as escorts to the westbound convoy ONS20. The convoy was routed on a course some 300 miles south of Iceland and there was another faster one (ON206) on a more or less parallel course 60 miles to the north. Neither was molested during the first fifteen or sixteen days but then several U-boats were detected by HFDF close to ON206. On the following day, there was evidence that ONS20 was also being shadowed. Air cover from Iceland was stepped up for both convoys and aircraft were soon reporting U-boat sightings. They began the offensive by sinking two of them and forcing several others to dive out of sight. At the end of the day, the Germans drew first blood by sinking the SS *Essex Lance* which had straggled behind ONS20. She broke in two but all her crew were taken off by the rescue ship.

Bentinck made contact with the U-boat responsible. It was making off on the surface so, calling for *Drury* to join him, Commander Chavasse set off in pursuit at high speed. The quarry dived when the two frigates were within visual range and fired a T5 as she did so. However, *Drury* and *Bentinck* did a neat double side step, which confused the torpedo's homing circuits and it passed harmlessly between them. The diversion had given the U-boat's CO time to dive deeper however and neither ship was able to gain Asdic contact. *Drury* was left to sit over the enemy position whilst *Bentinck* went back to join the convoy screen. During the ensuing night, several U-Boats were detected by radar but the escorts were only able to force the submarines to dive and abandon attacks. During that night it became clear that a whole U-boat pack was stalking ONS20, mostly from astern. According to Professor Rohwer, the German U-boat historian, at least twelve boats of the Schlieffen group were involved.

The defences of ONS20 had therefore been reinforced by B7 Support Group, detached from ON206, and whilst on their way, the corvette *Sunflower* had detected and sunk one more of the enemy (U631). The following day was hectic; the ships of B7 and 4th EG were continuously detecting surfaced U-boats and forcing them to submerge, even if none made successful attacks. The covering aircraft of Coastal Command were equally busy and sank one boat and inflicted severe casualties among the gun crews of two others.

Byard was in the vicinity of one of the boats when she was sunk and actually sighted some thirty German survivors in the water. She requested permission to rescue them but, with sincere regret, Commander Chavasse had to refuse. His first duty was to the convoy which was still under attack. The Commander was a God-fearing man and it was with a heavy heart that he ordered *Byard* to rejoin the screen. He records that it was the most difficult decision he had ever been called upon to make and in his words it was a sad Sunday for thirty Germans and for him. According to German records, this boat was U450 but there is doubt about this.

The refusal to allow *Byard* to be diverted was, however, instrumental in the destruction of yet another U-boat. On her way back to the convoy *Byard* made a firm Asdic contact and ran in to deliver a text book depth-charge attack. The boat was forced to surface and the crew attempted to man their gun but many were hit by *Byard*'s machine-gun fire. Eventually the Germans abandoned ship and a number were rescued. *Byard* continued to fire at the stricken boat with her 3″ guns but no one believes that these were responsible for her sinking. Commander Chavasse's version of the attack confirms that *Byard* hit the U-boat at the base of the conning tower with her first 3″ round, but he too doubts that this was the cause of her slipping stern first into the depths some time after. Their victim had been U841 and there were actually twenty-seven survivors. They learned, by sheer coincidence, that U841 had sailed from Trondheim on 10 October, the very same day that *Byard* had left Belfast. Her only officer to survive, Paul Voss, said that his wife was expecting a child that very day and, quite apart from this, his rescuers agreed that he deserved to live since, as he swam towards *Byard*, he was supporting a young lad who had been wounded in the stomach. This was no mean feat in a water temperature of below 40 degrees. Men of the Royal Navy have always been magnanimous to fellow mariners in distress, even enemies.

There was great pride and satisfaction in *Byard* after this action. Not only had she destroyed a U-boat during her very first real attack but she had also earned the distinction of being the first of all the Captains to fly the 'Jolly Roger' of success. One of the proudest of her company must have been her Gunner, Mr Love, who although he was one of the junior officers, had been the Officer of the Watch (OOW) and had directed the attack.

It was almost dark by the time *Byard* rejoined the convoy and meanwhile a Sunderland flying-boat JM712S had attacked and straddled two more U-boats, but accurate German AD fire had killed three of its crew and it was forced to put down in the sea. *Drury* was the closest ship and she was sent to the rescue. The two U-boats were still on the surface savouring their success but dived as soon as *Drury* appeared. She was able to rescue the remaining eight men of the aircraft's crew under difficult conditions but meanwhile the U-boats had escaped.

The pack attack continued through the night. One of the U-boats was run over by the convoy and was picked up by *Bentinck*'s Asdic but the Germans dived deep and eluded attack. During the forenoon, signals from the U-boats indicated that they were still lingering and following half heartedly astern but these signals gradually faded and it became evident that the enemy had been well and truly beaten and were abandoning the attack. The surface escorts were jubilant; they had only sunk two of the five U-boats destroyed but their alertness and efficiency had enabled them to form a virtually impenetrable screen around ONS20. Only one straggler had been lost and both the Admiralty and Western Approaches Command sent congratulory signals, appropriately enough on Trafalgar Day.

The 4th EG set out from Argentia with the return convoy HX263 on

28 October but the U-boats had seemingly withdrawn again and this voyage was without a single warlike incident. Eventually, in December, the Admiralty made a press release about the successful battle around ONS20 and there were banner headlines about it in the national papers but by this time the 4th EG had taken part in other successful operations.

During the month of November, 1943, the most concentrated actions against U-boats were taking place in the Bay of Biscay area where the Germans were making desperate attempts to sink troop and supply ships on their way to the Mediterranean theatre. The 4th EG joined the action when, on the 19th, they were ordered to sea with despatch to support Sierra Leone convoy SL139 which was under heavy threat from U-boats. They reached the designated point in the Bay by the 21st but by then the convoy's close escort had dealt so efficiently with the U-boats that they had retired to regroup. Commander Chavasse was ordered to sweep the reciprocal course of the convoy and break up any threatened attack. The group's next action did not involve U-boats however. This time it was a group of Heinkel 177's and instead of conventional bombs they were using the latest 'glider bomb' secret weapons. These had first been used at the Salerno landings and were later to be used with devastating effect off Anzio. Fortunately, the group which attacked 4EG did not appear to be very expert at guiding them. They only scored near misses and the single casualty suffered was one man on *Drury*'s quarterdeck who received minor splinter wounds. Commander Chavasse had read that radio experts suggested that any electrical device giving out even weak electro-magnetic radiations might interfere with the guidance systems of these bombs. He describes amusingly how he plugged in his electric razor and waved it at the approaching bombs but doubted very much whether this did much to defend *Bentinck*.

The main action began on the night of the 22nd when the second division diesels *Blackwood, Bazeley* and *Drury* made Asdic contact with a submarine which turned out to be commanded by a very experienced officer. Attack after attack made by the DE's was evaded with consummate skill. Each time the junior division ships lost contact but each time the determined A/S operators on one ship or another would find the quarry again and more depth charges would rain down. No less than twenty-two attacks were recorded before dawn and eventually, although there was no positive evidence that the U-boat had been destroyed, there were no more Asdic echoes and the three Captains put in a tentative claim that they had achieved a 'kill'. When their attack reports were later analysed by the Admiralty committee which decided such claims, the verdict was no more than a probable kill. After the war, when German records were consulted, it was discovered that the U-boat (U648) had definitely been destroyed and the official records now give equal credit to *Blackwood, Bazeley* and *Drury*. Because this final decision was so belated, it is probably the case that many men in the three ships are still unaware of this victory. (*Bazeley* and *Drury* were returned to the United States in August, 1945, before there had been time to consult German records and, as we shall see in the next chapter, many of *Blackwood*'s crew were dead by then).

During the following day, 23 November, the first division ships *Bentinck, Calder* and *Byard* were detached to cover another convoy OS59 and this splitting of the group posed certain problems. The lavish expenditure of depth-charges during the twenty-two attacks upon U648 had left the diesel ships with few reserves and the shorter ranged turbo ships, although having plenty of depth-charges, were running low on fuel. As the group was not far from the Azores at the time, Commander Chavasse decided to leave the second division to its own resources and take the turbos into Horta where they could refuel and possibly obtain depth-charges to bring back to replenish the diesel ships.

Left on their own, the second division continued the action. The following account describes one of those strange whims of fate which so often decide the border line between death and survival in times of war. It concerns the destruction of U600 which must have been the unluckiest U-boat victim during the whole war.

Drury had made a long range radar contact during the night 23–24 November and passed the bearing to *Bazeley* which was much closer to the surfaced U-boat. When she had reached the area indicated, *Bazeley* was still unable to pick up any target by radar or Asdic and fired a series of starshells on the suspected bearing but these revealed nothing. It began to look as though either *Drury*'s radar report had been wrong or that the U-boat had dived deep and escaped so, after some time, the search was abandoned. As it happened, there was still a starshell loaded in *Bazeley*'s 'B' gun and, since it is not customary for guns to remain loaded, the order was given to clear the gun. The starshell was fired off *on a purely random bearing* merely to empty the gun but, as the bridge personnel idly watched the parachute flare, they were astounded to see that the eerie glow revealed the clear outline of a U-boat. The hunt was on once more and *Bazeley* closed in to deliver Hedgehog attacks immediately after the sub had crash dived. Three attacks were made with no result but there was a gratifying explosion after the fourth and an even louder one a few seconds later. Meanwhile *Blackwood* had appeared on the scene and saturated the area with depth-charges for good measure. No Asdic contact could be found after this and the U-boat was presumed sunk. Regrettably this was only logged as another 'probable' since no tangible evidence in the form of wreckage or human remains had been recovered. However, as in the case of U648, the post war records confirmed that *Blackwood* and *Bazeley* had sunk U600.

Meanwhile the first division ships had successfully taken on fuel and depth-charges at Horta. There had been some reluctance to agree to Commander Chavasse's request for weapons but eventually our oldest allies, the Portuguese, although neutral, did break the rules and part with some charges. It had been intended to transfer these to the Evarts division at sea. However, by the time the Group was reunited, the weather had deteriorated so much that this was impossible. Their stocks of depth-charges were further depleted after their recent actions so the Leader sent them in to Horta, hoping that they too would be able to obtain depth-charges from the Portuguese. *Bazeley* and *Drury* set out immediately for the Azores on the 25 November but *Blackwood*, having slightly more fuel in reserve, was sent off to assist a crashed aircraft before joining them at Horta.

The first division were then ordered to sweep to the south-west in the direction of the next Sierra Leone convoy SL140. However, before long, signals from the almost weaponless second division reported U-boats in their vicinity as they sailed towards the Azores. Commander Chavasse changed course and the three turbo DE's made all haste to assist their diesel division. When they caught up with them *Bazeley* reported having sighted two U-boats in the area 40deg. 25mins N, 21 deg. 21 mins, W. *Drury* had attacked them but they had both dived deep.

Sending *Bazeley* and *Drury* on their way, Commander Chavasse took over the search with his turbo ships. After some time an Asdic contact was obtained with one or other of the two U-boats and a grim three hour battle then ensued. The German CO was obviously of the old school, well experienced at twisting and turning to evade the attackers. *Bentinck* and *Calder* each attacked six times and *Byard* five during this relentless hunt but, apart from a great mass of air bubbles which broke surface, which may have been a decoy device, there was no evidence of success. The contact was eventually lost and the three DE's resumed their course towards convoy SL140. It may well be that their attacks had been partially successful however. Post war German records show that two of the Weddingen Group U-boats had been damaged in this area at the time and the 4th EG's target may well have been one of them.

At the end of the day upon which this abortive attack had been made, the turbos of EG4 made yet another U-boat contact by radar. Commander Chavasse ordered the attack and they set off on a long stern chase. It was dark before they closed in on their quarry and, although a spread of starshell clearly illuminated the stern-on U-boat, it was much too small a target to shoot at. The ships plunged on towards it at full speed and the German commander was cool enough to let them get within two miles before he dived. *Calder* quickly made Asdic contact and made the first attack. *Bentinck* was not very far behind and was closing in for her turn when she suddenly staggered after what Commander Chavasse described as the biggest bang he had ever heard in his life. The U-boat had fired a T5 as she dived and it was this weapon which, for some reason exploding before contact, had gone off close under *Bentinck*'s stern. These torpedoes had contact fuses but fortunately this one had failed and the weapon had not actually hit *Bentinck*. It was a near thing however. Eyewitnesses swear that the after part of their Leader ship literally became airborne and Commander Chavasse writes that his ship twanged and whipped for at least two minutes after the explosion. Much of her internal furniture, but no vital machinery, was torn from its deck fittings and thrown into the air, as were most of her crew. To add to the confusion, the valve on the steam siren on the funnel jammed open and emitted an earsplitting blast until someone climbed the funnel and closed the valve. It must be said that this incident gave the lie to the fears that the all welded frigates would never stand up to any punishment. When *Bentinck*'s crew had recovered their composure and damage control parties had made detailed inspections, it seemed nothing less than a miracle that there had been no serious damage and as Commander Chavasse remarked, it did much to induce confidence in the sturdy construction of the DE's.

Whilst the Group Leader had been going through this traumatic experience, *Calder* had turned and made another determined attack on the elusive U-boat. She followed this by another after which there was a satisfying underwater explosion but Asdic contact was again made so there could be no claim of a 'kill'. The trail went cold some time after this and 4EG had to admit that another potential victim had got away with it. It could be, however, that this was the other damaged boat of the Weddingen Group.

Calder then developed some engine fault and, with her speed reduced, she was sent to join the close escort of the convoy when the group caught up with it at dawn. *Blackwood* also rejoined them briefly after her fruitless search for the crashed plane. Enemy aircraft shadowed the convoy throughout the day but no U-boat attacks developed. By nightfall they were joined by the redoubtable Captain Walker with the famous 2nd EG which took over the screening of the convoy on the port side whilst 4EG covered the starboard flank. A U-boat pack, presumably the Weddingen group, made bold attempts to get at the merchant ships during the night but the escorts maintained a tight screen and none broke through.

It was a similar story throughout the next few days and several of the 4th EG ships were in action again. *Blackwood* attacked a U-boat during the night of 27 November and *Byard* had a go at another on the following day. *Bentinck* chased one during the night of the of the 28–29 and shortly after *Blackwood* attacked another. Even the 'lame duck' *Calder* left the screen to follow up a firm contact at 0500; *Byard* joined her and both were counter-attacked by a T5 but, again, its guidance system was confused by having two targets and missed both, to explode harmlessly at the end of its range. None of these attacks were successful however. By the 30th the U-boats had apparently given up the chase and their radio signals soon faded astern.

Blackwood did eventually get her run into Horta; she did better than the others, in fact, since she had to wait a week until special lubricating oil was available. This is remembered by her surviving crew as a week of monumental hangovers but it marked her final connection with the 4th EG. When she returned to the UK it was found that she had internal structural damage. There were weld failures in fourteen of her forward ribs, probably due to the shock of so many DC explosions during the actions in the Bay. She was placed in dockyard hands for repair and missed the 4th EG's next operation. In fact, she never did rejoin them. Her place was taken by the 'supernumerary' *Burges* and she eventually joined up with the 3rd EG, a move which, as we shall see later, was to sound her death knell.

This exciting involvement in the Bay Offensive was to be 4th EG's last warlike foray for many months. On return to Belfast, they were given a task unique among the WA escort groups. As Commander Chavasse comments in his memoirs, the 4th EG were given the dullest job in the whole Command. They were to be the permanent escorts to the large liners acting as troopships from the UK to Naples. Such operations entailed great responsibility but were singularly devoid of contact with the enemy. In the following months the route they followed became so monotonous that it was universally known as The Tramline to Naples. It was important work but it did become repetitive and, time after time, when Commander Chavasse got back to report to Admiral Sir Max Horton, he requested that the 4th EG be sent back to the real task of hunting U-boats. Each time the C-in-C promised that the next trip would be the last, but it never was – right up to the time that Chavasse left the ship.

Most of the tramline voyages were so uneventful that it was almost as though the 4th EG had been opted out of the war and they became the envy of all other WA groups which were continuing the battle against the U-boats in the Atlantic. All the troopships used in the KMF convoys were large fast liners which could easily maintain an average convoy speed of up to 15 knots. This meant that they were virtually immune to U-boat attack. Even if they were sighted, no U-boat could possibly shadow them until nightfall at that speed. Furthermore, because of their vital importance, the convoys were given priority for air cover, which made daylight attack suicidal.

Many of the men were only too pleased that fate had virtually taken them out of the front line for a while but quite a few shared their leader's resentment of having lost the chance to be at close grips with the enemy as they had previously been. Even these had to admit, however, that although the KMF trips were boring and peaceful they did have their compensations. Even during the winter, the weather in the Mediterranean was usually considerably more pleasant than in the Atlantic but when spring came it was positively idyllic. There was no let up in the amount of sea time put in however; each round trip to Naples was the equivalent of a double Atlantic crossing and there was little respite between them. Naples was an extremely busy port and the turn round time after the troops had disembarked was kept to a bare minimum in order not to take up valuable harbour space. Similarly, at the Belfast end, the ships were given only a brief period to carry out maintenance and replenishment before they were back on the tramlines for another trip. Naples itself, which was the destination of every KMF convoy, was not a particularly pleasant place at which to spend time ashore; not only was it notorious for a particularly virulent strain of unsocial disease but it was packed with men of all arms of the Allied Forces, mostly Americans, whose shore patrols were renowned for the indiscriminate use of their night sticks. Thick heads were common from both the local wines and the frequent brushes with the US patrols. Sometimes, when suitable excuses could be made, the lads did get ashore in some of the better Mediterranean ports such as Algiers, Oran and Gibraltar. If, as sometimes happened, one of the watches got a bit of home leave during the Belfast stopovers, they were welcomed home with more than usual enthusiasm, because of the gifts they bore. They brought fresh oranges and other fruit long unseen in UK and various Mediterraean artifacts reminiscent of the presents which regular sailors took home after peacetime foreign commissions.

Even more reminiscent of the peacetime Navy was the occasion in October, 1944, when the Group actually put on a rowing regatta at Naples during a longer than usual spell there. It narrowly was won by *Bazeley* with *Drury* second and *Calder* last.

Pleasant though these trips were in many respects, Commander Chavasse bore tremendous responsibility during these months. Hundreds of thousands of Allied troops sailed under the 4th EG's protection but not a single man was lost due to enemy action. On one occasion, just before D-day, he had charge of just under half the total number of large troopships the Allies possessed, packed with 65,000 men on their way back from the Italian theatre to take part in the Normandy invasion. This was one of his last trips with the Group however. The 4th EG continued the KMF convoys for some time but Commander Chavasse got his wish at last and was taken out of *Bentinck* in July, 1944. He had been continuously engaged in the Battle of the Atlantic since early 1942 and his new appointment was in the yacht *Philante*, T. O. M. Sopwith's luxury yacht, which was being used as an escort group training ship. After that he joined the Western Approaches staff at Liverpool, an appointment which, sadly, was instrumental in ending his naval career. He was invalided out with tuberculosis after the war, a disease probably contracted during his spell in the poorly-ventilated underground bunkers at Liverpool. After recovery, he was ordained as a priest and had a second career in the Church before retiring to Cyprus where he spent many happy years until his death.

The Group was taken over by a new SO, Commander Garwood, and for several more months continued to plod along the well worn tram lines. During this period there was another change in the group's formation. *Burges* which had replaced *Blackwood* in December, 1943, was stricken with engine trouble which required attention in dockyard hands and her place in 4EG was taken by the newcomer *Pasley*, which remained with them until the end of the war. *Burges* went on to join the 17th EG.

Pasley, a diesel powered Evart, had a most remarkable early history. She was completed in November, 1943, at the time when the manpower pipeline ran into problems and there was no crew available for her at Boston. She was also fated to have three CO's, three crews and two different names, all in the space of three months. Her First Lieutenant had arrived at Boston on 1 Nov, 1943, the Engineer followed on the 4th and her first CO on the 5th; but, for some reason, he was changed the next day. More of her officers turned up on the 11th and were given to understand that the commissioning day was only ten days ahead. But there were still no signs of a crew. The ship was ready to receive stores on the 15th and a scratch crew had to be borrowed from other ships to complete this task. There were hopeful signs during the next few days as a few ratings turned up to join her but by the 19th there were only eight Canadian stokers, a Petty Officer Steward, a Sick Berth Attendant (SBA) and six seamen. Commissioning day was then only two days off and it was obvious that there was only one solution. There had to be a mock commissioning ceremony. A surrogate crew was assembled from men in Fargo who were allocated to other ships. Rifles and webbing gear for the guard, and even a White Ensign, had to be borrowed from another ship. The name allocated to her was *Lindsay* and no sooner had she been so christened than all her temporary crew disappeared back to Fargo, leaving only her officers and a few men on board. Clearly the Navy Yard wanted her out of the way as soon as possible and the NOIC had meanwhile made contingency plans to deal with this situation. The crew of the old 'four stacker' *Buxton* had just handed over their ship to the RCN and were immediately drafted to Boston where they manned *Lindsay* and steamed her to Halifax where she was laid up in care and maintenance (C and M). A third CO had arrived to take over at this stage but after reaching Halifax on 8 December, he lost all his crew again because they had been sent back to Boston to collect yet another crewless DE (*Hoste*). Then, shortly after being reduced to 'C and M', there was a further problem. Strange mail began to arrive and it transpired that there was another *Lindsay* in commission with the RCN! A report was made to Admiralty, and with no more formality than a signalled instruction, *Lindsay* was renamed as *Pasley*.

Eventually there were three other DE's laid up at Halifax and no one seemed to know how long they might be stranded there. It was rumoured that the RCN had been approached and was endeavouring to muster some merchant seamen who were capable of steaming the ships to the UK. However, nothing certain was known, until 13 January when *Pasley*'s CO was given two hours' notice to expect a crew to embark. He was uncertain what to expect but it is on record that he was staggered when a motley crowd of Canadians arrived, dressed in such a variety of flamboyant clothing that they resembled nothing so much as a gang of lumberjacks! *Pasley*'s officers soon discovered that they were all volunteers and that most of them had some experience at sea with merchant ships. Nevertheless, there were some who had never set foot on a ship before. They were all keen enough to learn though and it speaks much for their enthusiasm that within three weeks they had learned enough to be capable of taking *Pasley* to sea. Some had even mastered the rudiments of gun drill. Despite certain reservations and misgivings, *Pasley* sailed for the UK on 7 February, 1944.

There could not have been too many problems because she arrived safely at Lissahally on 16 February. Her RN crew arrived to take over two days later and, after a riotous time ashore, her Canadian crew departed back to Canada.

Most of the diesel-powered Evarts had been incorporated into one or other of the Belfast EG's by this time and no group seemed to need *Pasley*. She was given harbour training, did sea trials and even went to Tobermory on 12 March for the usual two week work-up but after this there was still no group allocation. She had one trip with the old V and W destroyer *Watchman* escorting SS *Empress of Russia* to Iceland and was then taken in hand at Pollock Dock for the usual conversion refit, during which her ship's company were much gratified to be given nineteen days leave to each watch. The refit ended on 2 June but while most of her sister DE's were at sea taking some part in the historic invasion of Europe, *Pasley* doggedly carried out post refit trials until 8 June, when she achieved at least some status by being attached to the 4th EG for training purposes. As we already know, this attachment became permanent when *Burges* went into dock with engine room problems and *Pasley* remained with the group for the rest of the war.

The first three months of *Pasley*'s time with the 4th EG was, of course, on the KMF tramlines. At one time it seemed likely that these would go on for ever but they finally came to an end in October, 1944. We now resume the 4th EG saga at this point, when they were returned to the reality of war in the Western Approaches.

Their new operational area was to be the inshore waters around Northern Ireland and the Scottish Isles. U-boats were making audacious attacks on many ships in these areas during the final stages of the war. All the famous aces had been lost by this time but one must admit that their successors in the remaining U-boats certainly did not lack courage, even if they were inexperienced. They had been driven from the broad reaches of the Atlantic but it must have taken just as much bravery to operate in these inshore waters, often within sight of what was, to them, the enemy coast.

The weather in those waters towards the end of the year, varied between rough and atrocious and whilst enduring endless watchkeeping on the bridge, lashed by gales and drenched by freezing spray, the crews looked back with longing to the more halcyon days in the Mediterranean, particularly as their hard work and discomfort all seemed to be in vain. U-boats seemed to be as scarce as they had been during the previous ten months on the tramlines. Their first taste of excitement came on 26 January, 1945. The Group had spent the previous day at Milford Haven and were now back at sea carrying out the usual monotonous A/S sweep somewhere east of Cork. Suddenly a signal came through reporting that the frigate *Manners* of the B2EG had been torpedoed east of Dublin Bay and was still in contact with the U-boat. The 4th EG plus *Aylmer* of the 5th EG were the closest ships to the scene of action and all set out at high speed towards this area. *Manners* was still afloat when they arrived but was totally disabled with her stern section blown off. Despite the trauma of damage and casualties, her Asdic crew had resolutely maintained contact with the U-boat. Its CO was no doubt ignorant of the damage his target had suffered and was lying motionless on the sea bed in an attempt to avoid detection. Medical attention was sent from the relief ships and *Manners* was taken in tow towards Liverpool. Her CO had given precise bearings for the U-boat but there were so many wrecks in this area that it was a long time before any of the newcomers made contact. Eventually *Calder's* A/S men picked up something positive. The CO decided to do a series of slow runs with the echo sounder to build up a profile of the sea bed and this revealed the undoubted presence of a U-boat. It was motionless on the bottom. *Calder* immediately carried out a hedgehog attack, scored a hit and was rewarded by seeing the sub suddenly rise to the surface. *Calder* was in a perfect position to engage by gunfire but just at the time *Aylmer* arrived on the scene and promptly rammed the U-boat which quickly sank.

This was certainly a confused 'kill'. Under the circumstances it may be difficult to understand why *Manners* shared in the credits. She had not originally detected the U-boat until after she had been torpedoed but the Domestic Committee at Admiralty, which investigated the several claims, concluded that it was a creditable performance for her A/S crew to have maintained contact with the enemy during the frightening experience of two torpedo hits which had caused much damage and many casualties.

The official credits for sinking the U-boat (U1172) acknowledge this and the honours were shared between *Manners* herself, *Calder, Bentinck* and *Aylmer. Bentinck's* part is somewhat obscure but it seems that she was credited with guiding *Calder* towards the target initially. Following this brief flurry of action it was back to the soul destroying grind for the ships of 4EG. Winter passed into spring and at least the weather improved but the monotony of the A/S patrols dragged on for three more months without another contact with a U-boat. All the ships, except the newcomer *Pasley*, had by now earned shares in credits for successful attacks but the war was obviously nearly over and everyone was convinced that there would be no more battle honours. Then, suddenly, just a few weeks before the war actually ended, two swift victories came their way. The first took place on 8 April when one of *Calder's* sharp eyed lookouts sighted a periscope during a sweep off the south-west coast of Ireland. A very long group search followed after the enemy made the usual deep dive but eventually *Bentinck* and *Calder* shared equal honours for a confirmed kill (U774).

Their next patrol took them to waters north Ireland and it was in this area that *Bazeley, Bentinck* and *Calder* hounded U636 to its destruction on 21 April and hoisted the Jolly Roger for the last time. *Pasley* had still not shared in any of the successes and her CO complained in the Group paying off journal that she had always been stationed on the fringe of any action and had had little opportunity to carry out attacks. Her failure to share in any official credits was no indication that she had not played her part in the group actions. She had only been with them for ten months and nearly half of this had been on the 'tramlines' where none of them saw action. A/S work, among all naval operations, is a matter requiring the highest degree of teamwork and it was often the case that while individual ships were given the lion's share of credits, non-scorers such as *Pasley* contributed significantly to the team victories.

Victory in Europe followed closely on the heels of the 4th EG's last kill and their final operation as a cohesive group was a convoy to Russia on 12 May. One may well ask 'why a convoy in peacetime?' but it must be remembered that although most U-boats had surrendered tamely, it was still possible that some fanatical Nazi commander might ignore the cease fire. There were still active minefields to be negotiated as well, so it was politic to continue to convoy merchant ships for some time after VE Day. This last trip was the Group's only venture into Arctic waters and it was, of course, quite uneventful. It did give the men an opportunity to appreciate that relationships between us and our Russian Allies were still far from cordial. There were official attempts at fraternization but it was quite evident that there was an underlying attitude of deep distrust among the majority of the Soviet forces. Our lads were perfectly willing to be friendly but there overtures were for the most part coldly rebuffed. They were invited to a grand concert in an army barracks in Polyarnoe but the jovial atmosphere was somewhat soured by the fact that they had passed an obviously used gallows on the parade ground on the way in. No one was sorry to shake the snows of Russia off their boots to get back to Belfast. Sadly the return voyage was the last time the six ships sailed together.

There were great expectations of them being sent east to join the Pacific Fleet and the first division turbo ships were even earmarked for refits to prepare them for such service by having better AD armament fitted but VJ-Day arrived before these were completed. The diesel ships were disposed of in almost indecent haste and by 20 August, 1945, they had all been returned to the USA – almost before the ink was dry on the Japanese surrender documents. The turbo ships were not far behind. *Calder* went back to the USA on 19 October, *Byard* following on 12 December. All traces of that gallant fighting unit faded away when the Leader, *Bentinck*, crossed the Atlantic for the last time on 5 January, 1946.

Much of their time had been spent away from the main cauldron of war but they had certainly made up for this during the remainder of their short career – as their final score of five U-boats shows. They had also been one of the hardest worked groups in WA Command. *Drury's* log shows that she had steamed 130,000 miles during her first two years and this must be typical for the whole group, apart from *Pasley*, since none had lost much time through defects or repairs. This figure is a somewhat meaningless statistic perhaps but to make it more understandable it should be noted that it would take a ship eighteen months to cover this distance at a speed of 10 knots sailing continuously day and night without a break. To have covered this distance in two years is a fair indication that the 4th EG were not often guilty of 'swinging round the buoy' or being tied up to the dockyard wall!

TABLE OF U-BOAT SINKINGS BY THE 4TH ESCORT GROUP

Date	U-boat No.	Ships Involved.
17.10.43.	U 841	*Byard*
23.11.43.	U 648	*Bazeley*
		Blackwood, Drury
25.11.43.	U 600	*Bazeley, Blackwood*
26. 1.45.*	U1172	*Bentinck, Calder.*
		(Manners, Aylmer of 5EG)
8. 4.45.	U 774	*Bentinck, Calder*
21. 4.45.	U 636	*Bazeley, Bentinck,*
		Drury

* This was actually U 1051. See note on page 103

– 3 –

THE 3RD ESCORT GROUP

*(Berry, Blackwood, Cooke, Domett, Duckworth,
Essington, Braithwaite and Rowley).*

Transfers of the Captains to the Royal Navy had been made in ones and twos during early 1943 and it was to be several months after the formation of the 4th Escort Group before there were enough of them for the next Captains group, the 3rd, to come into being. Even then it was not up to full strength until the end of the year. Two of the ships which were to become part of this group were among the earliest to have been completed. The first was *Blackwood* whose early days with the 4th EG have already been chronicled and the other was *Berry* (DE 3) which had been commissioned at Boston on 15 March, 1943. It may be remembered that it is recorded in the previous chapter how *Berry* had gained advantage from *Bazeley*'s early engine trouble and escaped the Bermuda work-up by taking over the urgent cargo from her sister ship and making an earlier return to the UK than had been scheduled. She was one of the Evarts diesels and one of the few Captains to have twin Bofors guns instead of the US quad 1.1″ weapons. Having had only preliminary training at Casco Bay before reaching Belfast, she was sent to undergo three weeks of working-up under Admiral Stephenson, known as 'The Terror of Tobermory', and became operational in early June.

For some time she was loosely associated with other groups and Harry Smith (who was one of her Telegraphists) recalls an early trip to Freetown:

> The trip was as close escort to a SL convoy and during the outward trip we contacted a U-boat and the charges dropped subsequently must have had shallow settings because the ship was much shaken up. The U-boat escaped but, after the attack, *Berry* suffered heavy vibrations down aft

which indicated that there was trouble with one of our prop shafts. We were diverted into Casablanca where divers had a look but they couldn't find anything wrong and we proceeded on to Freetown and even completed the trip back to the UK.

On returning to Liverpool *Berry* was put into dry dock as the vibrations were still quite ominous. This close inspection showed up some weld failure on one of the 'A' brackets but it was not serious and was soon repaired. Her next operation – also remembered by Harry Smith was:

> A very rough patrol in the Bay of Biscay in company with *Scylla* and another cruiser, with some corvettes. The weather became diabolical and after three days the big ships had had enough and retired to Gibraltar, leaving the frigates to endure it for another week.

Scylla was employed as AD guard ship for passing convoys at this time but it is not certain what the small ships were doing unless they were the A/S screen for the cruisers.

As there were still not enough Captains to start forming another Group, *Berry* then had a short spell with the 4th EG in August and it was during this time that she suffered the sad loss of one of her crew. She was alongside at Pollock Dock and, during the Middle Watch, it was discovered that her gangway sentry was missing. After a fruitless search in the ship and on the jetty, his body was found in the water between the ship and the dockside. No one will ever know how he fell overboard but his oilskin coat had snagged on a nail on the jetty below water level and the poor lad had suffered a lonely death by drowning, virtually within feet of his shipmates asleep on board in their bunks.

Meanwhile the other future members of the 3rd EG had been passing through the pre-operational phases on the other side of the Atlantic. *Duckworth*, which was to be the future Group Leader, had commissioned on 4 August, 1943, and *Cooke* followed closely on 30 August, *Essington* on 7 September and *Domett* a few days later, on the 10th. All these four ships completed their trials and the working-up period at Bermuda without many problems. *Essington* did have some very early excitement however. She had left St John's Newfoundland with a convoy on 8 November and there is a report in *The Chronology of the War at Sea* by Rohwer and Hummelchen that she attacked U967 on 21 November during a pack action against a Gibraltar/UK convoy (MKS30/SL139) in which 4EG were engaged. She was certainly not part of 4EG on this occasion but it is quite possible that she encountered one of the U-boats on the fringe of that group's action with the Weddingen group during the Bay Offensive. Surviving *Essington* crew members do not seem to recall this and although it was certainly not a successful attack, it was their first taste of real action. After the Pollock Dock refits, all but *Essington* had the checkered signal flag motif (Numeral 3) painted on their funnels in early December, 1943, denoting membership of the 3rd EG. *Essington* did not join them until her refit was complete on Christmas Day.

Braithwaite had been commissioned on 13 November. She was not destined to become a permanent member of the Group but from May, 1944, she was attached to them as a supernumerary for four to five months, so it is appropriate to mention her early days here. The most noteworthy aspect of these was the fact that she became notorious for an alleged mutiny during the trials period at Boston. Her First Lieutenant was an American serving as a Lieutenant RNVR. His name was Cherry, later famous as the author of the book *Yankee, RN*. He was a wealthy stockbroker and, unusually for an American in 1940, was an almost rabid Anglophile. More particularly, he hero worshipped British naval officers and long before the USA had been involved in the war was fired with a determination to fight against Hitler in RN uniform. Since he was an experienced ocean yachtsman and held navigational qualifications, he discovered that whilst it was strictly illegal from an American standpoint, the British would be quite amenable to giving him an RNVR commission. He therefore risked losing US citizenship by crossing into Canada and enlisting in the Royal Navy. This was a commendable attitude of course but unfortunately the man had extrovert, almost histrionic, tendencies. For example, his first act after completing basic training at the Royal Naval College at Greenwich was to request to Admiralty to spend his seven days' leave serving in a destroyer on East Coast convoy duty to get an immediate taste of action. Surprisingly enough, his request was granted and he spent a week in HMS *Whitehall* and had a due taste of action, since the East Coast, at this time, was notorious as 'Bomb Alley' by day and 'E-boat Alley' by night.

Later in his career, after serving in other ships, he eventually joined *Braithwaite* and achieved an ambition to become First Lieutenant of a Royal Naval vessel. Unfortunately his gratification was not shared by the officers and particularly the crew. He was unpopular in the wardroom for his egotism and hated by the lower deck as a viciously harsh disciplinarian. He not only became noted for handing out stiff punishment at the defaulter's table for comparatively trivial offences but he frequently handed out unofficial stoppages of leave to a whole watch of seamen if they had not performed a particular task to his liking. *Braithwaite* became a very unhappy ship. Those elements among the conscripts in her company who already had a tendency to buck against discipline found themselves almost permanently under punishment or stoppage of leave.

Matters came to a head one day when Cherry discovered that much of the ship's cutlery had been stolen from the cafeteria. The obvious conclusion was that it had been taken ashore and sold to some unscrupulous café owner for much needed cash to pay for a run ashore. Cherry cleared the lower deck and harangued the assembled crew in the most insulting and derogatory terms. Those who remember the incident recall phrases such as 'thieving scum' and 'unfit for the honour of serving under the White Ensign'.

It would have been bad enough to receive such insults from an RN officer, much less a foreigner, and it was the last straw for *Braithwaite*'s long suffering crew. They retired to the messdecks for the morning 'stand easy' ten minute break and remained there discussing their grievances instead of returning to work at the appointed time. This was a reprehensible breach of discipline of course, but Cherry, with his usual twisted view, looked upon it as nothing less than full-blooded mutiny. There was a British cruiser refitting at Boston at the time and he seriously contemplated sending for a squad of her Royal Marines to come over with fixed bayonets to march off the mutineers but fortunately had second thoughts about this. The Commanding Officer was ashore on business at the time and was perturbed to arrive back to find the confrontation still going on.

The matter was quickly resolved by sensible diplomacy, however, and the men were persuaded to return to duty. The ringleaders of the 'mutiny' were placed on a charge but even the NOIC advised the CO that there were hardly grounds for court martial proceedings. Some good conduct badges were confiscated and some stoppage of leave and pay awarded, which is hardly the scale of punishment for mutiny! As for Cherry, the NOIC clearly had an appreciation of his part in inciting the incident and had him transferred out of the ship. It was diplomatically suggested that his was not for punishment but for the benefit of his future RN career. The ship's company were well content to see the last of him, however, and from that time onwards *Braithwaite* became a normal, efficient and happy ship.

With trials complete, she departed to Bermuda for the customary working-up and eventually sailed from Norfolk Virginia as escort to HMS *Emperor* in early February.

* * *

To return to the account of the newly formed 3rd EG, the incomplete group, *Duckworth, Domett, Berry* and *Cooke*, plus two corvettes, began their career with a convoy to Gibraltar at the beginning of the month. This went through without complications and they arrived there on 10 December meeting up with *Blackwood* which was making a solo voyage back from Horta where she was last reported in Chapter 2. She joined up with 3EG for the return trip to the UK and, after her repairs, she became a permanent member of the group.

The only excitement during the return convoy was an incident on 28 December, when the group received orders to make an emergency change of course as they were passing through the Bay of Biscay. ERA Fred Barr remembers being on watch in the engine room where rumour had it that they were avoiding a U-boat wolf pack. In fact it was more serious than that. It was the occasion when ten large German destroyers had sailed from the Gironde to escort in the raider *Alsterufor*. These ships mounted 5.9″ guns and torpedo tubes and would have made short work of the frigates had they encountered them; so it was prudent to take avoiding action. The cruisers *Glasgow* and *Enterprise* intercepted this force, sank four, driving the rest back to harbour.

Since *Blackwood* and *Berry* had both been in commission for quite some time and *Blackwood* had also had experience of being temporary Leader of 4EG, there must have been expectation in both ships that one or another might become Leader of the new group. Commander C. P. Mills, who had been appointed Senior Officer, had the same opinion as Commander Chavasse however about the unimportance of speed and chose the Buckley class *Duckworth* as Leader.

A minor point of interest about *Duckworth* is that, although she was to become renowned as a successful U-boat hunter, the most lasting memories that most of her crew have are of quite trivial facts; first, that her Chief Stoker had two sons on board in his boiler room crew, and secondly, that the ship had a unique mascot in the form of a tame duck, dressed in a 'Donald Duck' sailor suit.

A few days after the return from Gibraltar the 3rd EG were at Scapa Flow to begin an unusual task for frigates. They were to escort five capital ships as far as Port Said, a duty normally performed by powerful Fleet Destroyers. The ships in question were *Renown, Valiant, Queen Elizabeth, Illustrious* and *Unicorn*. All were on their way to become part of the new East Indies Fleet (EIF) and 3EG's role was to escort them to the Suez Canal – after which they would meet up with EIF escorts. No doubt the crews were proud to have been appointed to this most responsible task, but they were soon disillusioned about the honour of the occasion. The ships sailed from Scapa on 5 January and headed straight into very filthy weather. This did not concern the big ships of course, but the 3rd EG was soon battling against gigantic seas to keep up with the fleet. Fearing serious damage to the upperworks, Commander Mills made tentative requests to the Flagship for a reduction in speed but these were not received with any sympathy. High speed was the best defence against U-boat attack and the admiral was not minded to risk his ships for the sake of a few frigates.

Fortunately, the seas did become calmer as they drove on southwards and the concourse reached Gibraltar for a brief refuelling stop on 7 January, pressing on to reach Port Said on the 12th. The entire trip had been almost uneventful. There had been one submarine alarm during the passage through the Mediterranean. *Essington* had investigated a suspected contact but found no target. After arrival at Alexandria, the Group were not allowed much time to enjoy the dubious attractions ashore. Fuel and stores were embarked rapidly and they set out for the return trip on 14 January. Their duty on this occasion was to escort *Ramillies* which was on her way back from the Eastern Fleet to the UK. It was another high speed voyage with one oiling stop at Algiers and they passed Gibraltar on 20 January, arriving back at Belfast on the 27th. The only event of note during this voyage was another attack on a U-boat made by *Essington*. It was apparently as abortive as the last one had been and the only record of it is a copy of a brief signal No271022 from Admiralty to Commander-in-Chief: '*Essington* reported attack on U-boat at 1247/26'.

Following this lightning trip through the Mediterranean and back, the Group had a fairly easy time during the next month. They had been on patrol into the Atlantic during early February, during which *Duckworth* is reported to have been narrowly missed by a torpedo from U445 and credited with possible damage to this boat in a subsequent attack on 13 February.

Although it was officially forbidden, Ron Collison, who was one of *Essington*'s crew, kept a continuous diary and he records that they were moored at Belfast or Larne with just one A/S sweep into the Atlantic between 21 and 27 February. They made up for this respite during the next weeks, however, and spent the entire period between 9 March and 5 April on continuous convoy support operations in the Atlantic, but there are no records of any actions during this time.

There is some evidence that *Ekins* was with the Group as a supernumerary during this last trip. Peter Elliott writes in *Allied Escort Vessels of WW2* that she did a number of six-week trips with 3EG before being allocated to Nore Command but Admiralty records do not support this. A Pink List records her sailing from Belfast with 3EG on 2 March and she was noted as unallocated and boiler cleaning at Liverpool on 19 April. Shortly after this, she was operational from Sheerness and no further mention of her will be made until the Chapter on the Nore Command.

The probable reason for *Ekins'* trips with 3EG was that she was a stand-in for *Cooke* which was *hors de combat* after a sorry event which took place in Pollock Dock. She had been due for maintenance work to be carried out by the base staff and the preparations carried out by her engineers were careless. One of the tasks involved the removal of a salt water inlet pipe in the engine room and they had failed to close the appropriate valve properly. The consequence was that during the night, when the ship took on a slight list due to the emptying of a fresh water tank, the engine room slowly flooded. An inquiry found her Chief ERA guilty of negligence and he was punished by being disrated and taken out of the ship. *Cooke* became non-operational for many weeks while the machinery and electrical circuits in the flooded engine room were dried out by base staff. She missed the next group operations which consisted of various A/S sweeps in the Western Approaches and the southern area of St George's Channel during April and the middle of May, 1944, none of which resulted in more than the usual number of spurious contacts. The Group's base of operations during this time was Devonport, which was much appreciated by the West Countrymen. *Blackwood* and *Domett* were both manned from this port Division and those of their crews who lived locally were able to enjoy an occasional evening at home when the ships returned for replenishment. The engine room and stores departments were not too pleased however. As in the case of some of the other Captains, they discovered that the authorities at Devonport were not very cooperative with those frigates which were not permanently based there. The dockyard did not cater for American type equipment and did not have the abundance of spares they were used to at Pollock Dock. They also found that the staff of the Victual-ling Yard were unsympathetic about supplying them with any but the bare essentials in the way of food.

Apart from the men who lived locally, there was relief all round when they returned to Belfast on 15 May, and had a ten-day period in which to get themselves prepared for the invasion which everyone knew must start soon.

It was at this stage that *Braithwaite* began her temporary attachment to the Group. Apart from *Berry*, which was under maintenance at Belfast from 2–18 June, EG3 was assembled, with many others, at Milford Haven during the days before 6 June and *Cooke* rejoined them there after having her engine room dried out. Unlike most of the WA groups, they did not get sailing orders until the day after D-Day. Their role was to join the vast fleet of escort groups which patrolled the Channel approaches against the expected influx of U-boats. The 3rd EG's patrol area was from Portland to Cherbourg and there were many false contacts during the first eight days after the landings in Normandy but nothing positive. Doenitz had planned to send large numbers of U-boats into the Channel to attack the convoys once the invasion had started but, in the event, the massive air patrols set up by the Allies made it suicide for the boats to surface and since the Germans only had about seven or eight U-boats equipped with Schnorkel devices, very few of their submarines were able to get into the Channel to approach the assault beaches.

The 3rd EG's first encounter with them was the tragic loss of *Blackwood*. She had been sent to Portland Roads to refuel on 14 June and Les Cheeseman, who lived in Weymouth, had fleeting hopes of an evening at home with his parents. But no leave was granted and Les recalls:

> After oiling, we moved into Weymouth Bay and anchored right opposite the road where I lived. Later in the evening, tenders came out to bring us depth-charges and some of the crews were well known to me. I managed to pass on a message through them to my parents that I was fit and well but we were under sailing orders and I could not get ashore. We sailed at 0700 next morning and by evening we were about 70 miles out into the Channel and at 1915 hrs, without any warning we were hit for'd by a torpedo. The explosion was extremely violent, possibly because the hedge-hog bomb magazine had been hit and the whole for'd part of the ship beyond the bridge was blown away. I was seriously injured and, with many other casualties, I was taken ashore by an air/sea rescue launch before the ship sank and I ended up in Weymouth hospital, where my parents were able to come and see me not all that long after getting my message that I was fit and well.

Casualties had been very high because the ship had been closed up at cruising stations and about two thirds of the men were down below in their messes at the time *Blackwood* was hit. Sixty men died and at least that number were injured to some extent but the ship did not immediately sink and all the wounded men were rescued. The remainder of the Group searched assiduously for her attacker (now known to have been U753) but they could not gain contact and this U-boat did, in fact, survive the war to surrender in 1945.

Chastened by the loss of their newest member, 3EG continued their patrols in the Channel for the remainder of the month but it was not until the last week that any of the few U-boats which had penetrated the defensive screen in Western Approaches crossed their path. A group of four boats had been active in the mid-Channel area south of the Devon coast on 25 June. Two of them (U1191 and U269) had been smartly despatched by DE's of the 1st and 5th EG's but U984 had torpedoed *Goodson* of the 5th EG. U988 broke away and sank two large merchant ships and the corvette *Pink* on the 27th. Large scale sea and air searches were set up and during 28 June, aircraft of 224 Squadron located a U-boat and delivered an attack in mid-Channel. Uncertain of success, the pilot alerted the 3rd EG and they were soon carrying out sweeps in the indicated area. *Essington, Duckworth, Domett* and *Cooke* all made positive Asdic contacts and carried out a number of heavy depth-charge attacks. However, none produced tangible evidence of a 'kill'. In the end, clear contact was lost and only occasional doubtful echoes came back from a considerable depth. It was presumed that the submarine had either deliberately bottomed or had been sunk. There is, in this part of the Channel, some 70 miles north-west of Guernsey, a narrow stretch of deep water, up to 600 ft, which is one of the few places in the area where a sub could dive deep. Suspecting that the U-boat might be lying motionless on the sea bed and having no charges which could be set to such depths, Commander Mills decided to report the situation to the C-in-C. As a result of his signal, a Canadian Tribal class destroyer was sent out from Devonport bringing one of the huge 1 ton depth-charges which could be fired from her torpedo tubes. After being given the position of the U-boat the Canadian destroyer made an attacking run and everyone on board the assembled frigates watched expectantly for the spectacular explosion of the huge charge. To everyone's surprise and disappointment nothing happened. For some reason the depth-charge pistol failed to fire. Flashing an apologetic signal, the Canadians departed back to port explaining that they had only carried one of the 1-ton charges.

3EG's U-boat problem remained. Without charges which would operate at greath depth their only solution was to wait in the area until the U-boat's endurance ran out and she was forced to surface. The Asdic crews were certain that she was still there but echoes were fleeting and to make certain that they were not wasting time, Commander Mills decided to use echo sounders to make up a relief map of the sea bottom. This was a laborious process but in the end they did locate the U-boat. She was lying on the bottom, as suspected, but the trace on the paper roll of the echo sounder clearly showed that she was already well and truly destroyed and was lying in two discrete parts some 30 feet apart. There was great jubilation in all the 3EG ships as the news spread. They all hoped that the U-boat had been *Blackwood*'s executioner but post-war records do not confirm this. Their victim had been U988. Allocation of official credits was difficult; four frigates and an aircraft had delivered attacks and there was no way of determining which had actually blown the U-boat apart and in the end honours were shared equally between *Duckworth, Cooke, Domett* and the aircraft of 224 Squadron.

After this mixed victory, the 3rd EG continued to operate in the Channel. Their sweeps regularly brought excitement and a colossal number of depth-charges were expended on suspicious echoes as the ships milled around chasing suspects. *Domett*, in particular, became notorious for spectacular changes of course to follow up a sudden asdic contact. Commander Mills eventually tired of her constant antics and sent a caustic signal: *Domett is to stop charging around like a rogue elephant* and, of course, this became her nickname in the group for ever after. She even had her private insignia painted on the wings of the bridge – an elephant sitting astride a jet propelled beer bottle!

One particular episode during this period is well remembered by both George Dyer and Sub-Lieutenant Jack Baggs of *Braithwaite*. A Mosquito aircraft returning from a sortie over France had sighted a U-boat but, having no weapons left, the pilot could only report the position to the 3EG ships which were nearby. *Essington* and *Braithwaite* were detached to investigate but were unable to make any sort of U-boat contact. Assuming that it had dived after the aircraft sighting, the two ships set about a box search. This was abandoned however! As other DE's which had strayed into these waters in sight of Guernsey had discovered, they soon found themselves under uncomfortably accurate fire from heavy calibre coastal batteries. Both ships were neatly straddled by the first salvo from the big guns and the CO's mutually agreed that discretion was the better part of valour and retired hastily out of range leaving the U-boat to survive another day under the protection of the shore batteries.

During these weeks of Channel operations up to early July, 1944, the Group had again been replenishing at Devonport. However, after a month away from Pollock Dock, there was urgent need to return for essential maintenance by the base specialists. With just one U-boat credit, 3EG returned to Belfast and rested on their laurels there from 6–11 July. There had been hopes of different employment on completion but there was no respite and they were back to scour the approaches to the Channel again. The first fortnight was almost without incident. U-boats were making great efforts to break through to attack the Normandy supply routes but they were being slaughtered mercilessly. Five had been destroyed by aircraft within the space of nine days and the famous 2nd EG had accounted for two more. Furthermore, the 3rd EG were soon to increase their score by another two.

The first of these victories went to *Cooke* which made a magnificent text book solo run to sink U-214 some 20 miles south of Start Point on 25 July. A couple of weeks later, when the group had been sent further south into Biscay, they were led to another kill by an aircraft of 53

Squadron west of Lorient where *Duckworth* and *Essington* shared credit for the destruction of U-618 on 14 August.

This particular patrol ended on 22 August and 3EG then enjoyed another welcome break at Belfast until the end of the month. When they were ready to return to the fray, the U-boat situation in the Channel had changed drastically. The Allies had captured all the French Atlantic coast ports and the submarines had been forced to retreat to Norway and other North Sea bases. Some of our escort forces could thus be relieved from Channel patrols and 3EG's next operation was a three-week period of convoy support work in the Atlantic which ended on 20 September. After a single day in harbour, they were off on another five-day A/S sweep off Northern Ireland. Both these last operations were devoid of action and the constitution of the group changed again on 1 October. *Braithwaite* was detached to join a newly formed mixed group (EG 10) and her place was taken by *Rowley* which had recently been released from Portsmouth Command. She was to remain with 3EG for the remainder of the war but a description of her early movements will be dealt with in a later Chapter dealing with ships of the Nore, Portsmouth and Devonport Commands.

The first ten days of October, 1944, were spent quietly at Belfast but ominous rumours about a Russian convoy run began to circulate when stocks of Arctic clothing were received on board. These rumours proved correct. The 3rd EG found themselves in Loch Ewe on 19 October and the news was released that they were to escort an important convoy to Murmansk. There were, in fact, two convoys (JW61 and JW61A). The larger consisted of twenty-nine ships with a large escort which included DE groups EG15 and EG21. 3EG was to go with the other section which consisted of only two large troopships, carrying liberated Russian prisoners back to the USSR. There was some disquiet about this operation; it was rumoured that the Russians were not exactly going back home of their own free will. They had been liberated from occupied territory and, as the Russian Government suspected them of being collaborators, the Allied decision to repatriate them by force was virtually a death sentence for them. That is by the way however; under such circumstances naval ratings have to do what they are told, not what they may think ought to be done.

Both parts of the convoy had a quiet passage for the first five or six days and it was not until they reached the approaches to the Kola Inlet that U-boats of the 'Panther' group gathered and attempted to attack. The escort forces (which included some modern 'S' and 'CA' class Fleet destroyers) were too strong for them however and not a single torpedo was fired at the convoy ships, although a number of T5s were loosed unsuccessfully at the frigates. As there were many U-boats involved in these attacks it might seem surprising that the strong escort did not sink any but as 3EG, newcomers to Arctic conditions, soon found, temperature layers in the water severely refracted Asdic beams and made Asdic operation a most difficult task. It was victory enough that all the convoy ships had been safely delivered.

They reached Polyarno on 28 October and had three days there to recover from the rigours of their first taste of merciless arctic weather before putting to sea again on the 30th to carry out preliminary sweeps to prepare the way for the next convoy departing for the UK. The U-boats were waiting in some force and the operation was again hampered by atrocious Asdic conditions. The most that could be achieved was to keep the U-boats down. Once again, the convoy passed through the danger area without loss. The only casualty was *Mounsey* of the 15th EG which received minor damage from a T5. She was able to limp into Polyarno. The 3rd EG covered the return convoy RA61 for three days but then returned to Murmansk and did not escape from those inhospitable waters until 9 November when they were thankful indeed to return to the haven of Pollock Dock on the 16th. There they remained for a maintenance period until the end of the month.

Many U-boats had been fitted with the Schnorkel devices by the end of 1944 and given the ability to operate submerged for long periods. In consequence, more of them were able to penetrate into our coastal waters in the Irish Sea and between Scotland and Northern Ireland. Torpedo attacks and sinkings began to increase significantly in those areas and several of the WA groups were operating there to defend the incoming convoys. 3EG was among these and for the next two or three months they hardly left the confines of the Irish Sea. This was not particularly arduous duty after the grind of long ocean patrols. For most of the time they acted as a support group, waiting in various places such as Holyhead, Milford Haven, Douglas, Isle of Man, and Belfast, ready to take off to support any threatened convoy or to go to the scene of any reported contact. Most of their sorties were of short duration, five to seven days being typical and their total sea time was remarkably short in comparison to that of other groups. *Essington*, for example, only clocked up some twenty odd days at sea in two months. This was partially accounted for by the fact that she had missed out on one group operation due to minor damage after a fire on one of her electrical switchboards. Even so, it does indicate that EG3 was having an easy time for a change.

Life was often hectic when they were at sea, however. A typical example is the time during January 1945, when five U-boats had penetrated into the Irish Sea and achieved a number of successes. The escort carrier *Thane* and a minesweeper were torpedoed off the Clyde by U481 on 15 January before being sunk by 22EG on the following day. U1055 also sank four ships further south in St George's Channel between the 9th and the 15th. A massive operation ('CE') was set up with a number of EG's scouring the Irish Sea for the next fifteen days. This sea looks comparatively small on the average atlas but it must be appreciated that Operation CE had to cover an area of some twenty thousand square miles and the forces engaged were kept very much on the hop to respond to attacks and reported sightings over such a vast area. Weather conditions were also bad and choppy seas made radar contact with targets as small as U-boats very difficult. *Duckworth* had a persistent but elusive radar contact during the whole of one night which turned out to be nothing but turbulent water caused by a tide rip in a shallow area.

One of the U-boats gave away its position by attacking and sinking a vessel off Holyhead and three groups, including 3EG, were directed in to hunt for it. Although they had been given a report that an aircraft had sighted the boat in Cardigan Bay a most painstaking search failed to make any contact during daylight hours. However, after dark, *Duckworth*'s submarine detector (SD) operators obtained a positive echo from a target on the bottom and she made a number of determined attacks. They did not obtain any positive evidence of a kill but Commander Mills was certain that the attacks had been successful and claimed a 'probable' sinking, but there was never any positive confirmation of this. Bottom searches are notoriously difficult and even experienced Asdic operators were often fooled into attacking targets which were nothing more than wrecks, rocks or even tide rips. On another occasion, *Duckworth* had expended a phenomenal number of depth-charges on such a target but when wreckage and bodies came to the surface they were horrified to see that the corpses were in an advanced state of decomposition and that they had been attacking a war grave consisting of an unfortunate merchant ship sunk by a U-boat on some previous occasion.

After the search in Cardigan Bay, alarms came thick and fast. 3EG were sent to investigate a loud underwater explosion ndear Llandudno but this was never satisfactorily explained. Then U1172 sank two merchant ships off the Clyde and both the 3rd and 18th EG's dashed to the vicinity but neither were able to get a fix on it. This boat had, in fact, escaped southwards and had met its end in the encounter with *Manners* described in the last Chapter. During the following day, U1051 was located off the coast of County Wexford where the DE's of the 5th EG put an end to its career. Only two of the U-boat group (U1055 and U825) had survived this audacious operation in the Irish

Sea but they had certainly caused a furore. One cannot help but admire the courage of the U-boat crews making such daring attacks right inside the inshore waters of the home ground of the Belfast escort groups. Their successes were minimal in comparison with their losses but it must be admitted that these U-boat crews must have required a higher brand of courage than their predecessors in the 'Happy Time' when ships could be sunk by the dozen in the Atlantic without much risk to themselves.

After Operation CE had ended at the end of January, 1945, EG3 had a ten-day rest and maintenance period at Belfast and when they next put to sea, there was a general feeling that the war was practically over. U-boats had again become troublesome in the Channel area though and the Group found themselves back in their old operational areas. *Berry* was undergoing a minor refit at Belfast until 23 February but the remainder of the Group set out for a ten-day patrol in the mouth of the Channel. Their search area was between Lands End and the Scillies and it was here on 24 Feburary that they made their first positive contact with the enemy for six months. *Duckworth* and the new group member *Rowley* picked up the trail of U480 and shared equal credit for its destruction, thereby restoring Group morale after so long without success.

They were back at Belfast by 4 March and their next foray took them southwards on the 21st to fight off the menace of a U-boat group (including U399, U315, U1195, U1002 and U953) which had been operating between Southern Ireland and the coast of Cornwall where they had already sunk four ships in quick succession. One of the boats had been reported off the Cornish coast and was believed to be seeking refuge in the inshore waters there so this became 3EG's first search area. It was not long before they had run the quarry to earth close inshore in Mounts Bay. Official credit for finding and destroying this boat (U399) was subsequently given to *Duckworth* as a solo victory but, as so often happened, other ships in the group had taken a hand in the hunt. Both *Domett* and *Essington* claim to have had good contact and were making an attack but that their Leader moved in at the last minute to actually deliver the fatal charges. It is the official record that counts, however, and this states that U399 was despatched single handed by *Duckworth*.

Two days after this victory, the Canadian frigate *Teme* was torpedoed off Lizard Point and the 3rd EG were again detailed to search for the U-boat responsible. Whether or not Commander Mills had an intuition or whether he was directed to the area is not clear, but he set an immediate course for Mounts Bay. The A/S crews thought it crazy to be seeking another U-boat there but, strange as it may seem, *Duckworth* gained another solo credit by sinking U1246 in almost the same place as U399 had met her doom.

This proved to be the last of the 3EG's victories. They remained operational in the Channel right up to the end of the war but during the latter weeks their patrols had been at the other end with Dover as their base. They were there to celebrate VE Day. With six U-boat kills to its credit, the Group was well up in the 'league table' of successful groups but strangely enough they were by no means the hardest worked. Ron Collison's diary (which checks out well against official Admiralty 'Pink Lists') shows that in sixteen months of active life *Essington* did only 270 days at sea. This is a 'sea time' record of less than sixty per cent which most groups would have considered to be a 'life of ease'. She only missed out on one group operation as far as I can establish, so it would seem that the remainder of 3EG's ships must have had just as much time in harbour. In one sense this makes the Group's record of kills even more impressive. If, for example they had spent as much time at sea as the 4th or 15th EG's had done, who knows how many U-boats they might have disposed of?

Duckworth, with 'shares' in five of the group victories, was undoubtedly the most successful of all the British DE's. Some would have it that Commander Mills did elbow the junior ships out of the way upon occasion in order to collect most of the glory but, after all, the war was about sinking U-boats and what matter if the team leader scored most of the goals? This was not the only group in which RNVR CO's complained of being kept out of the 'DSO Stakes' by cavalier action on the part of their Group Leaders. There was, it is true, great pressure on regular RN officers to get into the limelight as much as possible particularly at the end of the war. They were looking ahead to peace-time careers in the Service and the SO's, having reached Commander's rank were in the promotion zone which leads on to Flag Rank – or oblivion. It may well be, therefore, that some of them did push their juniors to the back of the queue when U-boat kills were in the offing but that is something which the bare records do not reveal.

With no more employment for escort vessels in the European theatre after VE-Day many of the Belfast escort groups were quickly disbanded. *Duckworth*, *Essington* and *Rowley* seem to have been the only ships on the 3rd EG to be earmarked for further service. The first two were taken in hand for refits to prepare them for Pacific service but the war in the east ended before the work was completed. *Essington* was reduced to reserve at Belfast until October, 1945, when she returned to the USA and *Duckworth* remained under 'Care and Maintenance' for even longer. A steaming crew took her across the Atlantic on 17 December.

Among other DE's, *Rowley* had been allocated to be modified as a 'floating power station' for use in occupied ports. This entailed the removal of all their armament but *Rowley*'s conversion was never completed. Her guns were hastily fixed back in place and she was returned to the USA on 12 November, 1945.

The diesel division *Domett, Cooke* and *Berry* were all paid off into the reserve fleet at Hull in June – even before the Pacific war was over and none of them put to sea again until they too went back to their 'home country' in February and March of 1946. The saga of another of the famous Belfast groups was ended.

TABLE OF U-BOAT SINKINGS BY THE 3RD ESCORT GROUP

Date	U-boat No.	Ships Involved.
28.6.44	U988	*Duckworth, Domett, Essington, Cooke* (and 224 Squadron RAF)
26.7.44	U214	*Cooke*
14.8.44	U613	*Duckworth, Essington.*
24.2.45	U480	*Duckworth, Rowley.*
26.3.45	U399	*Duckworth.*
29.3.45	U1246	*Duckworth*

SHIPS LOST FROM THE 3RD ESCORT GROUP

Blackwood torpedoed by U764 off Portland 15.6.44

– 4 –

THE 1st ESCORT GROUP

Affleck, Balfour, Bentley, Capel, Garlies, Gould, Gore, Whitaker.
(Hoste briefly)

S hips destined to join the 1st EG were handed over to the Royal Navy in September and October 1943.

Garlies, Gould and Affleck were handed over on 20, 23 and 29 September, 1943, respectively and were followed by *Balfour, Bentley* and *Gore* on 7, 13 and 22 October. There is no evidence that any of these ships suffered undue delay during the pre-operational routines on the other side of the Atlantic so it appears that the mechanical problems which plagued some of the earlier DE's had been ironed out by this time. The only events of note concerning these prospective 1st EG ships were early U-boat encounters by *Garlies* which took place during her first crossing to the UK. She took a southerly route which skirted the Azores and somewhere in mid-Atlantic, surprised a U-boat on the surface one evening. With starshell illumination provided by 'B' gun, 'A' gun was able to get off seven rounds before the U-boat dived. Asdic contact was established quite quickly and the crew in the Asdic cabinet controlled what they believed to be a text book attack but there was no evidence of success and the echo was never regained. Presumably the U-boat commander was more experienced than those in *Garlies* who hunted him. There was to be further excitement before reaching Belfast however. *Garlies* next ran into the fringe of an action by the 40th EG against U-boats of the 'Schill' group which had been alerted to join in the Weddingen group attack on convoy MKS30/SL139. Just as *Garlies* reached this area, *Chanticleer* and *Crane* of 40EG had located one of the pack (U515) and forced it to dive. As it did so, it loosed a defensive T5 which severely damaged *Chanticleer*. *Garlies* was called in to assist *Crane* in a search for the U-boat but no attacks developed and U515 slipped quietly away. When the search had been abandoned *Garlies* accompanied *Crane* and the damaged *Chanticleer* into Porta del Gardes, possibly taking the latter in tow. Medical attention was at hand to treat the many casualties in the crippled frigate but it seems that she was too badly damaged to leave Azores. *Garlies* took off her survivors and sailed the following day to deliver them to Gibraltar. This chance encounter with 40EG resulted in *Garlies* being temporarily attached to that group for a while. She accompanied them to Greenock, which was their operational base, and was appropriated by them as a temporary replacement for *Chanticleer*.

Garlies' first actual work with 40EG was a convoy escort operation skirting the Faeroes and Iceland but she did not remain with them for long. The weather was extremely rough and the pounding seas found a weakness in the welding in one of her forward seams and she began to take in water. The damage was by no means serious but the forepeak was flooded and some electrical circuits were put out of action. The convoy Commodore had no choice but to release her and she made for Iceland. The repair ship *Woolwich* was at Reykjavik at that time and *Garlies* moored alongside whilst emergency repairs were carried out and then returned to her rightful place in Pollock Dock where she remained in dockyard hands until the end of December 1943.

There is some evidence that she carried out one more convoy trip with an unknown group during January, 1944, but an Admiralty Pink List records her firm allocation to the 1st EG on 28 January, by which time her crew were certainly more seasoned mariners than those in the remainder of the new Group!

This date seems to have marked the inauguration of the entire Group apart from *Bentley* which was still being refitted after becoming a casualty during her first Atlantic crossing. She had originally sailed for the UK in company with *Gore* as escorts to the homebound convoy HX272 but she had been diverted to carry out a long fruitless U-boat search and lost so much time that she had no hope of rejoining HX272 and had to return to St John's to await the next. By this time the weather had deteriorated vastly. Most Atlantic convoys had a rough passage at this time of year but this one was to prove *extremely* rough. Within a few days of departure with HX273, the inexperienced *Bentley* had lost all visual contact with the convoy and as the weather beat her further off course she had soon lost radar contact as well and was utterly lost. Constant efforts on the part of the telegraphists operating the MWDF (FM12) set did eventually enable them to get a directional fix on the convoy but it was a very long way ahead and *Bentley* had to increase speed in an attempt to catch up. As they were plunging into head seas this increase had disastrous results. All but the most solidly constructed parts of her upperworks were severely damaged and by the time she caught sight of HX273 ships she was in a very sorry state indeed. Her gyro compass was useless and even the binnacle on the bridge had been bodily torn away from its deck fixings. Hardly any part of the superstructure had escaped serious damage and the convoy Commodore dismissed her from the escort and let her make her own way to Belfast at whatever speed she could. On her arrival at Pollock Dock it was so fully committed to carrying out the normal modification refits that it could not cope with extensive repair work as well so *Bentley* was sent across to Dunstaffnage (near Oban) and remained out of action there until 9 April. All the other five ships had been formed into the 1st EG by then and for its first operation the Group was assigned to take part in a six-week A/S patrol far out into the Atlantic, which was to bring their first battle honours and their first tragic loss. The first part of the operation was in support of convoys well out to the west of Ireland in latitude 26 degrees 30 mins west and on 25 February, 1944, they ran into their first U-boat action. *Gore* made the first contact at 2240 hrs from a range of 1200 yards and made an attack but her charges were not well placed. Apart from giving the enemy a good shaking, they only served to drive the boat deep. Single ships were not very successful at making attacks on boats which sought escape at the limits of their hull strength at depths of up to 600 feet. Depth-charges take a finite time to sink and experienced U-boat commanders, making expert use of the information passed by their hydrophone operators, could judge the very moment at which an attacking escort vessel was launching the deadly charges. A last minute change of speed and direction during the time it took for the charges to sink to his depth would thus enable him to get out of the danger zone of the explosions. Standard 500lbs depth charges needed to go off within thirty or forty feet of a U-boat in order to cause serious or fatal damage. *Gore* thus waited until Commander Gwinner in *Affleck* arrived on the scene to carry out a creep attack. This was a very effective tactic, developed by that ace U-boat hunter, Captain Walker of the 2nd EG. Two ships were needed to carry out such attacks. One stood off at a distance maintaining asdic contact but making no attempt to close in. She passed information about range, bearing and depth to a second vessel which made no Asdic transmission but which, directed by her group mate, slowly stalked up on the unsuspecting U-boat at less than six knots, at which speed her propeller noises could not be picked up by the German hydrophones. When she reached a position which the directing ship calculated was correct, she would drop her full pattern of charges. If the tactics had been carried out correctly the U-boat commander would have no inkling that the charges were on their way down. The method became the standard way of attacking deep submarines and had great success.

The first of these creep attacks was made at 0018 with *Affleck* controlling *Gould*. For some reason this failed and the ships changed roles for a second attempt half an hour later. This proved to be as unsuccessful as the first and, to make matters worse, both ships completely lost Asdic contact. *Affleck*, *Gould* and *Gore* then quartered the area for two hours before *Gore* again picked up the trail. Commander Gwinner once more acted as controller and it was *Gore* which did the creeping. This time the A/S crews heard the terrible grinding noises which followed the explosions indicating that the U-boat's hull was being crushed in by the great water pressure at 600 ft. Speeding in from the stand off position *Affleck* also dropped a full pattern of charges on the doomed submarine, probably quite unnecessarily but just to make sure. Surprisingly enough, the U-boat (U91) survived both attacks but was badly damaged and her Commander (Hungerhausen) was forced to bring his boat to the surface. He had no intention of surrender, even though his craft was mortally damaged. The U-boat broke surface at 0250 and seemed to be well down by the stern but Hungerhausen valiantly steered her towards his nearest tormentor, *Affleck* in a vain attempt to ram. The frigate had no difficulty in avoiding this brave manoeuvre and her gunners mercilessly picked off the German gun crew as they swarmed along the casing. The helpless boat wallowed about for another thirty minutes before she finally sank – leaving only sixteen survivors to be taken prisoner. Although *Gould* had taken some part in the early attacks, the final adjudication was that U91 had succumbed to *Affleck* and *Gore* and they shared equal credit.

Full of confidence after this first victory, the Group continued the operation in buoyant mood. A few days later, they were directed to proceed some 400 miles south and east in the direction of the Azores and had their second U-boat contact in position 45deg 46min N 23deg.16min W on Feb 28th. First contact was by *Garlies* at 0542hrs but unfortunately her Hedgehog developed an electrical fault and misfired. *Affleck* then dashed in to make her own Hedgehog attack but her salvo of bombs also missed.

Unlike depth-charges, which exploded at a set depth, the Hedgehog projectiles had two fuze mechanisms. The first was a contact fuze which exploded the charge as soon as the projectile hit something and the second was a sympathetic device which was set off by any violent shock wave. Thus if one bomb went off, the whole salvo of 24 would explode simultaneously. Silence after the attack therefore proved that it had been a total failure. Commander Gwinner blamed his A/S crew for failing to hit what had appeared to be an excellent target but events during the remainder of the day proved that failure was not the fault of the operators. Sea conditions were severely distorting the asdic transmissions. It was not only in arctic waters that temperature layers at various depths proved troublesome; such conditions could be encountered almost anywhere upon occasion and they most certainly existed in this area of the Atlantic during 1EG's search. Contact with the U-boat had been lost immediately after *Affleck*'s attack, giving the submarine commander (Manke of U358) ample time to take his boat down to the frightening depths where pressure in excess of twenty tons on each square foot caused every hull plate to creak and every submariner's heart to quail.

By 0612 the escorts had a reprieve from the intermittent temperature layer problems and obtained a firm enough contact to set up another creep attack. *Affleck* stood off as control ship and *Gould* ran in slowly to make the actual attack. All seemed to be going very well this time, but at the crucial moment during *Gould*'s stalking approach, just as she began dropping the first of a twenty-eight charge pattern, she was suddenly stricken with a bout of 'breakeritis'. The shock of the explosions had caused her main breaker switch to drop open and she lost what little way she had through the water and to everyone's disgust the attack had to be abandoned.

By the time that the ships were able to get back to the task of finding the U-boat again, the Asdic conditions had deteriorated badly and remained so for the rest of the day. Several times one ship or another would get a fleeting contact but always when she turned to make an attacking approach the echoes faded and disappeared again. Fortunately, the three ships were able to make enough of these unsatisfactory contacts to allow them to keep a fairly accurate plot of the U-boat's movements and they never entirely lost her. Time was on their side in this deadly game. Failing any successful attack, they only had to keep relentless contact and eventually the submarine's batteries would fail and her air supply become foul forcing her to surface.

As night fell at the end of the first twelve hours of this hunt, the ships were still getting vague echoes now and again. Commander Gwinner had surmised that the U-boat must surely surface during the night and gave orders for strict vigilance among radar operators and visual lookouts but, against all expectations, U358 remained submerged all night. Her commander was fortunate in that the Asdic conditions were so poor that not once were the escorts able to make a threatening attack and he could nurse his batteries by keeping his boat almost motionless at times.

Hopes of a quick end to this cat and mouse game were raised during the forenoon watch when both *Affleck* and *Gould* got clearer contacts than they had had for nearly twenty-four hours. Both dashed in to drop twenty-eight charge patterns but there was still no evidence of success. Some time later, at 1016 hrs, *Garlies* and *Gore* again picked up the trail but lost it once more even before they could try to attack. The odds against the U-boat were decreased slightly during the afternoon of 1 March when the Group received a signal from the Admiralty directing *Garlies* and *Gore* to proceed to Gibraltar but the remaining ships continued the search and maintained intermittent contact throughout the afternoon.

Conditions in the U-boat must have been almost beyond endurance by the end of the day. As the watches changed from Afternoon to First Dog, she had been submerged for about thirty-six hours. Her crew must have been at the point of exhaustion and practically suffocating but Commander Manke still hung on, grimly nursing his batteries in the hope of holding out until nightfall.

He almost made it, but the moment of truth came at 1723hrs. Physically and mentally exhausted Manke reluctantly gave the inevitable order to surface. He maintained an aggressive attitude right to the last however firing two T5's just as the boat rose towards the surface and had the savage satisfaction of seeing one of them strike *Gould*, blowing off her entire stern section.

The severed section of *Gould*'s stern continued to float stern uppermost for some time and caused some initial confusion. The weather had worsened and visibility was extremely poor and for some time *Affleck*'s gunners were firing at *Gould*'s dismembered stern under the impression that it was the U-boat's conning tower. They soon realized their error and changed point of aim to the real U-boat and a short gun duel ensued. During this action it is averred that the Leader ship very nearly became victim to a second torpedo. According to several eyewitnesses the track of this torpedo was seen heading straight for the stern by a sharp eyed Leading Torpedoman on the quarter deck. It is said that this man, without waiting for any orders, used commendable initiative and rolled a shallow set depth-charge over the stern. His intention was to explode the torpedo before it hit *Affleck* but in the event it didn't pan out that way. The exploding charge is reputed to have lifted the DE's stern clear out of the water and the torpedo passed harmlessly underneath. This deed is said to have resulted in the award of the DSM to the Leading Torpedoman but the author has found no confirmation of this tale. *Affleck*'s gunfire only caused superficial damage to the surfaced U-boat and the *coup de grâce* was delivered by approaching to close quarters and firing a pattern of shallow charges which virtually blew the submarine apart. She sank at 1945 hrs leaving only one solitary survivor. After the U-boat had been finally dealt with, there was time to try to rescue some of *Gould*'s survivors. Frank Owen who was one of them remembers:

> Fierce fires broke out amidships after our stern was blown off and with no power we had no hoses with which to tackle the flames. All the survivors (and there were quite a few to begin with) were mustered on the foc'sle to abandon ship in good order. Unfortunately the majority of our Carley rafts were stowed aft and had been lost and there was very little for the men to cling on to once they had gone over the side. The sea had become very rough and, sadly, by the time the other ships tried to pick us up, there were not many who had survived.

Able Seaman A. Penwarden who served in *Affleck* still has nightmare memories of the forlorn attempts to pick *Gould*'s survivors out of the water. The sea was extremely rough and there was no possibility of launching the sea boat and he is very critical about the lack of training that *Affleck*'s crew had received to deal with such a dire emergency. He still firmly believes that the absence of such training during the working-up period was the main reason why so many of *Gould*'s men were lost. However, in all truth, it is difficult to imagine what training could have been given. The inexperienced youngsters were shown how to put scrambling nets over the side in time of emergency and to launch sea boats and Carley rafts if sea conditions permitted but there was little else they could have been taught. When put to the test, inexperienced seamen made herculean efforts to rescue survivors but in the case of *Gould*, the heavy seas made their task almost impossible and, in any case, by the time that rescue operations could be mounted, most of the men, with no means of support other than their blown up lifebelts, had already perished.

When the roll call was taken, there were only three officers and thirty two ratings left from *Gould*'s complement of about 180, a greater loss of life than was suffered by any other Captain class frigate.

So ended what proved to have been the longest submarine hunt in which any RN ships were involved during the whole of the Second World War. Although the final accounting gave *Affleck* the credit for the actual kill, the official record acknowledges the part played by *Garlies* and *Gore* and posthumously to *Gould* herself. She was, incidentally, the first of our DE's to become a casualty less than six months after commissioning and with less than six weeks with an operational group.

After this long action, the remainder of the group were sent in to Gibraltar to refuel and restock depth-charges. They then continued their interrupted operation by being sent to act as support group to a number of convoys in the Bay of Biscay and the Straits of Gibraltar. It was in the latter area that they were involved in further excitement on 16 March.

* * *

Two American Madcat aircraft had detected a U-boat attempting to run the gauntlet into the Mediterranean off the coast of North Africa and made several unsuccessful attacks. As the instruments and weapons used by the Madcats were quite unusual, it is pertinent to explain them here. Their method of detecting submarines was by using a magnetometer device known as a magnetic anomaly detector. This reacted to distortions of the earth's magnetic field caused by the lines of forces being concentrated through the U-boat's hull. Unfortunately it could give no reaction until the aircraft was directly above the target and by then it was too late to attack with conventional weapons, since bombs and depth charges fall in a curved trajectory due to the residual velocity imparted by the plane's forward movement. The Madcats were therefore equipped with 'retro-bombs'. These had small rocket motors which fired ahead and theoretically neutralized the bomb's forward motion, causing them to drop vertically onto the target. This was the principle of the new method of attack but, like so many innovations, it often did not work.

The unsuccessful aircraft gave up the chase and handed over to the destroyer *Vanoc* which was operating in the vicinity. This old veteran, of First World War vintage, delivered a Hedgehog attack but she also missed. *Affleck* then appeared on the scene and, possibly pulling rank, Commander Gwinner led her into the fray. By this time the U-boat was less than 20 miles off the African coast and, in those shallow waters, stood no chance of escape. Conditions were ideal and *Afflecks*'s first pattern of Hedgehog bombs landed neatly around the target. Three of them exploded on contact and the remainder went off on hitting the bottom. The U-boat (U392) disintegrated in a most satisfying explosion. So much oil came to the surface after the attack that there were suspicions that their victim had been one of the 'milch cow' refuelling boats but this is hardly likely. Such vessels were only needed in the wide Atlantic and it is not reasonable to conclude that one would have been sent into the Mediterranean.

This third victory ended the 1st EG's most momentous first operation and on 22 March they made a triumphal return to Belfast. Their fame had preceded them and, since it was a rare occasion for a group to enter harbour with three Jolly Rogers flying, they were accorded a heroes welcome, with all ships manning the side to cheer them in amidst

1. Fargo Barracks, Milk Street, Boston. The first accommodation for DE crews standing by ships at Charlestown Navy Yard or Hingham Shipyard. The food served there was 'fabulous' and in sharp contrast to home fare at that time.

2. Frazier Barracks, Charlestown Navy Yard accommodation for crews standing by Evarts class DE's. The messing rivalled that of Fargo Barracks. *(Both photos: US Navy Collection, Boston National Historical Park)*

3. Hingham Shipyard. This vast facility was built by Bethlehem Steel for the sole purpose of constructing the Buckley class DE's. About fifteen ships would be under construction at any one time. (Photo: US Navy Collection, Boston National Historical Park)

4. DE - 278, at that time USS *Tisdall*, is launched at Charlestown. Although so called because she was originally allocated to the US Navy, she became HMS *Keats* on commissioning, having been reallocated to the Royal Navy. *(Photo: US Navy Collection, Boston National Historical Park)*

5. HMS *Calder* - handover and commissioning ceremony. 15 July, 1943 *(Photo: Private collection Electrical Artificer Ron Ayres)*

6. HMS *Holmes* dressed over all for her commissioning. *(Photo: Private collection Lieutenant Bill Wood RANVR)*

7. Commander C Gwinner DSO★, DSC
RN. Senior Officer 1st Escort Group
and CO HMS *Affleck* and HMS *Balfour*.
(Photo: IWM A28246)

8. Commander D Macintyre
DSO★★DSCRN. Senior Officer 5th
Escort Group and CO of HMS
Bickerton. *(Photo: IWM A16768)*

9. Lieutenant Commander R Hart DSC★RN. Senior Officer 21st Escort Group and CO of HMS *Conn*. His four U-boat victories with 21EG earned him his bar to his DSC.

10. HMS *Conn* flying the Jolly Roger from the masthead. A typical Buckley class DE. Whilst Group Leader in 21EG, she escorted convoys to Normandy and took part in three successful anti-submarine actions in the Minches. (*Photo: IWM A28197*)

11. HMS *Inman*. Evart class. The last DE to be handed over to the Royal Navy. Served in a mixed Escort Group (B1). *(Photo: IWM A23706)*

12. HMS *Lawford*. Served as a headquarters ship in the Normandy Invasion and was off GOLD Beach on D-Day. On D plus 2 she was sunk by air attack, the only Captain to suffer this fate. This picture shows clearly how extensive were the modifications which had to be made to those Captains employed as headquarters ships. *(Photo: IWM A2187)*

13. HMS *Bickerton* crippled by a U-boat's torpedo during Operation GOODWOOD. She was later sunk by friendly fire in order not to make increased difficulties for the surviving escorts, who were already having to cover the stricken escort carrier HMS *Nabob*.
(Photo: *Author's Collection*)

14. HMS *Duckworth*. The Buckley class Leader of the 3rd Escort Group after one of her many successful forays. She had shares in the destruction of six U-boats, making her 'the Champion' of the Captains. *(Photo: IWM A28186)*

15. HMS *Holmes*, a Nore Command frigate. This picture is reproduced from a painting in the possession of Mrs Wood whose late husband, Lieutenant Bill Wood RANVR, was her First Lieutenant. Note the pom-pom bowchaser fitted to all CFCF's for use against E-boats.

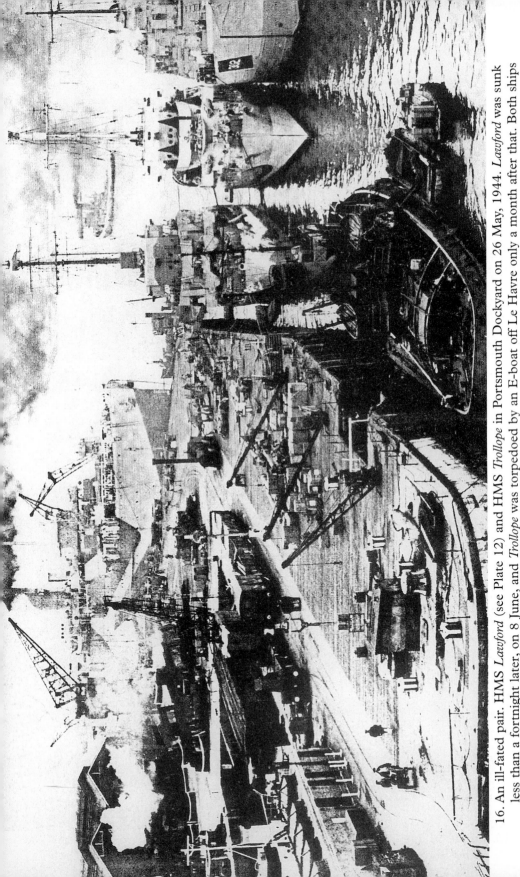

16. An ill-fated pair. HMS *Lawford* (see Plate 12) and HMS *Trollope* in Portsmouth Dockyard on 26 May, 1944. *Lawford* was sunk less than a fortnight later, on 8 June, and *Trollope* was torpedoed by an E-boat off Le Havre only a month after that. Both ships suffered heavy casualties. (*Photo: IWM 25517*)

17. The horrific damage suffered by HMS *Whitaker*. In the foreground is a group of her survivors: *(all names left to right) (Front)* Able Seamen Stanley and Costello, Leading Seaman Lancaster, Able Seaman Meers and Leading Seaman Northcott. *(Rear)* Able Seamen Paultor and Rowell, (unidentified), and Able Seaman Brady.

18. On the bridge at sea. Lieutenant Bill Wood RANVR, First Lieutenant HMS *Holmes* and later CO of HMS *Cotton*.

19 & 20. *(Left)* HMS *Goodall*. Looking aft from the forecastle. *(Right)* Sub-Lieutenant Paul Mallet SANF, *Goodall's* South African Gunnery Officer. He was at home on leave when she was sunk, which in all probability saved his life.

21. *Goodall's* wheelhouse. Note the utility ship's wheel – brass, with plastic rim and no spokes! *(All photos: Author's collection)*

22, 23 & 24. HMS *Goodall*. *(Top Left)* A fine view of her forecastle and A and B gundecks. *(Top Right)* Looking aft from the funnel top. Note the additional racking to hold up to 200 extra depth charges. *(Bottom)* A view from the mast of the bridge area. These three photographs from the Author's collection are very typical of an Evarts class DE.

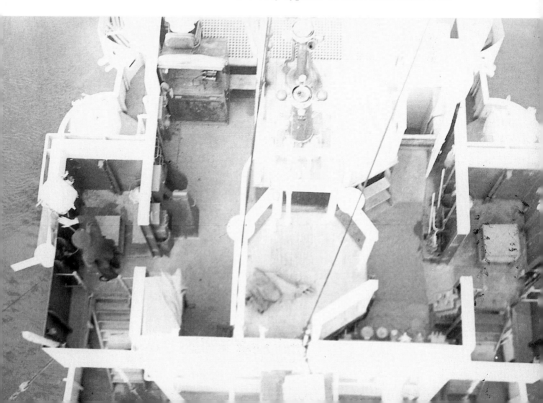

25. HMS *Cubitt* at Harwich in August, 1945. In March she had been refitted at Tilbury. Shields had been fitted to her 3" guns and her two for'ard 20mm Oerlikons had been replaced with two single 40mm Bofors guns. *(Photo: Author's collection)*

26. Ordnance Artificer 3rd Class Donald Collingwood, HMS *Cubitt*, March, 1945.

27. Sick Berth Attendant Will Patey in his Sick Bay in *Cubitt*. Mentioned in Despatches for his outstanding work tending MTB casualties during an E-boat action in the North Sea. *(Both photos: Author's collection)*

28. Paying off at Brooklyn Navy Yard, 19 October, 1945. HMS *Calder*.

29. Although no DE was given an Admiralty approved ship's badge, many had badges designed by their crews, based upon the family arms of the man whose name they bore. This was *Calder's*. (*Both photos: Electrical Artificer Ron Ayres, HMS Calder*).

a cacophony of hooters and sirens. Nonetheless, the occasion was sadly marred by the absence of their group-mate *Gould*.

* * *

Bentley, which had been refitting at Dunstaffnage, had now had all her storm damage repaired and most of her modifications were complete. She at last became operational with 1EG on 9 April, 1944. To make up for the lost *Gould*, another of the Captains, *Capel*, was recruited into their number.

Capel was senior to all her new group-mates having commissioned ahead of them on 24 August, 1943, but she had not had any previous operational experience. As explained in Chapter 1, a number of the Captains were ferried across the Atlantic by RCN crews and taken over by RN personnel at Lissahally who had never even seen one of the new frigates before. Though this was not a problem for most departments, which were soon able to familiarize themselves with the US equipment, the engine room staff did need some pre-commissioning training. To provide this, two of the earlier ships (one Buckley and one Evarts were partially decommissioned and used as floating classrooms for ERA's and stokers earmarked for ships being brought over by Canadians. *Capel* had been one of these (*Duff* was the other) and her only sea experience had been fourteen-day trips out of Liverpool with the trainee engine room ratings. When enough men had been trained, she went into Pollock Dock for a short refit, had her complement restored to operational levels – and was just in time to become *Gould*'s relief – bringing the 1st EG up to full strength for the first time.

For some weeks before D-Day the Group operated in the waters off the Scottish Isles and in the Irish Sea but found no opportunity to enhance their reputation. Many charges were expended on suspect echoes but the only casualty was one of their own number. The newly repaired *Bentley* unwisely dropped shallow set charges at too slow a speed. Some of her internal fittings were severely shaken up and she was back in Pollock dock hands again for minor repairs.

As the pre-invasion tension built up, the 1st EG joined many others of the Belfast frigates in Moelfre Bay in Anglesea to await their sailing orders. They left there on 5 June to become part of the vast A/S screen set up in the Western Approaches to bar the way for the U-boats which were expected to appear in large numbers when the first landings had been made. Their first period with this defensive force lasted for thirteen days but the anticipated battle against the U-boats just did not materialize. So without having seen further action, the 1st EG went back to Belfast for a maintenance period on 18 June.

By the time the Group returned to the Channel, which was to be their main theatre of operations for the remainder of the year, a few of the Schnorkel U-boats were making an appearance and 1EG's ego was much bolstered when they encountered one of these (U1191) in mid-Channel south of Lyme Bay on the very first day of their renewed patrol. *Affleck* and *Balfour* promptly added to the group score by sharing equal credit for sinking it on 25 June.

During the next few weeks, they made no more positive contacts with U-boats but they did come under fire, on one occasion, from shore batteries in the Channel Islands. Norman McElroy, an ex-Gunnery PO of *Affleck*, describes this attack, which was the only time that these guns caused casualties in any of the Captain class:

> We had received a report of a periscope sighting by the RAF and were diverted to sweep the area but to keep out of gun range of the island. I often wonder if we were advised what this range was. I think the guns were 188mm. We swept the area through that evening and night – but with no joy. By the time daylight came, the batteries must have worked out who was the Leader. When the sun was right for them, they opened fire with shrapnel shells. The first salvo was short but the next was pretty accurate. I had just reported the forenoon watch closed up and was on my way down to the mess to collect a jacket (as it was chilly). That was when I heard the first salvo. There was a gallop on deck by all present and the first two through the screen door caught fragments from the next salvo. Both were Messmen and the first, who was a stoker, lost an arm and the seaman who was with him was hit in the chest. I was No. 3 and the Messman's height saved me. The bit that hit me bounced off the bulkhead and passed through my side without hitting anything vital. I think that in all about ten of us were caught, the masthead lookout having the back of his leg torn away but we all received the best of attention in the RN hospital at Portland.
>
> I believe that the Germans came off second best though, as I have heard that their Lordships sent over the *Nelson* plus another battleship a couple of days later and these two gave the battery a hammering.

* * *

Boredom began to set in again. Life had become a monotonous routine of endless patrols, the only respites being the occasional visits to Plymouth for replenishment of fuel, stores and weapons. Then on 18 July, *Balfour* signalled a submarine contact in mid-Channel south of Portland, not far from the scene of the Group's last kill. She delivered a faultless solo attack which so severely damaged her target (U672) that its commander was forced to surface and abandon ship. All escort ships' CO's dreamed of the kudos attached to the capture of a U-boat intact and *Balfour*'s skipper was no exception. However, even before a sea boat could be launched with a boarding party, the U-boat swiftly sank.

The total score of the group was now confirmed at five but, sad to relate, this was the peak of their success. They were never fated to gain another victory and the remainder of the war brought them only a series of disasters. The pattern of operations changed after the surrender of Cherbourg. The port was quickly cleared and refurbished to augment the Mulberry Harbour as the Allies' supply terminus and instead of roaming A/S patrols the 1st EG became increasingly involved in convoy escort work to and from Cherbourg.

Their operational base was still Plymouth and it was common knowledge that U-boats were still active in the Channel and Biscay areas. There was disappointment in the Group that their escort role kept them out of the main actions. They were impatient to be let loose amongst them again but it was not to be. At the end of September there was a slight change in the Group's membership. *Balfour* was detached to operate with the 18th EG (*Hoste, Stockham* and a miscellany of other frigates) and her place with 1EG was taken by *Whitaker*. She had been among the last of the Buckley class to be delivered to the RN on 28 Jan, 1944. She had been one of the ships which was ferried across by RCN crews and her British crew did not join her until she reached Lissahally in February. Her immediate fate was similar to that of several of the last Captains to be handed over. She remained as an unallocated unit for several months. There was a number of Atlantic convoy duties with an assortment of sloops, First World War V&W destroyers and other frigates but they hardly ever worked with the same group twice. Her D-Day role had been to escort two troopships through the Irish Sea and across to the Normandy beaches and she remained in the Channel area, still, unallocated, to carry out a number of escort and patrol duties until August. Permanent allocation to a group was delayed until October as she was first sent to Pollock Dock for the usual modification refit before joining 1EG. The Group was having a respite from Channel convoy work when *Whitaker* joined them and her first operation in their company was as support group for convoys passing between Northern Ireland and the Scottish coast. Shortly after midnight on 31 October - 1 November the convoy and support ships were off Malin Head. Just as the middle watchmen had taken over in *Whitaker*, without any warning or alarm, she was shattered by a terrific explosion which blew off the entire forward part of the ship including the bridge.

All the officers had been killed in this blast, together with the senior ratings who lived in the forward part of the ship. Many of the PO's who lived aft were also lost as they customarily had midnight poker sessions in the Gunner's store, which was right for'd where the explosion took place. With no one to really take charge there was some confusion about what to do at first. The most senior rating left alive was the Ordnance Artificer B. Harrop but he tells about being temporarily trapped in his mess for some time after the calamity. By the time he reached the upper deck, he discovered that most of the ship's survivors had abandoned ship. It appears that one of the Petty Officers had taken charge and, being convinced that even *Whitaker*'s aft section was about to sink, he had encouraged the men to abandon ship. After a short time the survivors realized that the remaining section of the ship showed no signs of sinking any lower in the water and somewhat shamefacedly they began to return to their stricken ship. It is to be noted however, that the PO who had instigated the panic abandonment was not among those who clambered back on board. He apparently continued to paddle away in a Carley boat.

Meanwhile the remainder of the Group were carrying out sweeps around the convoy to try to contact the attacking U-boat. It was assumed that it *was* a U-boat since losses by mines were not frequent in this area. *Gore* was sent to assist *Whitaker* and was able to go right alongside her remains and many of her officers and men went across to assist the casualties and carry out damage control work. These men vividly remember the grisly sight of an officer's head, still wearing its peaked cap, lying on the depth charge rails aft. They also recall that there was no MO available and all the work of tending the many wounded had to be done by the Sick Berth Attendant, who carried out rudimentary surgery in the seamen's bathroom since the sick bay in a Captain class was little more than a cubby hole.

By morning, *Whitaker*'s stern section was under tow towards Belfast and a hospital ship was sent out to meet her and take off the casualties. Not a sign of a U-boat had been found by *Whitaker*'s group-mates that night. A Court of Inquiry reached no positive conclusion about the loss. There were also court martial proceedings to deal with the PO who had prematurely ordered abandon ship but the outcome of that cannot be told since such proceedings are not released for public information until a period of seventy years has passed.

Post-war German records have established that it *was* a U-boat that was responsible. The attack was made by von Morstein in U483 who reported that he had aimed at 'two steamers and a monitor in the convoy but the torpedoes missed and hit one of the convoy escorts.'

One may well ask why there had been no U-boat alarm prior to this attack. It might even be suspected that inexperience of *Whitaker*'s Asdic team might be to blame but John Brady, who was one of them, sensibly refutes such suspicion. He had been on watch in the Asdic cabinet until midnight and the men who relieved him were two of the most reliable SD's in the ship. Able Seaman Deanes had already been awarded the DSM and Bar for A/S operations and his partner was a survivor from the second HMS *Hardy* and clearly no inexperienced new entry. Such men would not have failed to react to the slightest suspicion of an Asdic echo and under normal circumstances would have also heard the telltale propeller noises as the torpedo approached the ship. From Von Morstein's account, it would appear that the attack had probably been made from the side of the convoy opposite to *Whitaker*'s position however. The torpedoes would thus have passed between the convoy ships whose prop noises would have masked that of the torpedoes. The buoyant morale in the 1st EG was somewhat depressed by the loss of this second member in the space of seven months and when they were sent back to the Channel again soon after this incident there was grim resolve among them to exact vengeance – but no such opportunity would come their way.

Antwerp was the main Allied supply port by this time and it was at that end of the Channel that the 1st EG mainly operated, using Portsmouth as a base for replenishment. They resolutely patrolled the convoy routes for about a month, but the main menace during this phase came from the E-boats and as these were being kept away from the convoys by the CFCF patrols (see Chapter 6) 1EG had no further chance to wreak vengeance right up to the time they returned to Belfast for maintenance on 1 December, 1944. There had been great hopes that WA Command would have taken pity on them and extended this maintenance period to include Christmas – but that was mere wishful thinking and long before the festive season began, the 1st EG were back on their old beat in the Channel. They spent a cheerless Christmas Day patrolling off Cherbourg, particularly *Gore* whose CO did not believe in Christmas and forbade even the limited celebrations that were possible in a ship on active service. His daily orders for Christmas Day were no different from those for every other day of the year.

The Group's final tragedy took place on Boxing Day, 1944. A German submarine (U486) had crept unobtrusively into the patrol area and her commander could hardly believe his good fortune on sighting no less than three enemy frigates through his periscope. What was more amazing was that, from their behaviour, not one of them seemed to be aware of his presence. No such opportunity had come the way of a U-boat commander since the early days of the First World War when the renowned Weddingen had found and sunk three old British cruisers within the space of half an hour off the Dutch coast.

With cool deliberation the U-boat commander loosed off two T5's against the nearest targets *Affleck* and *Capel*, then manoeuvred into position to fire a salvo of G7's at the third (*Gore*). Both the T5's found their mark. *Capel*'s damage was mortal and she sank but *Affleck* survived – but only as what is recorded as a 'Constructive Total Loss'. Meanwhile U486's commander had fired his salvo of torpedoes at *Gore*. They were well aimed and, but for prompt action by her CO, she would have completed the U-boat's 'hat trick'. He handled the ship in textbook fashion and 'combed' the salvo of torpedoes as calmly as if it had been a peacetime manoeuvre. He had never been a popular captain; his crew had found him remote, uncommunicative and generally 'a miserable so-and-so' but all that was forgotten. As Telegraphist Bill Garland has said:

> I, like most others on board, had never had any reason to like the man, but he undoubtedly saved our lives by his superb seamanship on this occasion – and this made up for a thousand previous sins!

Seen from the enemy side this double tragedy was the culmination of a week of great success for Lieutenant Meyer in U486. He had sunk a large supply ship on 18 December, the troopship *Leopoldville* in which 600 troops were lost, on Christmas Eve, and now two frigates were added to the bag. As a matter of interest, Lieutenant Meyer and his crew did not survive the war; U486 was sunk by the British submarine *Tapir* west of the Shetlands on 12 April, 1945.

To return to the stricken DE's: *Capel* sank with great loss of life but *Affleck*'s damage was not so severe and miraculously she had only nine fatalities. She was eventually towed back to Portsmouth and written off as a fighting unit. After being patched up, she had all her armament removed and was converted into a floating power station. She was operating as such at Teneriffe until as late as 1957.

* * *

As 1EG was now under strength, *Hoste* and a previous member (*Balfour*) were seconded back from the 17th EG. Commander Gwinner took *Balfour* over as Group Leader for the remainder of the war but the final stages of the Group's career were almost uneventful. The ships continued to carry out patrols from Portsmouth and, later, Dover but the only event of note during these last days was when tragedy nearly struck again. This happened off the Isle of Wight and the near-victim was *Balfour*. She was leading the group in an A/S sweep after a U-boat sighting close to shore. All ships were prudently streaming their 'Foxer' devices (noise making machines to decoy T5's) and, for once, these much maligned contrivances actually worked and the T5 was successfully decoyed to explode alarmingly against it.

The 1st EG virtually ceased to exist during the final stages of the war in Europe. In anticipation of the final surrender of U-boats, many groups had been dispersed around the British Isles to round them up. *Balfour* performed this task off Rosyth and when all the surrendered U-boats had been shepherded into Loch Ryan and Scapa, she had a short spell as target towing ship for the Fleet Air Arm at Invergordon. Her crew believed that this was just to kill time before joining in the Pacific war but it was the last stage of her useful life. By September, 1945, she was placed in Care and Maintenance at Hartlepool, where most of her crew were paid off and she went back to America on 25 October, 1945.

Garlies had similar duties shepherding surrendered U-boats in the Western Approaches but her career came to an abrupt end on VJ-Day and, like many of the Evarts, she was hastily returned to the USA on 20 August.

Gore was on patrol in the Biscay area in late April and lingered there for some time after VE-Day. Ostensibly, she was patrolling and searching fishing vessels to ensure that no Nazis escaped via Spain. None were ever found, however, and her only brief excitement was a U-boat scare when a lookout reported a periscope sighting. They had been warned that perhaps not all U-boat commanders would meekly surrender and so this sighting was taken very seriously with all the old familiar tightening of the bowels until, that is, the 'periscope' turned out to be a floating broomhandle, discarded by one of the Spanish fishing vessels! She was back at Belfast in mid-May but there is no evidence that she was ever again operational. By September she was at Hartlepool and had a long spell in the Reserve Fleet before returning to America in May, 1946.

Bentley was the only ship of 1EG to be definitely earmarked for further service. Immediately after VE-Day she went into dock at Cardiff for an extensive refit and conversion into a fighter direction ship for Pacific service. However, when Japan surrendered, this work slowed down and eventually stopped. During October, 1945, there were hasty moves to put all her loose parts back on board. This was done so hurriedly that some gun mountings were merely lashed in place with wire ropes and in this state the once proud ship made her final crossing to Brooklyn Navy Yard on 5 November, 1945.

Hoste having had as little excitement with 1EG as she had previously with *Balfour* in EG18, ended her unspectacular career quite suddenly after the Japanese surrender and was among the first Evarts to return to the USA in August, 1945.

Thus passed what had been the unluckiest of all the DE groups. Their score of victories had been creditable but had only been achieved at the loss of four of the eight ships which had served in the Group. The balance sheet of their victories and losses shows that at five against four they were only just ahead of the enemy but all those men who served with the 1st EG are still very proud of their connection with it.

TABLE OF U-0BOAT SINKINGS BY THE 1st ESCORT GROUP

Date	U-boat No.	Ships Involved.
25.2.44	U91	*Gore* and *Affleck*
1.3.44	U358	*Affleck, Garlies, Gore* and *Gould.*
16.3.44.	U392	*Affleck* (+ 2 USN aircraft)
25.6.44	U1191	*Affleck* and *Balfour*
18.7.44	U672	*Balfour*

SHIPS LOST FROM THE 1st ESCORT GROUP

Gould sunk by U358 off the Azores 1.3.44
Whitaker torpedoed off Malin Head by U483 (CTL) on 1.11.44
Capel torpedoed by U486 off Cherbourg on 26.12.44
Affleck torpedoed by U486 off Cherbourg (CTL) on 26.12.44.

NOTE: The only casualty list for *Affleck* which I have seen mentions but one fatality – but ex-Petty Officer McElroy tells me that he believes that there were nine casualties – including a pair of brothers.

– 5 –

THE 5th ESCORT GROUP

*Aylmer, Bickerton, Bligh, Grindall, Keats,
Kempthorne, Tyler and Goodson.*

5 EG was the last of the groups formed on the basis of three Evarts
and three Buckleys. Although an Admiralty Pink List records
ships being allocated to this group on 28 January, 1944, it was
not operational until April. Eight ships were to be associated with 5EG
during its existence but the original six were *Aylmer, Bligh* and *Bickerton* (Buckleys) and *Keats, Kempthorne* and *Goodson* (Evarts). *Aylmer*
was the first of them to commission on 30 September, 1943, and she
had finished all her trials and working-up routines by 10 December,
giving her crew fond hopes of being home for Christmas, which indeed
they should have been if all had gone well. Their wishful thinking was
foiled, however. Shortly after leaving Bermuda, en route to her first
convoy rendezvous, she had an engine failure and returned unhappily
to Bermuda.

The defect turned out to be more serious than the Bermuda dockyard
staff could deal with and all hopes of Christmas at home faded when
she was routed back to Charlestown Navy Yard for expert attention.
The whole of the Christmas season was spent there and she was not
finally fit for sea again until New Year's Eve when she departed for
Argentia, for a delayed Atlantic crossing.

Goodson had similar problems. She had been commissioned on 16
October 1943, and completed the Bermuda work-up just a few days
behind *Aylmer* on 15 December. Like her sister ship, she too had an
engine breakdown on the way to the convoy departure point and had
to go back to Bermuda. The problem was less serious than that of
Aylmer and the Bermuda dockyard staff were able to carry out the
repairs fairly quickly. She sailed for Halifax again on 20 December and
departed for Britain with convoy HX272. Shortly after this convoy

89

sailed, there were U-boat alarms in the vicinity and the convoy Commodore detached *Goodson* and *Balfour* to carry out a search. Their orders were to continue searching until 30 December. If no contact had been made by then, they were to return to catch up the next convoy. Their search *was* fruitless and the disappointed pair turned back as ordered.

Meanwhile, *Bickerton, Bligh, Keats* and *Kempthorne* had successively commissioned on 17, 23, 28, and 31 October, 1943. Unlike their predecessors, none of these four had any problems whatever, either at Boston or Bermuda. They all departed for the UK within a couple of weeks of one another. *Aylmer* had left with HX 273 on 3 January, 1944, *Goodson, Bligh, Keats* and *Kempthorne* were with HX274 and *Bickerton* followed with HX275 on 17 January.

With six frigates arriving so closely together, the base staff at Pollock Dock were unable to cope with their modification refits all at once. Four were taken in hand but *Aylmer* and *Bligh* had the unusual experience of being sent to Liverpool for their modifications. *Aylmer* had the misfortune to be delayed by a foolish and unsuccessful attempt to sabotage her engines. Just as she was ready for sea trials after the refit, her ERA's discovered a quantity of sand in the lubricating oil tank. The damage could have been serious if the abrasive material had found its way through to the turbine bearings but the vigilance of the ERA's had forestalled this. Even so, there was a considerable delay to the ship's programme while the oil tanks and all distribution lines were meticulously cleaned and flushed to remove every last grain of sand.

It must be emphasized that attempts at this kind of sabotage were extremely rare in ships of the Royal Navy and were never inspired by sympathy with the enemy. More often than not they were irresponsible acts of thoughtless vandalism aimed merely at prolonging a ship's stay in a particular port for as simple a reason as to continue to enjoy home comforts or to dally with a girl friend. One of the Stoker PO's was court martialled and the man was probably disrated and spent the remainder of the war in the cells. Fortunately, the incident did not delay *Aylmer*'s operational schedule too much and, by the end of March, she was ready, with all the other five original members of 5EG, to undergo preliminary group training. The officer appointed to lead the new group was Commander D. McIntyre, a dour Scot and renowned disciplinarian who had just completed two years as Senior Officer of the B2EG in the destroyer *Hesperus*. This had been a close escort group and the transfer to the role of support group with a more roving commission to hunt out the enemy much appealed to him. He chose *Bickerton* as Leader and set about getting the new 5EG into operational shape.

McIntyre was a hard taskmaster and it was much to the relief of all when he was eventually satisfied that the ships were in an efficient state by 21 April. They were then allocated their first duty. This was as support to an outward Atlantic convoy (ONS233) and the first days were notable only for the truly abominable weather. In the words of Commander McIntyre those days were 'More of a throw up than a shake down!' By the time everyone was coming to some sort of terms with the characteristic but unpredictable motions of the ships, the convoy had progressed without incident to beyond the point where U-boat activity could be expected. So when an enemy report was received from a different area, 5EG were detached from ONS233 and sent to investigate the sighting report. A whole day was spent quartering the allocated search area without them gaining the slightest Asdic or radar contact and on the following day, 26 April, the Group's orders were changed. They were sent to rendezvous with the escort aircraft carrier *Vindex* and the Canadian EGC9. This group had been sent out with the specific task of hunting down a lone U-boat which had been sending regular weather reports. Such reports were of importance to both sides in view of the impending invasion and the Admiralty had considered it well worth while to try to silence this particular boat. The whole operation was a thorough test of HFDF techniques as the only clues to the U-boat's position were its regular wireless transmissions back to Doenitz's headquarters. By the time 5EG had made rendezvous with *Vindex* on 2 May, the Turbo division were getting desperately short of fuel, although the longer ranged Evarts still had adequate reserves. With some reluctance, Captain Bayliss in *Vindex* agreed to give a limited amount of fuel to the Buckleys from his own tanks. The Canadian ships of EGC9 were also nearing the limit of their endurance and when a further U-boat sighting was reported in the Western Atlantic this Group was ordered back to Nova Scotia to refuel and to investigate the U-boat en route. It is on record that Captain Bayliss was not particularly impressed about this change. EGC9 had at least been a well experienced group but what of these strange frigates which had only recently joined in Atlantic operations? His confidence in them was soon very much diminished when *Bligh* sent his aircraft on a wild goose chase on a reported HFDF bearing. *Bligh* hotly denied the accusation but Captain Bayliss was firmly convinced that the inexperienced DF operator had read off the reciprocal bearing of the target instead of the true one.

After this initial gaffe, the two divisions of 5EG separated. *Keats*, *Kempthorne* and *Goodson* took over the task of close escort while the Buckley group pressed on into the area where the weather reporting U-boat was believed to be. Three days passed without any transmissions being picked up on the frequency which had been in use before. Swordfish and Hurricanes flew continuous patrols from *Vindex* and on

6 May they lost their first pilot, a New Zealander, whose Hurricane had engine failure, forcing him to bale out. One of his companions dropped him a dinghy but in his frozen and exhausted state he was unable to clamber into it. *Vindex* and the frigates were some 70 miles away so it was quite a considerable time before *Goodson* got to the scene and pulled the unconscious pilot on board. She carried no MO and the SBA was unable to revive the survivor, nor could the doctor from *Vindex*, who arrived later. The young pilot died without ever regaining consciousness.

Later that same day, the U-boat surfaced just as it was getting dark and one of the Swordfish was able to get a radar fix on it. Being short of fuel, the pilot jettisoned his depth-charges to prolong airborne time and made towards the U-boat. Although visibility was now almost nil, he did manage to sight the enemy but having no weapons could only mark the position with a flare. Fog began to hamper further flying operations so 5EG first division homed in on the aircraft's position report and by 0400 *Keats* made radar contact and fired starshell but an almost immediate Asdic echo indicated that the quarry had dived. *Keats* began the action with a number of DC attacks. *Bickerton* joined in at 0518 but by then the U-boat was too deep for conventional attack. Commander McIntyre thus set up a creep attack with himself controlling *Bligh*. This was progressing well up until 0558 and two minutes later *Bligh* began to drop the first of the pattern of charges. With only four left to drop there was sudden confusion and pandemonium on *Bligh*'s quarterdeck. The explosion of her charges had thrown reload charges from their stowages and these were careering about the quarterdeck, buckling the flaps on the stern rails. To add to the confusion, one of the charges already dropped exploded at extremely shallow depth and threw everyone off their feet. A cloud of soot belched from the funnel and a 100ft column of water from the shallow charge descended and drenched the now bewildered DC team!

However, the exercise had been successful. Soon after this foreshortened attack, the U-boat broke surface some half a mile astern of the two ships. Both *Bligh* and *Bickerton* opened fire immediately but, although the gunners' aim was good, Commander McIntyre, who had always doubted the despised 'elephant guns', had his fears confirmed as the 3" shells were seen to be bouncing off the U-boat's pressure hull. Here was a ridiculous situation! Two frigates had a damaged U-boat on the surface at their mercy – but how were they to sink it? The Oerlikon gunners were sweeping its decks to prevent return fire but beyond this things were at an impasse! The problem was soon solved however; one of *Vindex*'s Swordfish zoomed into the action, dropped two charges which accurately straddled the target and literally blew it into two parts. The official records credited *Bickerton, Bligh* and *Aylmer* and 825 Squadron with the destruction of U765 and Commander McIntyre was much satisfied that his inexperienced group had justified their existence so early in their career. Quite uncharacteristically, he even made a local signal that the group should henceforth be known as 'The Fighting 5th'.

The destruction of the weather reporting boat had been the sole purpose of the operation and now that this had been achieved there were great hopes that they could return to base for some well earned rest and replenishment. Interrogation of U765's commander Werner Wendt began to cast doubts upon this possibility however. He admitted that his observation patrol had been practically at an end at the time of the sinking but that another boat was due to relieve him at any time. Consultation with the Admiralty confirmed that they would be ordered to stand fast until this information could be tested. Wearily, the aircraft crews and the men in the frigates set up the monotonous search routine all over again. These efforts were not in vain. Another U-boat *did* turn up and began making regular transmissions about the ambient weather conditions to the meterologists at U-boat Command. The signals were strong and clear and a good HFDF fix was made during the first day of the new search. Moreover, on the second day *Bickerton, Bligh* and *Aylmer* all made Asdic contact with the new enemy. It had dived deep and creeping tactics were again necessary. *Bickerton* acted as control ship and *Bligh* began her stalking approach. Perhaps they were over confident after their last successful use of this ploy but they certainly bungled this one. Due to the heavy weather, *Bligh* was having difficulty in keeping steerage way at the slow pace of her creeping approach and her CO, Lieutenant-Commander Cooper, pleaded with McIntyre to be allowed to speed up 'just another couple of knots'. Now, as every good gambler knows, if you are working to a system you *must* stick to its rules but on this occasion the Group Leader gave permission for *Bligh* to increase her speed and the whole attack failed. The slight increase of propeller noise had warned the U-Boat's CO of the impending danger and a rapid alteration of course took him out of range of the deadly charges. To exacerbate matters, Asdic conditions deteriorated and the frigates were quite unable to locate the enemy again. By this time the 5th EG had been at sea for over three weeks and the Buckley division's fuel tanks were almost empty. *Vindex* could not afford to let them have more oil from her so on 9 May, *Bickerton, Bligh* and *Aylmer* were released to return to Belfast. The Evarts division still had some endurance left however and remained with the carrier. Three ships were insufficient to look after *Vindex* and continue the search so the Admiralty called in the 2nd EG from some nearby operation and it joined forces with the three frigates.

No more enemy contacts were made during the next two days of the search and it was reluctantly decided to call it off. The operation ended on a sad note with the loss of another aircraft. A Swordfish had crunched a wing whilst landing on in very rough weather and crashed over the side. *Goodson* was acting as crash boat at the time and although she was only five cables astern of the carrier, the weather was so bad that it took them two hours to locate the ditched fliers. She lowered her whaler in almost impossible seas and picked up the plane's observer but he died of exposure soon after. Another of the plane's crew was then sighted close to *Goodson* and the tragic events which followed are described by Able Seaman Smith:

> A scrambling net was lowered over the stb'd side. Petty Officer James and myself clambered down to assist the airman. PO James had secured himself by means of a line but I had to hold on as best I could by twining my legs in the net. We both managed to get a hold on the man but we couldn't lift him because of the weight of his water-logged flying suit. We tried to help him get a hold of the net and he kept muttering 'Good lads, Good lads!' – but eventually a huge wave broke our hold on him and he was swept away into the darkness for ever.

The whole force returned to Greenock after this long operation and the two divisions of the 5th EG were reunited again after their first foray.

After replenishment it was not difficult to guess what their next operation was going to be. They moved down to anchor to Moelfre Bay during the last few days of May, joining company with what seemed to be the entire frigate strength of the Royal Navy, all under orders for the imminent assault on mainland Europe. From D-Day onwards, the 5th EG joined several other WA groups in carrying out massive A/S patrols in the Western Approaches. Their particular area was from Ushant to the Cornish coast but they patrolled it regularly for two weeks to no apparent good effect. They found plenty of Asdic echoes but most were spurious. There had been great expectations of real action when the invasion began but, as each day passed without any sign of a U-boat, life became almost unreal. It was difficult to realize that although just across the Channel one of the greatest battles of all time was being fought, here in 5EG's patrol area action was being sought but not found.

This period of peaceful patrols came to a violent end on 15 June. It was one of those rare summer days at sea with not a breath of wind and the surface of the water was as smooth as a mill pond. The Group was on patrol in the usual line abreast formation and the River class frigate *Mourne* was also in company about a mile on *Bickerton*'s port side. None of the ships had any radar or Asdic contact but an alert bridge lookout suddenly gave the alarm and reported seeing a wisp of smoke rising from the mirror like surface of the sea some distance ahead. It was soon established that this was the exhaust fume emitted from a Schnorkelling U-Boat and all ships were alerted to A/S action stations. *Mourne* was the first to make Asdic contact but no sooner had she made range and bearing reports than she almost instantly disappeared in a huge explosion which left nothing but some floating wreckage, human remains and a few floundering survivors. The sudden violent disintegration of a ship is always a terrible experience but on this occasion such an event, on a perfect summer's day, was particularly horrifying.

Mindful that other torpedoes might have already been fired, Commander McIntyre ordered the Group to make a course change and then turn back towards the enemy bearing to make an Asdic sweep. This slight, but prudent, delay may well have given the U-boat commander the one chance he needed to make his escape and he certainly made use of it. None of the 5th EG frigates was able to pick up any trace of the U-boat during many hours of search. German records indicate that it had been U767, which was sunk three days later by the destroyers *Fame, Inconstant* and *Havelock* west of the Channel Islands. During the abortive search, *Aylmer* was detached to pick up *Mourne*'s survivors and take them into Plymouth. EG5 continued their Channel patrols for quite some time after this latter incident and their next unusual experience was a strange contact with the French Resistance movement. A carrier pigeon, complete with message capsule, landed on *Aylmer* in mid-Channel during one operation. The capsule was retrieved and taken to the CO and all sorts of wild rumours circulated about the secret message it contained. The most popular had it that the pigeon had carried information about VI launching sites in France but Lieutenant A Shepherd (*Aylmer*'s Engineer) remembers the true facts. He was with the ship's doctor when he was given the message to be translated from French and says that:

> The message consisted of two pieces of paper roughly torn. One carried a plan of Nogent le Rottreau showing the position of the château, the garden 'summer house', the *utile de panage* and the road system. The other was a description of the plan and gave details of German troop movements. It also said the château was a German Army HQ and that the owners lived in the summer house. A footnote asked that seventeen

Spitfires be sent and (in English) a plea that 'When you come, don't send us all to perdition – we shall be there soon enough'. The note was signed 'Hubert No 17'.

Lieutenant Shepherd has tried many times to discover whether any action was taken as a result of the note. *Aylmer* was released to take it straight to Portsmouth but it remains a mystery. He has contacted M. J. Buckmaster but the latter merely admits that he remembers the particular note and 'believes that it was of some tactical use to the Allies'.

Not long after this pigeon incident, *Keats*, which had missed the chance of sinking the U-boat during their first operation in the Atlantic, believed that she had been given a second chance. Proceeding cautiously in thick fog in an area reputed to be devoid of any friendly shipping, she picked up a clear radar contact. After reporting to the group by TBS (radio telephone), she suddenly added an excited postscript 'Submarine in sight on the surface!' The excitement was short lived, however. Just as the gunners were about to open fire, the target was recognized as an Allied landing craft. The embarrassed young Sub-Lieutenant in charge of it admitted to being utterly lost and without any navigation charts. He probably never knew how close he came to being peppered with 3″ and close range fire!

Following these light relief incidents, 5EG were back in real action again on 25 June. Whilst on patrol about 35 miles south east of Start Point, *Bickerton*'s Asdic crew picked up a positive echo amongst a multitude of spurious ones. Commander McIntyre had just retired to his sea cabin and was a bit annoyed when recalled to the bridge. In his considered opinion the echo was much too good to be true and he dismissed it out of hand as 'non sub'. *Bickerton* had passed right over whatever it was whilst McIntyre was making this judgement but the contact was immediately picked up directly astern. When the new position was plotted it was discovered that the object had moved by an amount commensurate with the speed of a submerged U-boat and even Commander McIntyre had to agree that they had indeed found a submarine echo. *Bickerton* swung round on to an interception course and ran in at the maximum attack speed (20 knots) to deliver a well placed pattern of charges. It had all happened so quickly and smoothly that everyone was amazed when the U-boat broke surface after this first swift attack. Figures were clambering out of the boat's conning tower and the close range gunners were grimly picking them off. The 3″ 'elephant guns' again came in for some caustic comment from the Commander though; as usual they were making hits but the shells simply bounced off harmlessly. There was no need for an aircraft to come along to finish the job this time, however. In the dramatic light of the searchlight beam, all the uninjured Germans were seen to be abandoning ship with great alacrity and within minutes the U-boat (U269) had slid sternfirst into the depths. The whole episode had taken scarcely ten minutes. *Bickerton* picked up survivors but many were wounded and, despite the efforts of the MO, several died almost immediately. Leaving *Goodson* in charge of the group *Bickerton* returned to Plymouth with the living survivors and buried the dead en route.

This ended the career of U269, but she had not been alone. U1191 from the same group had been sunk by 1EG the same day. However, a third boat (U984) still lurked in the area and was soon to wreak vengeance on the 5th EG.

After the departure of the Leader, Lieutenant-Commander Cooper in *Goodson* continued to organize the patrol and by the following afternoon they were in the usual formation, line abreast, 4,000yds apart carrying out a search not very far from U 269's last resting place. It was another fine day with the surface of the sea mirror calm. Because of these unusual conditions, one of *Goodson*'s Oerlikon gunners was able to spot a periscope about 1000 yards off the starboard quarter. The sighting was reported on TBS and several of the group hopefully opened fire on the periscope. The submarine had already fired a T5 however and this homed in to explode under *Goodson*'s stern. *Bligh* at once turned to attack with a ten charge pattern but the U-boat escaped damage. For some time the group milled about the area trying to regain contact; at one time it was suspected that she was hiding under the crippled *Goodson* but in actual fact she was long gone after discharging a second T5 which failed to find a target. For some reason, the torpedo which struck *Goodson* had exploded prematurely and so although her damage was quite severe, it was not fatal and, by a miracle, none of the crew were killed. She listed to starboard and water was flooding into her after compartments faster than it could be pumped out, so the CO called for volunteers to dive down into the filthy waters in these flooded compartments to attempt damage control. ERA Simpson and Able Seaman Cribb came forward and, after plunging into the oily water several times, were eventually able to plug the holes and stem the inrushing sea sufficiently to get the flooding under control. *Bligh* then took her sister ship in tow into the dockyard at Portland. If *Goodson*'s crew had expected any sort of wounded heroes welcome they were most definitely disappointed. The base staff did not exactly ignore her presence but neither did they make much effort to provide even the rudimentary comforts to the stricken ship's crew. Some shipwrights came on board to check the damage and carry out enough jury repairs to ensure that *Goodson* didn't sink and arrangements were made for Naval stores to provide basic clothing for those who had lost all their possessions in the flooded after messes. Yet no one thought to deal with their creature comforts. It was hoped that, at the very least, the men would have been taken into the nearby Naval Base where they could clean up and enjoy a hot meal but no such simple humanitarian arrangements were offered. With no power in the ship, the galley was unable to operate and their only meal consisted of dry bread and bully beef, which was eaten sitting in darkness around the hatch leading down to the flooded mess deck. When someone found a few shillings in his moneybelt and suggested that they could do much better ashore in the dockyard canteen, four or five of them trooped over the gangway, despite being clad only in ragged overalls and seaboots. Unfortunately for them they were soon spotted by a carload of base officers on the way down to peer at *Goodson*'s damage. They were lined up and castigated for being in 'piratical rig' and when they could produce no identity cards they were marched off and placed in custody by the Dockyard Police. One of *Goodson*'s officers came along to identify them and they were released to go back to the ship, still hungry and dirty and very much incensed at being told that they were in serious trouble. The senior officer of the base staff had made it very clear to *Goodson*'s CO that he expected to get a full report of the disciplinary action taken against the miscreants next day.

The majority of *Goodson*'s ship's company got away on the customary five days 'survivors leave' very soon but the defaulters suffered a delay. Arrangements had been made for a USN tug to tow *Goodson* away to Belfast where she belonged and their punishment was to remain on board as towing party whilst their shipmates disappeared on leave. Pollock Dock authorities declared that *Goodson* was too much damaged for repair attempts to be worth while and when her crew returned from leave, they were paid off and she was declared a Constructive Total Loss.

This action was to be the last in which the 5th EG was involved during the remainder of its operations in the Channel and they were all back in Belfast in July. After having their outstanding defects dealt with in Pollock Dock, they were then ready for their next operation. Being under strength, their numbers were restored by *Grindall* joining them. Her origins had been contemporary with the others in 5EG since she had commissioned on 30 September, 1943, and she had actually finished work-up and reached Belfast in advance of the 5EG ships on 3 December. According to an Admiralty Pink List entry she was actually appointed to join 5EG on 28 January, 1944, but for some reason this affiliation did not take place. She joined B7EG instead and, after some convoy work with this group, she was sent in lonely exile as one of the weather observation ships far out into the Atlantic. This monotonous duty lasted from mid-April up to D-Day. She then went into Pollock Dock for a delayed conversion refit and was one of the very few Captains which took no part in the historic landings in Normandy. After her refit, she exercised with submarines off Rothesay for a while and, on being pronounced fully operational, she was conveniently ready to take her place with the 5thEG as *Goodson*'s relief.

The Group's next operation was to be very different from Channel patrols. They were ordered to Scapa Flow where they were to join the Home Fleet units in operation GOODWOOD, a diversionary aircraft carrier attack on the *Tirpitz*, as cover for a Russian convoy. The Group set out for Scapa on 12 August and, as the weather was exceptionally good during their progress through the Minches, Commander McIntyre ordered that all the Group were to paint ship on the way. This was in order to give a good impression when the frigates came under the scutiny of the several Flag Officers at Scapa but many wondered whether this had been a worthwhile exercise. When they passed through the lines of battleships, cruisers and fleet destroyers, all famous ships with names that were household words, they were amazed to see that these great ships of the Home Fleet looked as disreputable as the 5EG ships normally were! The hulls and upperworks were rust stained and salt encrusted and many of the funnels had heat blistered paint, all honourable marks indicating the long hard periods the ships had spent at sea. Their crews must have been looking askance at the smart appearance of these strange looking little ships and concluded that they must have been enjoying a peaceful life in harbour somewhere!

When GOODWOOD began, the 5th EG's task was to act as A/S screen and general tenders to the light carriers *Nabob* and *Trumpeter*. After being 'masters of their own fate' for so long, the frigates found it hard going to be constantly dashing about and changing course to keep station with the carriers as they manoeuvred into the wind every time their aircraft were landing on or taking off. At least it was exciting to be in a different part of the world for a change but nerves grew taut as they steadily approached Norway and reached areas of known U-boat activity. The Asdic crews in particular began to get a little apprehensive; having been warned about the temperature layers that played havoc with Asdic beams in these northern waters. They constantly made test transmissions on the hulls of the other ships and the results were not at all encouraging. No U-boats had been encountered so far but it was a worrying thought that when they did turn up it would be a matter of chance if 5EG could make contact with them. In the event, their worst forebodings came true. The carriers had reached the attacking area and when their aircraft returned, the force was due to turn west to make a refuelling rendezvous. The undetected enemy chose this moment to deliver their long expected attack. *Nabob* was the first victim, hit by a torpedo and seen to be rapidly settling down by the stern. McIntyre rapidly ordered his second division Evarts to screen *Trumpeter* and the cruiser *Kent* and also gave the signal for 'Foxers' to be streamed. But for *Bickerton* this was too late. A torpedo hit her in the stern and wrecked the whole of the after part of the ship. To add to the confusion, her steam siren jammed open and the smoke generating apparatus between the depth charge rails began belching out dense clouds of acidic white smoke. Some of the younger and less experienced ordinary seamen were quite convinced that *Bickerton* was in a sinking condition. Without waiting for orders, they began lowering the whaler. Commander McIntyre screamed at them to desist but his voice was not heard in the general din and he had to dash down from the bridge to calm the youngsters down.

When a calm appraisal of the damage was possible, McIntyre was much afraid that his ship was indeed finished. What remained of her stern was under water and she listed badly. A volunteer party (Stoker Petty Officer (SPO) Taylor, Ordnance Mechanic Chapman and Able Seaman Steele) had investigated the aft engine room however and reported that so far the bulkhead was showing no sign of giving way. Commander McIntyre had fleeting hopes of salvaging *Bickerton*. *Kempthorne* was called alongside to take off the casualties and all non-essential personnel but at this point McIntyre had no immediate intention of abandoning his ship. *Nabob* had by now reported that she hoped to be able to get under way again within a couple of hours and, realizing that his first responsibility was to screen the fleet ships and that none of 5EG could be spared from this task to stand by *Bickerton*, McIntyre reluctantly agreed to transfer himself and his staff to *Aylmer* and watched sadly as a fleet destroyer delivered the *coup de grâce* to *Bickerton* with a torpedo.

According to signalman Bernie Wheardon, who was on *Aylmer*'s bridge at the time, when McIntyre came on board to take over command, his first action was quite characteristic. He looked gloweringly at *Aylmer*'s bridge staff and growled at them all for their unseamanlike appearance and sent them, including the CO, below to shave and get changed into the rig of the day. Most CO's of small ships relaxed dress and shaving regulations whilst at sea, but obviously *Aylmer*'s crew were going to have to toe the line in future.

The remaining ships of 5EG had formed a sound screen around *Nabob* and the U-boat (U354) was unable to penetrate for a second attack. No contact with it was ever obtained. (It was sunk by aircraft from *Vindex* some three days later). The carrier was able to get along under her own steam again and the whole force returned to the Clyde where 5EG lost their bluff Scots commander. The Admiralty considered that over two continuous years of U-boat hunting plus the loss of his ship was enough for any man and he was given a shore post. The Group was then placed under the command of Commander B. W. Taylor on 30 August and, once again being short of one ship, the Captain class *Tyler* joined the Group.

Tyler was another of the ships delivered to Lissahally by an RCN crew on 25 February, 1944. After going through the normal Western Approaches work-up at Tobermory during April, she was on temporary loan to Nore Command for the invasion operation. She began her operations by taking part in general coastal convoy work in the North Sea until D-Day and then joined with other Nore Command ships in the shuttle service of convoys between Southend and Arromanches. Some ships engaged on these tasks had encounters with German coastal forces in the Channel but there are no records that *Tyler* saw much action during this busy part of her career and she was one of the first of the Nore Command Captain class frigates to be released back to Belfast in time to be co-opted into the 5th EG to make up its full number again.

Tyler's crew must have thought that they had joined a very fortunate group because her first operation with them was one of the renowned peaceful runs with a KMF convoy to Naples and back during September. This was more of a holiday cruise than a wartime convoy and was much appreciated by all, apart from the foolish individuals who ignored the MO's warnings and contracted an unsocial disease in the bordellos of Naples, but it was the last time that 5EG enjoyed one of these trips. On their return from the Mediterranean, the Group was back to the usual routine of long A/S patrols but now the operational area was around Northern Ireland and the Scottish Isles. This remained their role for the remainder of 1944 but the harsh monotony of battling against the weather in these regions was not relieved by any action with the enemy.

However, the New Year brought them new battle honours during two actions in quick succession. The first of these was a controversial victory for *Aylmer*. The group had been at hand when *Manners* was torpedoed off the Isle of Man and arrived on the scene just as *Calder* and *Bentinck* of the 4th EG had flushed U1172 to the surface (see pages 53–4). There was a confused gun action which ended by *Aylmer* closing in to ram the submarine. There are reports that the U-boat caught fire after this rough handling and there were fears at one time that it might blow up but, before this happened, it sank out of sight.

One eyewitness in *Aylmer* herself avers that the ramming was not altogether intentional. He believes that in the noise and general confusion of the gun duel, *Aylmer*'s coxswain misheard orders from the bridge and put the helm over the wrong way! It would be difficult to verify this after all these years but there is possibly some truth in this allegation. The tactical situation did not warrant such action and some time before this the Admiralty had issued instructions that ships were not to ram U-boats except in dire circumstances. *Aylmer* limped off to Liverpool where she remained out of action for three months having her bows rebuilt.

Immediately after this action, Commander Taylor had transferred to *Grindall* and the remaining ships of 5EG continued operations to the east of the position of *Manner*'s loss and searched for another U-boat which was suspected to be still in the vicinity. This search was not protracted as the Group made contact with that U-boat (U1051) the very next day (27 January). A combined attack by *Keats, Bligh* and *Tyler* earned the Group's fourth 'Jolly Roger' of success.

* * *

Whilst *Aylmer* continued to enjoy a relaxed existence in dry dock at Liverpool, the Group endured a frustrating period of patrols off the coasts of Ireland and Scotland which produced no tangible results. *Kempthorne* and *Grindall* were now the only two which had earned no share of the official credits for U-boat sinkings. As February and then March passed with no signs of action, they were losing hope of ever having individual success.

Aylmer's repairs were completed in early April and she resumed group leadership for one of their last operations of the war. This was a sweep into the Atlantic west and south of Ireland and against fading expectations they *did* notch up another victory. They discovered U285 some 125 miles south-west of Ireland and it was efficiently despatched by *Grindall* and *Keats* on 15 April, 1945.

That really was the end of the war for 5EG. Germany surrendered three weeks later, leaving *Kempthorne* still without any share of battle honours and the Group slowly drifted apart. The ships of the 'Fighting Fifth' gradually faded away into separate obscurity.

* * *

Aylmer spent some time after VE-Day shepherding surrendered U-boats into captivity, operating variously from Belfast, Lochalsh and Scapa Flow and then carried out exercises and trials off the Isle of Man to prepare her for Pacific service. When Japan surrendered, she became attached to the Rosyth flotilla which really did not have any operational duties to offer and she made her final return to the USA on 5 November, 1945.

Grindall also took part in receiving the surrender of U-boats but paid off at Chatham in July and, together with *Kempthorne*, was among the first of the Evarts to be sent back to America on 20 August, 1945.

Tyler was put into dock to be converted into a floating power station at Portsmouth but this work was never completed and she went back to the USA just a week after *Aylmer* on 12 November, 1945, just over two years after her handover to the Royal Navy.

Keats was the last of the Group to disappear to the land of her origin. She ended up in the Reserve Fleet at Hull in August, 1945, and remained there awaiting a steaming crew for the last Atlantic crossing. This last voyage was on 27 February, 1946.

TABLE OF U BOAT SINKINGS BY THE 5th ESCORT GROUP.

Date	U-boat No.	Ships Involved.
U765	6.5.44	*Bickerton, Bligh, Aylmer* (and *Vindex* aircraft)
U269	25.6.44	*Bickerton*
U1172*	26.1.45	*Manners, Aylmer* (with *Bentinck, Calder* of 4EG)
U1051*	27.1.45	*Tyler, Keats, Bligh*
U285	15.4.45	*Grindall, Keats*

*These details of the sinkings of U1172 and U1051 are recorded in Roskill's *History of the War at Sea* but eyewitnesses report that on the conning tower of the U-boat sunk on 26 January, 1945, there was a badge which showed a continental figure 7, the cross stroke of which was a fish. This positively identifies this boat as U1051 (confirmed in Rohwer and Hummelchen's *Chronology of the War at Sea*). Hence, to keep the records straight, the details of these two sinkings must be transposed.

(See also *Battle in the Irish Sea* by The Reverend Sir D Gibson (Asdic Officer of *Manners* and published by Maritime Books, Liskeard.)

SHIPS LOST FROM THE 5TH ESCORT GROUP

Goodson - torpedoed off Start Point by U984 26.6.44 (CTL)
Bickerton - torpedoed by U354 during Operation GOODWOOD 22.8.44
(Abandoned and sunk by own forces.)

– 6 –

THE COASTAL FORCES CONTROL
FRIGATES (THE CFCF's)

Duff, Riou, Retalick, Seymour, Stayner,
Thornborough, Torrington, Trollope
(Later, Cubitt, Rutherford, Dakins, Ekins)

One of the major problems facing the planners of Operation
NEPTUNE was how to protect the huge invasion armada and
the subsequent supply convoys from the menace of the German
E-boat forces. These had been a major hazard to our coastal convoys in
the North Sea and Channel right from the early days of the war. Their
low profile, high speed and good sea keeping qualities had enabled
them to make daring night raids on our inshore shipping lanes which
resulted in major losses from our coastal convoys whose escorts found
the E-boats to be exceedingly elusive targets. In size and armament they
were roughly equivalent to our own Coastal Forces' Motor Torpedo
Boats (MTB's) and Motor Gun Boats (MGB's), but it must be admitted
that the German designers had produced a better type of vessel. Most
E-boats had a top speed of over 40 knots, which was slightly better
than our own MTB's and, being built with rounded bilge hulls, as
opposed to the planing type hulls of MTB's, they were capable of
maintaining higher speeds in rough weather and could easily travel at
36 knots in sea conditions which restricted MTB's to about 18 knots.
With these advantages, the E-boats destroyed some quarter of a millon
tons of our coastal shipping during the war, some by torpedo and some
by mines dropped in the path of the convoys.

There were five flotillas of E-boats deployed in the Channel ports of
Brest, Cherbourg, Le Havre, Boulogne and Ostend in 1944. Each
consisted of nine boats, six of which were normally operational with
the others undergoing maintenance or training. The Allied Naval staff

were much concerned about the real threat that these flotillas posed. They were very vulnerable to air attack but since they confined operations to night time sorties and retired to concrete pens during the day, they were extremely difficult to locate except on moonlit nights – when they obviously stayed in port. Our own Coastal Forces were quite capable of dealing with them at close quarters but lacked the radar sets to detect them. Frigates and destroyers had this radar capability but lacked the speed to intercept them.

It was eventually decided to combine the advantages of frigates and MTB's to form patrol units which could be deployed along strategic lines specifically to deal with E-boat forays. Each Coastal Forces Control Frigate (CFCF) had tactical command of up to six MTB's or MGB's so that when E-boats were detected at long range, the light craft could be directed on to an interception course and, if possible, drive the enemy units towards the heavier guns of the controlling ships. There were initial problems about co-ordinating these tactics. The Coastal Forces were accustomed to being free agents and resented being under the control of officers who did not really understand their methods of attack. However, this problem was solved by using experienced Coastal Forces officers in the frigates as Control Officers to advise on tactical matters. Once the CFCF groups had trained together and had operational experience, the system was a great success and by their use we at last gained the upper hand over the E-boats.

After the formation of the first four all-Captain escort groups, the urgent need for ships in the Western Approaches Command had receded. As there were a large number of Captains of both types still to arrive from the USA early in 1944, it was decided that a number of them could be spared from duties away from the Western Approaches. Some were allocated to local flotillas in the three Home Commands and eight became the CFCF's nominally attached to the 1st Destroyer Flotilla (DF) at Portsmouth. All were the Buckley class turbo type since their extra speed of 24–26 knots would be more suitable for this sort of work than the slower Evarts. In addition to their standard close range armament, all were given a 2pdr Pom Pom as a bow chaser.

The first of the CFCF's in order of commissioning was *Duff*, inevitably to be affectionately known as one of the Pudding Class frigates and, unlike most of the new group, she had been in operation for some time. Her commissioning had taken place at Boston on 23 August, 1943, and she had been contemporary with *Duckworth* and *Essington* of the 3rd EG during their Bermuda training in October. Had she sailed with them to the UK it is quite possible that she might have also been one of the 3EG ships. However, minor engine room problems had delayed her passage and she made a solo run to Belfast later. During this first voyage, her inexperienced crew missed the chance of flying the Jolly Roger even before they were properly operational. Two days after leaving the United States she had a positive radar contact with a surfaced U-boat at night. The first embarrassment was the failure to burst of her first spread of starshells. This resulted in mutterings about defective American ammunition, but there were very red faces among the Gunner's party when B gun's crew began to examine the contents of the ready use lockers. The one allocated to contain starshell had nothing but fused HE. Obviously the Gunnery PO had forgotten to replenish properly after their last practice shoot at Bermuda and this carelessness had lost them the chance of a gun action. By the time that the supply party had produced starshells, the submarine had long since dived. They did gain Asdic contact fairly quickly but the U-boat commander was obviously more experienced at A/S warfare than a crew making their first real attack and he evaded the probing Asdic beam and disappeared into the depths.

By the time *Duff* reached Belfast, 3EG was already up to strength and she was condemned to a boring six months running fornightly trips from Liverpool as a training ship for engine room staff waiting to join new Captain class frigates. She is mentioned as being a member of the 4th EG during this time but this was probably only an attachment for administrative purposes. At the end of this training stint, her complement was restored to operational strength and she departed to Portsmouth to join the CFCF's in early April, 1944.

The next in succession was *Riou* commissioned on 14 December, 1943. For reasons explained below, she was not an original member of the CFCF's and did not join them until some time later. Her early days at Boston were without problems but her progress towards operational status was delayed when she reached Casco Bay. *Fitzroy* had been acting as Base Training Officer's (BTO) ship there for some time but with *Riou*'s advent she was sent on her way to Bermuda and much to the disgust of *Riou*'s crew, they found themselves allocated as BTO's ship until 16 March, 1944. The notorious author of *Yankee RN*, named Cherry (see Chapter 3 page 59) joined her as 1st Lieutenant and actually achieved his burning ambition to command an RN ship in her, but only for the short trip back to Boston when the ship's period as BTO expired and he was promptly relieved by Lieutenant F. L. Boyer before the Bermuda work-up started. Her period of training there ended in April and she sailed in company with *Hotham* to Norfolk Va. where they met up with HMS *Indomitable* on the 20th and escorted her back to the UK via the Azores. On arrival home, *Riou* was sent to await further orders at Greenock.

The next three of the embryo CFCF's rolled off the Boston production lines during December, *Retalick* on the 8th, *Seymour* on the 23rd, and *Stayner* on the 30th. All three were ferried to Britain by RCN crews on their way to commission River class frigates. The RN crews for the Captains arrived to take them over at Lissahally on 16 February. Some key RCN ratings remained for a while to instruct engine room crews but this did not last long. After a few shake down days at sea, all three ships were sent to the Clyde for their conversion refits after which they suffered miseries on the infamous Tobermory work-up course. This was followed by further intensive gunnery training, mainly at high speed splash targets towed by MTB's and when these were completed, on 15 April, they were inducted into the CFCF group at Portsmouth.

Only three other Buckleys were original members of the CFCF's – *Thornborough*, *Torrington* and *Trollope*. These all commissioned at Boston in the normal manner within a couple of weeks of one another, 31 December, 1943, 10 January, 18 January, 1944, respectively. *Torrington* had finished the initial training period slightly ahead of the other two and had begun her voyage to the UK on 20 March, 1944, encumbered by a precious deck cargo of some 40 tons of manganese bars temporarily welded to the deck. There is a Pink list record that her Pollock Dock refit was complete by 2 May and she then joined the CFCF's at Portsmouth.

Meanwhile, *Torrington* and *Trollope* had left Bermuda on 25 March, 1944, and sailed in company to the Azores. There they joined a small UK-bound convoy as escorts. They left the convoy at the Channel entrance and proceeded into Devonport where they were reminded in no uncertain terms that there was still a war on. Their first night home coincided with an air raid on the port and they spent most of the night closed up at action stations with the gunners adding their tiny 3″ bursts to the general barrage. *Torrington* sailed for Newhaven the following morning but *Trollope* was diverted to Pollock Dock for her modification refit which lasted until 20 April. As soon as this was over, she was despatched immediately to join the CFCF's and plunged straight into their operations by meeting *Torringon* off Cherbourg on the 22nd to carry out their first CFCF patrol.

These early operations in April were more or less training exercises to enable the CFCF's to perfect their tactics. Nevertheless, they were training exercises under action conditions. The ships had to learn quickly or fall victim to the very E-boats they were to hunt. There were only about nine nights during the month when weather favoured the E-boats but on each occasion two or three enemy flotillas would make forays. A number of destroyers, *Whitshed, La Combattante, Middleton, Stevenstone* and *Volunteer*, made contacts and several E-boats were sunk or damaged during the month but there is no record that the

CFCF's had any successes in those early days. During May, the CFCF's settled down into a regular pattern of patrol routines which was to continue for many months. The ships operated from Portsmouth but, apart from replenishment, they spent most of the time anchored off Ryde pier when not at sea. The patrols themselves were nightly affairs with the frigates putting to sea during the dog watches to rendezvous with their MTB's and arrive on their designated patrol line before midnight, which was a favourite time for the E-boats to set out on their raids. The patrols would continue during the hours of darkness when the ships would return to Ryde for the day. Some of the men who had served in ships in the Atlantic escort groups were under the impression that this Channel patrol business was going to be a sinecure but they soon changed their minds. Although spared the long weeks at sea endured by Western Approaches groups, the CFCF's routine became very demanding on physical endurance. Whilst sailing towards the patrol area, it was customary for the ships to be at cruising stations with only a third of the personnel closed up. However, when actually on patrol, the rule was to close up to full actions stations. For the rest of the night, the men might occasionally be partially stood down but even then they had to remain on the upper deck in the vicinity of the guns, so sleep was a rare commodity during the hours of darkness. Then, on return to harbour, all the normal daywork tasks had to be performed around the ship and maintenance carried out on weapons and machinery. On occasions when the night had been particularly gruelling, the non-duty parts of the watches were permitted a few hours to rest and sleep during the afternoon but this was by no means the norm. Thus although the ships spent much time at anchor in full view of shoreside attractions, the crews suffered much from lack of sleep and looked forward to nothing so much as the rare one night stand down from patrol duties when they could enjoy a few hours ashore and all night in their bunks.

The month of May was almost as devoid of CFCF actions as April. There were only seven nights when various enemy flotillas put to sea and most of them were on minelaying operations during which they seem to have avoided the CFCF's successfully for most of the time. There was one encounter on 12–13 May when a large E-boat group attacked a convoy off Selsey Bill. The escort drove off this attack and the retiring E-boats ran into the patrol line which included *Stayner* and *Trollope* with the French *La Combattante* in company at 0100hrs. The MTB's were directed into action with the frigates and destroyer providing starshell illumination and gunfire support. In these engagements, the forces were only in contact with one another for about ten mintues at the most. During this time the night sky was rent with angry tracer and then all would go silent as the enemy force broke away and retired, usually under smoke screen. Not all the E-boats escaped on this occasion though. One E-boat was hit and sunk, and one of our own MTB's and several of the enemy received damage. After the attack, *Stayner* picked up the survivors from the German boat and *Trollope* went to assist the stricken MTB and take off her casualties. This was the first time that most youngsters in the DE had seen the ghastly wounds caused by HE cannon shells and a few of them had quite different attitudes during future actions. Lookouts' eyes became that much sharper and gun crews were more alert now that they knew how quickly a quiet patrol could turn into ten minutes of death and destruction. Although the CFCF patrols were devoid of E-boat activity during the latter part of the month, they did come under air attack several times, but not from the enemy! On two successive patrols, *Riou* and her MTB's had been attacked with anti-personnel bombs dropped by USAAF Black Widow fighter bombers. Fortunately these attacks did not result in any British deaths. The only casualty was the respect of the RN for the USAAF, which suddenly plummeted.

During the early days of June, 1944, practically all the DE's were under sealed orders to take some part in Operation NEPTUNE and the CFCF's were no exception. All except *Seymour*, which had been sent to Sheerness, were in the Portsmouth area. When the great invasion armada set out *Stayner*, *Thornborough*, *Trollope*, *Duff*, *Torrington*, and *Retalick*, with destroyers of the 1st DF, acted as part of the screening force on the eastern flank of the assault fleet. *Seymour*'s role was to join ships of Nore Command to escort four troopships from Southend to Normandy after the first wave had gone in. The Germans had destroyers, U-boats and E-boats available in the Channel ports but they put up no opposition whatever during the first stages of the landings. Subsequent actions were many but not all will be chronicled in the following pages. British ships did not keep war diaries but after any action the CO was obliged to make a detailed report to the Captain(D) of his group or flotilla. Most of the accounts which follow are taken from such reports held in the Admiralty files at the Public Record Office. Unfortunately, these have never been indexed and it is extremely difficult to identify the exploits of particular ships. Another problem is that many of these reports and signals were destroyed before being transferred to public records. However, enough information is here to provide a good outline of the CFCF activities.

Riou was last mentioned waiting for her D-Day orders at Greenock. She was still not destined to become a CFCF but to complete the records of her movements it is to be noted that her invasion role was to escort *Warspite* and *Rodney* during their passage through the Irish Sea to take up their bombardment positions off Normandy. She remained with them to witness the awesome softening up of Hitler's West Wall which began at 0530 hrs and although her gunners had hopes of joining in the general destruction, it was not considered that the 3″ guns would add much to the damage and they were ordered to remain silent. *Riou* remained in a passive role until *Rodney* ran out of 16″ shells and needed to be escorted to Milford Haven to replenish her ammunition. On return to the beachhead area, *Riou* was co-opted into a number of patrol and convoy activities which kept her busy in the invasion area for the next six weeks but she still did not operate with the CFCF's at this stage.

Although there had been no E-boat activity in opposition to the landings, it was fully expected that they would be out in force when night fell on 6 June. The entire CFCF force was organized into tight defensive patrol lines around the vital landing areas but to everyone's amazement, the expected E-boat attacks were not as concentrated as had been expected. The two flotillas, 5th and 9th, at Cherbourg and Le Havre, did make determined attempts to get at the massed shipping off Normandy but three other flotillas made sorties elsewhere. The 2nd and 8th Flotillas put out from Ostend and proceeded on a sweep into the North Sea and the 4th Flotilla, from Boulogne, sortied in their immediate area but naturally found no targets there. It may seem strange that the Germans sent three whole flotillas on fools' errands when so many fat targets awaited them off Arromanches but one must remember that our invasion plans had been so closely guarded that for some time German High Command was convinced that the landings were a feint and that the real invasion was to take place elsewhere. The three wasted flotillas were very likely sent to probe other areas of possible invasion activity.

Two of the E-boats which did attempt to attack off Normandy ran into a minefield and were lost; others ran into *Stayner* and her MTB's and were driven off after a swift indecisive action. After regrouping, six of them returned to attack but were intercepted by *Trollope*. This was her first serious encounter but there was no time for apprehension. Having illuminated the enemy she opened fire at 3000yds but with a combined closing speed of 55knots this was soon down to 1000yds and then point blank. All her close range weapons were in action including a Lewis gun on the bridge manned by the Gunnery PO and all hell was let loose for some moments until the enemy had zoomed past and were out of range again. *Trollope*'s gunners had gained their first blood however. The two leading E-boats were hit repeatedly and one of them caught fire and sank. Thus ended the first night of the running battles that were to become the norm for the CFCF's. Only two of the many

E-boats in action had gained any success, sinking an LST and an LCT off St Vaast. On the whole, the CFCF patrol lines had effectively prevented any serious losses among the invasion forces.

On the following night, there was a redeployment among the E-boats. Some were moved down from Ostend to reinforce those at Boulogne but again these units did not attempt to attack the main forces off Normandy and were merely able to sink two LSTs from an incoming convoy. E-boats from Cherbourg and Le Havre went into action off the beach areas but there they encountered *Stayner* and *Retalick* plus their MTB's and were forced to break away after a brief action during which three of them were seen to take many hits.

Frustrated by attempts on the eastern flank, the E-boats tried to break through the USN Dixie patrols on the west flank the following night but had little luck there either and by the night of 10–15 June the attacks were resumed in the British sector. Some twelve boats put out from Cherbourg and actions took place over a wide area. *Stayner* and MTB's of the 35th Flotilla were again in the thick of it and in a brief spell of fierce fighting one E-boat and an MTB were sunk. The saddest loss of the night was that of *Halsted* one of the Nore Command frigates. She was with a convoy in mid-channel approaching the beach areas and, whilst defending it against a determined E-boat attack, she was torpedoed and lost her bow section.

West of Le Havre, the 4th [E-boat] Flotilla had successfully laid mines in the Seine Bay but then ran foul of *Duff*. She was unable to close with them and had to be content to send in the MTB's. One of our boats was damaged but all the enemy seem to have escaped. By then *Duff*'s radar had detected another group and she turned towards them at 24 knots. Whilst both forces approached one another at high speed, a salvo of torpedoes forced *Duff* to veer off course but they all missed. The weather conditions were such that the frigate was able to outstrip the MTB's on this occasion and she took part in a solo action against the E-boats on her own account. After a brisk exchange of fire, one E-boat veered off and sank. Some time later, *Duff*'s MTB's were again able to engage and after two more E-boats had been severely mauled, the whole enemy group retired behind smoke at high speed and the night's encounters were over.

Duff had hopes of more action the next might as well. Some E-boats had penetrated the USN defences and sunk the USS *Nelson* but on their return towards Cherbourg they crossed *Duff*'s patrol line. They travelled at such high speed that even the MTB's could not intercept. *Duff* followed at her full 24knots, hoping that the E-boats might turn and give fight again but had to turn away in disappointment when, as her CO reports, she came under fire from heavy shore batteries. It was the same story on the 12–13th. *Duff* and her light forces intercepted a group of enemy boats again in Seine Bay but the CFCF's only success was to drive them back into harbour.

Peter Scott, son of the antarctic explorer, joined *Duff* as MTB control officer shortly after this and during the first patrol his charges had to deal with forces much larger than E-boats. First interpretation of the radar echoes was 'destroyers' but when the enemy was illuminated by starshell they turned out to be three minelayers. The MTB's had no difficulty in bringing these slower ships to action and achieved such surprise that two of the enemy began firing at one another in the confusion. Leaving them to fight it out, the MTB's made short work of the other one but then had to retire as they were dangerously close to enemy minefields.

All E-boat action virtually ceased during the latter part of June. From the 19th, the Channel suffered the most violent gales that had ever been known at this time of year. The Mulberry Harbour and the shipping therein suffered grievous damage, much greater than any inflicted by the enemy.

The storms had abated by 27 June, when the Allies captured Cherbourg. During that night, when *Trollope* was on patrol off Cap D'Antifer, the Cherbourg E-boat flotilla retreated hastily to Le Havre. *Trollope* made contact with them at 0100hrs but the enemy kept to inshore waters and only the MTB's could engage. They managed to give two of them a severe mauling before the whole force gained the security of the Le Havre defences. *Trollope* then had a five-day stand off, as her three-monthly boiler cleaning period was due. Normally this was an occasion to give part of the crew a few days leave but the only advantage her crew gained was five nights of very welcome undisturbed rest in Portsmouth dockyard. Leave was a rare commodity during the invasion period!

During *Trollope*'s absence, the remaining CFCF's were kept busy. Both *Stayner* and *Thornborough* made contact with separate E-boat groups on 3–4 July, but found the enemy more reluctant than usual to allow close action. This was the first sign that the E-boat commanders were beginning to realize the formidable power of the CFCF patrols.

Trollope was back on patrol the following night off Cap D'Antifer and intercepted some E-boats which were attempting to sneak in from Dieppe to reinforce the Le Havre flotillas. None were sunk but the whole force was successfully chased back to Dieppe. On the following night, her place in the patrol line was in the area of Seine Bay, known as North Tunny, and she had the two 1st DF destroyers *Stevenstone* and *La Combattante* in company. There was considerable E-boat activity after midnight and *Stevenstone* had been involved in a particularly hot action some time after 0100hrs. When the enemy had retired out of range, she turned back and joined *Trollope*. The tragic events which then followed were graphically described in a signal from *Stevenstone*. There are some unexplained aspects of this sad loss. In the first place, neither ship appears to have been in radar contact with any enemy forces at the time, which seems quite puzzling if there were E-boats within torpedo range, since both ships had excellent surface radar sets.

Then there are certain anomalies in *Stevenstone*'s report to the Flag Office British Assault Area (FOBAA). After *Trollope* was hit, she reports having opened fire on suspected enemy forces to the east but desisted when these turned out to be friendly forces. Under the circumstances it is difficult to envisage any friendly craft being between *Stevenstone* and the French coast apart from the CFCF MTB's. It thus could have been the case that during a general mêlée at high speed the controlling ships' plots had confused friend and foe. Perhaps they could see the echoes on their radar screens but believed that they were their own light forces.

The German version of what happened does not help very much either. Strangely there was no report whatever about *Trollope*'s loss in the first edition of Rohwer and Hummelchen's *Chronology of the War at Sea*. It appeared in the reprint issue but with a date which is a day late compared with British documentary evidence.*

Trollope had her entire bow section blown off, killing sixty of her crew and wounding another thirty. The bow section continued to float upside down but what incensed her survivors is that while rescue was being carried out by *Stevenstone*, the destroyer *La Combattante* rushed in and sank it by gunfire, despite the fact that several survivors averred that they had heard shouts indicating that some men were still alive in this severed portion of the ship. One can understand such drastic action perhaps; there were still confidential documents plus secret radar and Asdic equipment in this part of the ship which could not be risked falling into enemy hands if it drifted on to the French coast. The decision to sink it was probably one of those difficult and terrible decisions which had to be made in time of war.

A small towing party was left on board when all casualties had been

---

* Author's Note - Correspondence with Dr Hummelchen some years ago revealed other anomalies. He reports the time as 03.21 which is two hours late but possibly explained by different zone times used by Germany and ourselves. More surprising is his contention that the two E-boats S176 and S177 were at Quadrat BF3682 at the time they fired torpedoes. He translates this as 49 degrees 29 mins N, 0 degrees 15 mins W. but this position is 17Km southwest of *Trollope* according to *Stevenstone*'s signal and quite obviously no torpedo attack would have been attempted at a range of over ten miles.

taken off and *Stevenstone* towed *Trollope*'s remains towards Arromanches where they were taken over by a salvage tug.

The loss of *Trollope* as a CTL reduced the CFCF numbers to six frigates and as a replacement the unallocated *Riou* was at last appointed to join their ranks. It was to be some time before she was in action with them, however, as during August she was involved in a collision with the Liberty ship *Dan Baird* off Portsmouth and although the damage was not serious, she had to wait several weeks before Portsmouth dockyard could take her in hand.

The Germans introduced new weapons in the attempt to attack the Allied ships off Normandy during July. The two man 'Neger' piloted torpedoes appeared together with the 'Lentil' explosive motor boats and a new type of mine known as 'Oysters' was used. These were exploded by a pressure device which detected when a ship was passing over them and were quite deadly in shallow waters. To combat the Negers and Lentils a new defence known as the 'Trout Line' was set up around the Normandy anchorage. This consisted of a large number of landing craft (LCG's, LCF's and LCS's) formed up into a continuous double line at half mile intervals each night and a new duty for the CFCF's was to provide patrols outside this barrier. It was a most unpopular duty since, to avoid destruction by the Oysters, the ships had to sail at a snail's pace to prevent a pressure wave building up and they became sitting ducks for any form of enemy attack.

However, the chief problem for the CFCF's was still the E-boats. Nine of them put to sea on 7–8 July and there was a fierce battle in Seine Bay in which *Thornborough* with the destroyers *Cattistock* and *La Combattante* successfully drove the enemy back into Le Havre. None were destroyed but several suffered damage and casualties.

Duff was in action again on 17–18 July. Boats from the 6th Le Havre [E-boat] flotilla sortied out and ran into *Duff*'s patrol but once again they did not force a close action and the only casualty was MTB361. On the following night, *Stayner* and the destroyer *Forester* found action further along the Channel. E-boat units from the 8th Flotilla were escorting the German destroyer T28 from Boulogne to the Hook of Holland when *Stayner*'s radar picked them up. A stern chase developed but the enemy force steered clear of trouble inside their own coastal minefields and not even the MTB's could catch up with them in the prevailing choppy seas.

This was *Stayner*'s last CFCF action for some time. After the fall of Cherbourg, the USN had some spare PT patrol boats which had been working with their Dixie patrols and these were seconded to work with the RN CFCF forces. *Stayner*'s task was to exercise with them off Portland for a while to train the Americans to the CFCF methods. It still involved much night work but at least it was a respite from more desperate action.

It was *Retalick*'s turn to be in the line of fire on 26–27 July. Five E-Boats had sortied out of Le Havre and made the most determined efforts to break through the CFCF lines. They doggedly refused to give way against the MTB's which were deployed against them and a fierce dog fight took place at such close quarters that collisions took place. MTB430 was rammed by S182 and her next in line MTB412 collided with 430's wreck and both sank as did the E-boat. *Retalick* had to refrain from fire during this close action but loosed off a few rounds when the enemy eventually withdrew, but the targets were too fast for them and the enemy all escaped.

* * *

The next episode in the CFCF saga was unique in their records. It was the sinking of a U-boat. *Stayner* had finished the training with her USN PT boats and was on the way out from Newhaven for the first real patrol with them on 4 August. U671 was also in this vicinity on passage back through the Channel after an Atlantic patrol and *Stayner*'s bored A/S crew were galvanized into life when they contacted the U-boat off Beachy Head. Eager to demonstrate that they had not forgotten the art of submarine detection, they concentrated hard on the attack but it turned out to be a long chase. Many unsuccessful patterns of charges were dropped and the weary DC crews on the quarterdeck began to suspect that the Asdic crew *had* got rusty but, in the end, they were rewarded to see three human figures floundering in the vicinity of the last DC explosions. On picking them up, they discovered that they were all that was left of U671's crew – the Commander, the Engineer and the Coxswain. No other CFCF frigate was ever to earn the right to fly a Jolly Roger and *Stayner*'s crew were rightly proud of their unique feat.

Stayner did not get away scot free from this encounter however. After the attack, it was noticed that something had gone severely wrong with her steering. She could no longer perform the tight turns for which the DE's were noted. In those days individual ships did not carry shallow water divers and no investigation could be made until her next boiler cleaning period at Chatham, when it was discovered that all the cladding plates of one of her rudders was missing, leaving the bare frame ribs. Obviously, some of the charges she had dropped had been set very shallow but this slight damage was negligible in the face of the success of her attack.

The next bit of CFCF excitement fell to the lot of *Seymour*. She had just completed fifteen consecutive nights on the dreaded Trout Line patrols and had survived unscathed until, on the sixteenth night, she was shaken by a tremendous explosion directly under her which caused her to lose all power and come to a dead halt in the water. No one had any doubts about the cause. It had clearly been one of the pressure operated Oysters and the damage control parties fully expected to find a flooded compartment or two. But once again, the sturdy construction of the DE's had prevented damage. The loss of power had merely been 'breakeritis' and she was soon under way again with everyone congratulating one another on their lucky escape. Nevertheless, it is on record that many of them needed clean underpants!

The month of August had started fairly quietly as far as E-boat attacks were concerned but activity soon increased and it was to turn out to be one of the CFCF's most hectic months. Both *Thornborough* and *Retalick* had been given USN PT-boats (the equivalent of the British MTB) and by this time each had had brisk encounters within the first week of August. The first was a sharp action with minesweepers off Cap D'Antifer on the 5–6th and they then encountered an E-boat group off Le Havre the very next night. Neither of these actions resulted in sinkings but there was evidence that some severe damage had been inflicted before the enemy units withdrew. Then *Retalick* and her PT's ran into units of the German 14th Minesweeping Flotilla on the 7–8th and had another inconclusive action. It was noted that the USN PT-boats did not seem to put up any better performance than our own MTB's during these encounters and two of them were, in fact, severely damaged in the battle with the minesweepers.

With the British and Canadian forces advancing out of the beachhead area to the east, threatening Le Havre, the ships stationed there began to evacuate on 23–24 August and to move further east to Boulogne and Dieppe. The first of the German units to move out were a motley collection of trawlers, submarine chasers, minesweepers and KFK assault barges. *Thornborough* and *Retalick* were on their usual patrol lines in Seine Bay that night but since the escaping German ships were hugging the coastline up to Cap D'Antifer, they could only engage them at long range and were frustrated at not being able to stop this mass evacuation. The nightly exodus continued until the end of the month, harried as far as was possible by the CFCF patrols of *Seymour*, *Retalick* and *Thornborough*. It is known for certain that they sank E-boat S91, a KFK assault barge and two minesweepers whilst damaging many others, but at long range it was difficult to assess the damage. On the 29–30th, some E-boats turned up to cover the retreat and these were eagerly engaged by *Retalick* and the destroyer *Cattistock*, which pursued them so relentlessly that they were eventually within range of coastal gunfire. *Retalick* escaped harm but the destroyer was badly damaged and her CO was killed before both ships retired.

The Allied break out from the Normandy beachhead and the swift advance along the Channel coast completely changed the pattern of the CFCF activity. By 4 September the E-boats had all been driven eastwards to such bases as Rotterdam and Ijmuiden and their actions in the Channel virtually ceased. When Antwerp was captured and refurbished as a usable port, the main Allied supply routes were those funnelled into the Scheldt Estuary and when the E-boats had time to reorganize, the convoys in that area became their prime targets.

The CFCF's had moved as well. Portsmouth was now too far away from the action to be useful as their base and they had all moved eastwards to operate from the Nore Command bases at Sheerness and Harwich. Nore Command DE's also became more involved in E-boat hunting and some of them were to be incorporated into the CFCF force in the New Year, but their exploits will be dealt with in Chapter 7.

One of the last actions in the Channel area was on 18–19 September when *Stayner* intercepted a group of E-boats escorting a supply force on its way to the surrounded Dunkirk. Bad weather restricted the MTB's speed but they did cripple one of the enemy which was promptly finished off by *Stayner*. Two other E-boats then collided, enabling the frigate to catch them up and both were sunk; a triple victory which earned decorations in *Stayner*, including a DSC for the CO.

However, the E-boats were to have some revenge. They successfully laid mines on 28–29 September and *Duff* struck one at 0750 hrs on her way into Harwich after a night patrol. The explosion was under the for'ard boiler room and the only casualties were the SPO and two Stokers on watch there. Nevertheless, there was severe flooding for'ard and *Duff* limped slowly into Harwich with her bows practically under water. There were no repair facilities at Harwich and most of her crew were paid off before Christmas, leaving only a Care and Maintenance party to look after her until she was towed down to Chatham in the New Year. The damaged boiler room had been sealed up at Harwich and, sad to relate, the bodies of the three men were not recovered until the ship docked at Chatham. They were buried in the cemetery of the Royal Naval Hospital at Gillingham – Stoker Petty Officer G. Bishop, Stoker 1st Class E. O. Donovan and Stoker 1st Class E. Hannah.

Some repairs were carried out to *Duff*'s external plates but she was treated as a CTL and ended her days as a derelict at Rum Wharf in the East India Docks until taken to the breakers' yard after the war.

During December, 1944, the E-boats had become well established in their new bases and were attempting to harry the Scheldt convoys with as much vigour as they had shown off the Normandy coast. Their determination to get at the merchant ships had not abated but, probably because their numbers were growing less, they became more wary of the CFCF patrols which consequently found them more difficult to bring to close action. In the early days, they had been quite prepared to mix it with the patrols but now there was more of a tendency for them to retire and re-group in order to probe elsewhere when the CFCF's detected their approach.

Seymour was in trouble again before Christmas when, during a Scheldt patrol which was quiet as far as E-boat activity was concerned, she had a minor collision with a merchant ship. Her Yeoman of Signals, Dave Murray, recalls:

We were somewhere near NF4 or NF5 areas and the skipper was in the chartroom when we saw a large tanker bearing down on us from dead ahead. There really was no problem as there was plenty of sea room and the ship was perfectly visible but the young Sub on watch made a hash of things. By the time I had shouted for the skipper to come up quickly, it was too late to avoid disaster. The 'old man' did what he could but the tankers bow just scraped our stern wrenching off depth charge racks and letting a bit of daylight into the tiller flat.

The damage was slight and was all well above waterline but everyone expected a long wait to get into Chatham for repairs and Christmas leave suddenly became a great possibility. A survey by the base staff at Harwich decided that docking was unnecessary though. They had sufficient welding equipment to do the job alongside Parkeston Quay and the reprieve from action lasted for only eight days with five days leave for one watch and three for the other.

*   *   *

One of the fiercest battles at this period was two days before Christmas, 1944, when newspaper headlines announced 'E-BOAT FLEET ROUTED!' The action began off the Hook of Holland when some MTB's encountered an E-boat group and claimed one probably sunk and two damaged. The remainder of the enemy eluded them and made towards the Scheldt where *Torrington* was running the CFCF patrol with *Curzon* and *Walpole* of Nore Command in company. This group managed to bring the E-boats to action again and two more were sunk and three damaged, completely breaking up this attack. Later, during the same patrol, *Torrington* was in contact with another enemy group but these retired without the CFCF's being able to engage them. It had been a most successful CFCF night, four E-boats sunk and five badly mauled and all attempts to attack our convoys thwarted.

Undaunted by this defeat, the enemy forces were active again the following night with two strong groups. One was shadowed by Wellington bombers which drove the E-boats towards a Nore Command patrol including *Rutherford* and two of them were sunk and several others hit. The second group ran into *Torrington*'s patrol line later on and two of them were severely damaged before the rest retired behind smoke. Keeping up this Christmas offensive, the E-boats were out yet again on the 24–25th but all their attempts to reach the shipping lanes were blocked by *Thornborough* and her MTB's. None of the enemy were sunk but all their attacks were driven off. Unfortunately, despite these CFCF success, Christmas 1944 was a sad one for the Captains as a whole. As recorded elsewhere, *Affleck* and *Capel* were torpedoed on Boxing Day and *Dakins* of Nore Command, became a CTL after striking a mine on Christmas Day.

Seymour was soon in action again after her stern damage had been repaired in the New Year. She was on patrolling Area 16 in the Scheldt on 14–15 January, 1945, when radar detected six E-boats at a range of 5½ miles at 0135hrs. Ten minutes later, one of her MTB's, MTB695, illuminated the enemy with flares and caused them to manoeuvre violently to avoid close action. Frustrated by the inability of her MTB's to catch up with the enemy in the prevailing sea conditions, *Seymour*'s CO signalled the coastal craft to clear the range to let his gunners have a go. At 0151 hrs they opened fire at 1700 yards range but, sadly, the action was marred by sudden confusion around B gun which resulted in an unexplained cessation of starshell firings and the enemy contact was lost. The CO's report to Captain(D) merely states that one of B gun's crew lost his head and was discharged to hospital some days later. A case of nervous breakdown? The most likely explanation is that this was another case of the sticking firing plunger in the 3″ breech. In the heat and excitement of action it would be understandably frightening for a loading number to have the gun fire immediately he had pushed the round home and in all probability he was struck by the ejected shell case and became firmly convinced that he had been hit by the enemy! A nervous breakdown would be fairly excusable under these circumstances!

A few minutes after this incident, at 0154hrs, the radar plot indicated that one of the E-boats had fallen out of formation and stopped but an assiduous search failed to find it. The thwarted gunners liked to think that it had sunk but there was no confirmation of this in the way of survivors or wreckage.

It was not only in the Scheldt estuary that the E-boats were active.

They continued to operate in all their old stamping grounds in the coastal areas of the North Sea which had in the past become notorious as E-boat Alley. On 22–23 January for instance, five of them sortied close inshore off the North Foreland. *Seymour*'s group intercepted them and, in desperation, the enemy force fired off their entire arsenal of torpedoes at them – eight conventional G7E's plus two T5's. *Seymour* and the sloop *Guillemot*, which was in company, were hard pressed to avoid all these and the delay occasioned by their change of course gave the E-boats a chance to elude them but they didn't escape scot free. They were engaged by the Royal Artillery guns on the Tongue Sands fort which sank one, S199, and when *Seymour*'s group made contact again some time later the MTB's got within such close range that collisions occurred and both MTB495 and S701 were damaged. The German vessel was a write off.

During this same night of 22–23 January, *Riou* and *Stayner* had a sharp battle with another group further along the coast to the south and two more E-boats were destroyed and an unconfirmed number damaged. This too was an extremely close encounter; one of the E-boats actually tried to ram *Riou* and passed so close astern that some of her quarter deck guard rails were torn off. A number of decorations were awarded that night.

At one time, the Germans were so desperate in their attempts to attack the Allied supply routes that even miniature submarines were brought into action. Dick Ford of *Torrington* remembers an encounter with one of them one morning off Ramsgate. The asdic operators had no idea what the target was, of course, and all on deck were amazed when the first pattern of charges brought the tiny two man craft bobbing to the surface. *Torrington* disposed of another of the miniatures in the same area a few days later. Dick avers that this was not such a quick victory and earned them a black mark from Captain D for expending a total of forty depth-charges on it!

Another E-boat foray into our coastal waters took place on 17–18 February, when a large E-boat force managed to get through the patrol lines and successfully laid mines off the Humber, one of which sank one of their arch enemies of very long standing the Free French *La Combattante*. Another group made a similar breakthrough and dropped mines further south off the North Foreland. Then, three nights later, the minelaying operations switched back to the Scheldt estuary. *Riou* made contact with four of these boats at 2330hrs and, after a short, fierce battle, forced them to retire hastily. By 0031hrs, this same group made another thrust and this time ran into *Thornborough*'s patrol. But the enemy were not eager for close combat. The frigate could only attack from 3000 yards range and the German force again retired. A few minutes later, a different group started an attacking run against a supply convoy in *Riou*'s area but she also had difficulty in getting close to the E-boats. She did manage to get within just over a mile of them and opened up with a 3″ HE barrage. On this occasion the enemy beat a very hasty retreat and circled round to make two more attack attempts at 0050 and 0111hrs but *Riou* repulsed both of these by using the same tactics. The gunnery officer's report on ammunition expenditure for this night of 20–21 Feburary emphasizes the long range nature of the night's work. 147 rounds of 3″ were fired and nearly a hundred rocket and starshell flares, but not a single round of 20mm or 2pdr!

On the following night, *Torrington* was once more in action. Her CO's report to Captain D pinpoints the area as being between buoys HK2 and HK4, some 20 miles north of Ostend/Zeebruge, where radar contact with E-boats was established at a range of 8 miles at 0130hrs. The sea must have been rather choppy because MTB's 677 and 726 were ordered to close the enemy at 23 knots, presumably the fastest they could manage in the prevailing conditions. They exchanged fire with the enemy at fairly long range, 1000 yards, but the action was inconclusive on both sides. At these speeds *Torrington* had been well able to keep up with the light forces and at 0148hrs she too engaged the enemy with all her armament. Hits were obtained on all four of the enemy by 20mm cannon fire and one was also actually hit by a 3″ round. Though none of them sank, they all retired hurt at great speed. The action had only lasted for a short time but *Torrington*'s gunners had got away 83 rounds of 3″, 1000 rounds of 20mm and 20 rounds of 2pdr. This last figure throws an interesting sidelight upon the Pom Pom bow chasers mounted in all the CFCF's. Being right in the eyes of the ships, these guns had a marvellously clear arc of fire and their two pound HE shells were able to tear nasty holes in the hulls of E-boats. However, on nights such as this, when the DE's ran at full speed into moderate seas, they were almost impossible to man. With seas and spray breaking over the foc'sle, the gun crews practically needed diving suits and it is no wonder that *Torrington*'s 2pdr was almost unusued on this occasion!

Riou had another disappointing night on 24–25 February when she caught up with an E-boat group at 0244 hrs. This was much later than most of the actions and indicates that the enemy were probably on their way back to base after an operation. They were certainly not eager to join action and *Riou* could only engage with 3″ at long range to break up the formation. The group immediately dispersed but the radar showed that one seemed to be in trouble and left behind by her flotilla mates. *Riou* sent in MTB's to locate and destroy this straggler but before they had reached it, the German crew had set demolition charges and abandoned ship. *Riou*'s gunners like to think that this was one of theirs, but the German records claim that the E-boat in question (S167) was lost after collision with another E-boat. Twenty two survivors were picked up and made prisoner, only one short of a full E-boat crew, so whatever happened, the boat could not have been severely damaged.

The next positive destruction of an E-boat was on 1–2 March and the victim was S220 one of the latest 1944 class. The victor in this case was *Seymour*.

This is the last of the actions I can find attributable to the original band of CFCF's. The patrols continued right up to the bitter end, since Holland was the last of the occupied countries to be liberated and the E-boats had their bases there right up until the war ended. During the last couple of months, it seems to have been the CFCF's from among the Nore Command DE's that enjoyed all the action and these will be dealt with in Chapter 7. Perhaps it was that those who were running the war considered that the original group deserved to rest on their laurels; for nearly a year they had been involved in almost continuous night patrols with only very occasional one night stand downs and the five-day boiler cleaning periods which came around about every three or four months.

What of the successes they achieved? It would be invidious to attempt to allocate individual honours. It is difficult to obtain accurate figures for the number of E-boats destroyed or damaged. One of my correspondents, whose hobby is collecting data about German naval actions and losses, has found that the German light forces were not renowned for keeping full war diaries but at a conservative estimate it seems that the CFCF's were responsible for at least twenty E-boat sinkings and many more than this received damage and casualties to some extent. Not a very impressive figure perhaps but the success of the CFCF patrols was not measured entirely by the number of sinkings they achieved. E-boats were cheap and fairly easy to build in almost any small shipyard and it was never believed that the attrition due to CFCF action would ever outstrip production and reduce the number of boats operational with the flotillas. Their primary success was to curtail drastically the depredations against the vital convoys carrying troops and supplies to maintain the Allied offensive and in this they did very well.

Immediately after VE-Day the CFCF patrols all enjoyed a number of interesting trips to the liberated ports of Belgium, Holland and Norway as well as to the occupied German ports such as Brunsbüttel and Cuxhaven. One of the first of such trips was that of *Riou*. She was at Portsmouth for minor repairs on VE-Day but sailed from there on 9 May to visit Hamburg and collect a number of surrendered U-boats from Baltic ports. She claims to have been the first Allied ship to pass through the Kiel canal after the war and also to have been one of the few RN ships to have had a Field Marshal's Inspection. The place was Hamburg and the VIP was Monty himself. Personal opinions about this man vary but *Riou*'s ship's company voted him a popular hero, especially as he authorized the CO to Splice the Main Brace after his inspection!

Riou's return trip with the captured U-boats began somewhat unhappily; the submarines were, of course, disarmed but one or two of the CO's were still truculent enough to cause minor problems by pretending to misunderstand orders and got deliberately out of station. *Riou*'s CO had orders to stand no nonsense however and ended this mutinous attitude by threatening to sink the U-boats there and then by gunfire. This had the desired effect but with the knowledge of the shortcomings of the 3″ pop guns, I imagine *Riou*'s CO was pleased that he didn't have to try to put his threats into action!!

After this jaunt, *Riou* was sent to join Portsmouth Command and was used as a general maid of all work for some time until the Admiralty decided to put her into dockyard hands for conversion into a torpedo recovery vessel. This work was to be carried out at Liverpool and the ship's company were very much looking forward to a long period in dock or to be returned to the Royal Naval Barracks (RNB) to join the 'demob' queue. However, they were frustrated on both counts. One of the other frigates *Curzon*, had already been paid off but, for some reason the Admiralty decided that they wanted her back in commission again. Thus no sooner had *Riou* arrived in Liverpool than her entire crew was transferred to *Curzon* for a bit more sea time!

Riou did complete her refit and conversion but, for some reason, her performance as a torpedo recovery vessel was not much thought of at her subsequent trials and, after languishing around for some time, she was sent back to the USA in February, 1946.

Seymour was transferred to the Rosyth local flotilla in August, 1944, and unlike several other DE's banished thence she did actually put in some more sea time there. On one occasion she went to German ports to shepherd back some forty merchant ships which had been commandeered as war reparations. She then had a pleasant month at Christiansands as floating headquarters ship to Lord Tennyson who was Acting Admiral, Coast of Norway, but Rosyth seemed to lose interest in her after that and she was sent south to join the Devonport local flotilla. From there she visited Barry Island and Barrow-in-Furness but there her career ended. The welding on one of her propeller A brackets gave way and she was sent to Birkenhead, ostensibly for repairs, but in the event she remained there until she too was sent back to America on 5 January, 1946.

Stayner and *Retalick* were also both banished from Harwich once the Pacific war had ended and they too were sent to Rosyth but to the best of my knowledge they did little, if any, running from there. By September, both ships were being prepared for return to makers and sailed for the USA, *Retalick* on 25 October, 1945, and *Stayner* on 24 November.

Thornborough and *Torrington* had both been decommissioned together and placed in reserve Fleets at Hartlepools and Londonderry respectively but they both had a long wait before steaming crews could be spared to take them across the Atlantic. *Torrington* got away on 11 June, 1946, but *Thornborough* had to wait another six months and it was January, 1947, before she returned to America.

TABLE OF ENEMY SHIPS SUNK BY COASTAL FORCES CONTROL FRIGATES

E-Boats	Approximately 20. Number damaged not recorded.
U-Boat	U671 by *Stayner* off Beachy Head 4.8.44.

SHIPS LOST BY CFCF's

Trollope	Torpedoed in Seine Bay 5.6.44. CTL
Duff	Mined off the Dutch coast 30.11.44 CTL

– 7 –

DE's OF THE NORE COMMAND

Cubitt, Curzon, Cosby, Dakins, Ekins,
Holmes, Rutherford, Halsted

The ships dealt with in this chapter are those which were permanent members of Nore Command. There were others, *Conn,*
Deane, Redmill, Byron and *Fitzroy*, but these were only seconded to the Nore for a few months and were then returned to Belfast
and formed the 21st EG. For completeness, the whole stories of those
five ships have been included in Chapter 11 (21st EG). Similarly,
Cranstoun, which served briefly at the Nore, from April - August, 1944,
before she went on to the 17th EG, has been covered in Chapter 12
(Mixed Escort Groups).

To return to the main theme: once the WA escort groups were up to
operational strength and the CFCF's had been designated, there were
still a number of Buckleys unallocated. Since it was accepted that the
south and east coast forces would be called upon to provide strong
support for operation NEPTUNE and subsequent convoys, a number
of the frigates were transferred to the Nore Command. They were
nominally attached to the local flotillas, 21st DF at Harwich and 16th
DF at Sheerness, both of which, up to this time, had consisted of Hunt
class and old V and W class destroyers.

All the Nore Command Captain class, apart from *Holmes*, had been
completed and commissioned at Boston within six weeks of one
another. *Halsted* on 3 November, 1943, *Cubitt* on 17 November,
Curzon on 20 November, *Dakins* on 23 November, *Ekins* on 29
November, *Rutherford* on 16 December, *Cosby* on 20 December and
finally, *Holmes* on the last day of January, 1944. All except *Cosby* were
commissioned in the usual manner by men who had travelled to Boston.
Cosby's crew had, however, come mainly from the cruiser HMS
Uganda. This ship had suffered damage from glider bombs at Salerno

during September and had been sent to the USA for extensive repairs at Charleston, South Carolina. As repair work was expected to last for about six months, only certain technical ratings were left on board to liaise with the American repair crews and the remainder of the ship's company were sent to the Drafting Pool at *Saker*. According to Leading Stoker Alan Whalen, most of *Cosby*'s crew came from these ex-*Uganda* ratings.

By the time this group of frigates were passing through their trials and working-up programmes most of the earlier teething problems had been ironed out and there were few breakdowns and hold ups. All the Nore Command group passed through the post commissioning routines with only minor snags. *Halsted* had her initial trials delayed by a couple of weeks due to minor engine room faults and later on *Rutherford* was in trouble after hitting some submerged wreckage on the way from Bermuda to the homeward convoy rendezvous. This damaged her propellers but repairs did not delay them for long. The only other mishap was the failure of an electric drive motor in *Holmes* during her Bermuda work-up. Her engineers were of the opinion that this was going to be quite a long job. Replacement was beyond the resources of the Bermuda dockyard and she had to go back to Charlestown Navy Yard where there were ample spares and specialized staff. Her engineers estimated that there would be at least another week at Boston to enjoy the bright lights but this was not the case. The Navy Yard personnel proved that they were just as adept at repairing ships as they were at building them. Large sections of deck plate were burned away with acetylene torches, the faulty motor removed, a new one fitted and the deck plates replaced, all within the space of twenty-four hours.

Although *Cubitt, Curzon, Dakins, Ekins* and *Halsted* were all at Bermuda at the same time during December and January, none of the crews knew at that time that they were destined to operate in the same flotilla some months later. It is sad to recall that of those five ships, which worked and played so hard together at Bermuda, only two were to survive the war unscathed.

Cubitt and *Curzon* were the first of the group to complete working-up. *Cubitt* departed on about 24 January, had a brief couple of days at New York and then sailed to the UK in company with *Cotton* on 31 January, 1944, arriving at Belfast about a week later. *Curzon* followed on as escort to convoy SC152 from Halifax on 2 February and was at Pollock Dock with *Cubitt* and *Cotton*.

Halsted and *Dakins* were not far behind the first pair and were operational in time to collect the Lease Lend escort carrier HMS *Emperor* and the LSI *Empire Anvil* for passage to Argentia on 10

February where they joined with a large convoy of US troopships bound for the UK.

Ekins is recorded as being available for escort duties in a signal from the British Resident Liaison Officer, Norfolk Virginia on 7 February, 1944, and probably left for Britain with one of the HX convoys close behind *Halsted* and *Dakins*.

Rutherford and *Cosby* both reached Bermuda just as their five predecessors had left and their working-up progressed throughout February, 1944. Having kept pace with one another throughout the commissioning and working-up period they should both have departed for the UK with the same convoy from Halifax in early March but, as already related, *Rutherford* hit some submerged wreckage and was left behind in Nova Scotia for repairs whilst *Cosby* made the Atlantic crossing and arrived at Belfast in mid-March, 1944. *Rutherford* got to Belfast before the end of March, so by this time all the Nore Command ships except *Holmes* had arrived there.

It is not certain whether the Admiralty had already determined their future deployment but for some weeks these ships operated with various established WA escort groups. *Ekins*, as we have seen in Chapter 3, was temporarily attached to the 3rd EG but although this group was to become quite successful in later months there was nothing spectacular in their operations during the time that *Ekins* was with them between the end of March and early June when she was released to become one of the Nore Command frigates.

Halsted was initially incorporated into the 11th EG together with *Conn, Deane, Redmill, Byron* and *Fitzroy* but this group had a very brief existence. After a period of operations in the Atlantic from Belfast, it was disbanded and the ships sent on temporary loan to the Nore Command. As already explained, the others will be dealt with in detail in the Chapter 11 but *Halsted* did not survive to join them in this new group and she is thus included in this present chapter where we note her arrival in Nore Command in April, 1944.

Cubitt and *Curzon* were sent across to Liverpool for a period as supernumerary to the B4EG at the end of February and sailed with them as escorts to a convoy to Gibraltar. This was to be an uneventful voyage and the only enemy presence was the inevitable Focke-Wulf aircraft which shadowed them for a large part of the way. Fortunately for them, there did not seem to be any U-boat group within striking distance and they arrived on about 6 March. The return trip with convoys SL150/MKS41 was not so peaceful, however. As they crossed the Bay on 9 March a flurry of U-boat transmissions was picked up, indicating that there were a number of them in contact. From later

German records it seems that several U-boats of the Preussen group were shadowing the convoys but only one, U575, appears to have penetrated the outer screen to get into an attacking position. One of the B4EG corvettes *Asphodel* was soon in Asdic contact with this intruder and was actually able to get away a signal that she was on an attacking run, but U575 had fired a defensive T5 torpedo which struck the gallant little vessel and literally blew her apart. The remainder of the night passed without any more attacks, so presumably the escorts had formed into a tight enough screen to prevent U575 or her sister boats from getting at the convoys. Fleeting Asdic contacts were still being made after dawn and *Cubitt* was detailed to patrol at the rear of the convoy for some hours during the forenoon. But there was never a firm enough echo to warrant an attack. *Cubitt* and *Curzon* returned to Belfast after this one convoy experience and by early April they had been sent round to Sheerness to augment the 16th DF and become permanent members of Nore Command.

Holmes had meanwhile arrived from the USA in early April and, after the Pollock Dock refit, she had been sent to undergo concentrated gunnery exercises in the Clyde area. Bill Wood, her Australian First Lieutenant, recalls with some pride that her weapon crews had displayed remarkable skill and application during her training period. Not only had the A/S team dropped a practice hedgehog bomb squarely into the conning tower of a target submarine at Bermuda but her gunners had shot down an AA drogue with the very first round of 3″ gunfire during the Clyde practice shoots but, like many of her sister ships in the Nore, *Holmes* was never fated to have much opportunity to show off her prowess against the enemy. After this extra training, *Holmes* did not receive orders to join the Nore Command yet and she remained in the Clyde awaiting orders which everyone fully expected would involve them in some aspect of the forthcoming invasion of Europe.

The influx of the Captains into Nore Command must have been a welcome relief for the veterans of the 16th and 21st DF's and the Rosyth groups which had been the sole protectors of shipping in the North Sea up until this time. The newcomers, to their disgust, began to take over the lion's share of the convoy and patrol work and their crews frequently bemoaned the fact that the veteran destroyers were having an easy time. *Garth*, which was Captain(D) of 16DF, for example, seemed to be permanently moored to the dockyard wall at Sheerness. With due respect, however, these ships deserved a respite from action and if the new frigates were to be fully prepared for their part in the forthcoming invasion it was to their operational advantage to get in as much sea time as possible.

During April and May of 1944, all the East Coast frigates were kept extremely busy. As far as action was concerned, it was a fairly quiet period compared to what it had been like in this area in the past. This part of the world had long been notorious among mariners as 'E-boat Alley' by night and 'Bomb Alley' by day. No one who sailed those East Coast waters during the war will ever forget the ghastly Graveyard of Ships which stretched endlessly along in the shallow coastal waters; wrecks of hundreds of vessels of all shapes and sizes, some with only their masts showing above water, some with funnels and upperworks still uncovered. They were the victims of the many air attacks and E-boat onslaughts of the earlier years of the war and were a permanent reminder to the newcomers to keep their eyes peeled at all times.

Fortunately, air attacks on coastal convoys had become almost a thing of the past by 1944. There were still frequent mine dropping raids at night but the RAF kept the skies clear during the day. E-boats were still active but these too confined most of their activities to laying mines and there are grounds for belief that during these two months before the invasion, only one ship, a rescue tug, was sunk by direct E-boat action along the East Coast.

Much of the employment of the Captains during these pre-invasion weeks was as escorts in the East Coast convoys or as E-boat patrols further out at sea during the night times.

* * *

Before describing some of the operations following D-Day, it may be of some interest to note that among other tasks performed by the Nore Command frigates prior to that historic event were some convoy duties which crews found extremely puzzling until they saw the mysteries solved off the Normandy beachhead. Apart from conventional landing craft of various kinds, which were often shepherded from the Thames estuary round to south coast ports such as Newhaven, there were often strange slab-sided concrete objects which, in security ignorance, could only be guessed to be some sort of makeshift landing barges. Even stranger were contraptions which looked like giant floating cotton reels whose purpose confounded even the most imaginative of the lower deck know-alls. These things were, of course, the pre-fabricated concrete caissons which were to form part of the Mulberry harbour breakwater and the huge hose reels from which PLUTO (the Pipeline Under the Ocean) was to be unwound to provide petrol lines from Sandown on the Isle of Wight to the Normandy coast. In retrospect, it is impressive confirmation of the highly successful security that surrounded the invasion preparations to recall that no one had the slightest inkling of the purpose of these strange objects which were to play such a vital role in the establishment and maintenance of the force in the beach head.

Immediately prior to the invasion the Nore Command Captains were split into two groups. *Cosby, Cubitt* and *Rutherford* were stationed at Harwich and *Curzon, Dakins, Ekins* and *Halsted* were at Sheerness. None of them were destined to take part in the first historic assault on 6 June, 1944. They had a secondary role. Some collected laden troopships from the Thames estuary and escorted them down the Channel to reinforce the men already landed whilst others, like *Cubitt*, formed up to make an offensive sweep from the Dover Straits down to Arromanches to clear the way for these subsequent convoys.

In common with most of the RN ships involved in operation NEPTUNE, the Nore Command frigates found the actual event very much of an anti-climax. With the destroyers, E-boats and miniature submarines which the enemy had available in the Channel ports, there had been an expectation of determined German attacks from surface vessels, aircraft and submarines. When, therefore, the ships reached the landing area that evening without a sign of opposition of any sort, it was difficult to believe. It was awesome to witness the bombardment still being carried out on targets ahead of the troops. This holocaust, which was evident such a short distance away, made such a contrast to the peaceful progress the ships had enjoyed down Channel that crews felt almost shamefaced at not having suffered their share of the general onslaught.

Cubitt and others of the Nore Command contingent remained at the anchorage until morning and then escorted empty convoys back up the Channel and into the Thames estuary where more troopships and transports were awaiting their turn to join the endless procession of traffic to and from the Normandy beachhead. This task became the main routine for several weeks after the landings but taut nerves unwound considerably as each trip proved to be as uneventful as the first. One of the East Coast Captains which *was* present at the Normandy beachhead at the time of the first assault was *Holmes*. The last mention of her was that she was waiting in the Clyde for her Operation NEPTUNE orders. When these arrived, her allotted task was to escort HMS *Nelson* down through the Irish Sea to her bombardment position off the French coast to soften up the defences with 16 inch shellfire before dawn on D-Day. *Holmes* then remained in the area as part of the A/S screen for the bombarding ships for the remainder of June with brief replenishment trips to Portsmouth on the 23rd and 29th. When this duty came to an end in early July, she escorted a convoy back to the Thames estuary and was assimilated into the Nore Command.

*   *   *

The next event in the story of the Nore Command frigates was their first sad loss. *Halsted* had sailed from the Thames estuary on D-Day to escort a convoy of miscellaneous landing craft and arrived off Arromanches without incident. She too spent the night at the anchorage and returned to Southend next day ready to bring back more troopships on 10 June. By the night of the 11th, her convoy was in mid-Channel approaching Normandy when it was attacked by E-boats from the Cherbourg Flotilla. The Hunt class destroyer *Fernie* was also in the escort and her CO's report to Captain(D) states that six E-boats were detected by radar at 0140 hrs. They were in the vicinity of 58B and 58C buoys ahead and to port of the convoy and were contacted by *Halsted*. *Fernie* detected the others on the port wing. Events then developed rapidly, as described by Able Seaman Bill McCoy, who was trainer of *Halsted*'s after 3" gun:

> E-boats attacked from our port bow but the close range guns fought them off. By 0200 the enemy had re-grouped and made another attack on the port side of the convoy. The moon was on our starboard side and suddenly an E-boat could be see between us and the convoy ships. Petty Officer Darby Allen, who was captain of Y gun, got a glimpse of this boat and shouted a target bearing to me. Frantically I turned the training handle to swing the gun round quickly to bear on the enemy – but it was too late. A torpedo hit us somewhere for'd and the whole ship lifted out of the water and came down stern first so that we on Y gun were almost submerged for some seconds and when the ship seemed to have regained an even keel we noticed that she was going round in circles. Some order may then have been passed to the engine room because the engines stopped and we wallowed helplessly in the water. Fortunately, *Fernie* was not far distant and when no further attacks seemed likely she came to our assistance.

The torpedo had struck forward of the bridge and the whole fore part of the ship from B gun deck was blown away with the B gun deck itself bent up and back towards the bridge. As in the case of several other Captains similarly torpedoed, *Halsted*'s for'ard bulkheads remained firm. Miraculously, she remained afloat and her remains were towed back to Portsmouth. The detailed report of the damage makes fantastic reading in Admiralty File 199/2070 and there is a photograph in P. Elliot's book *American Destroyer Escorts of WW2* which gives stark evidence of the amount of damage these ships could sustain without sinking. Since the torpedo had struck for'ard of the bridge, her casualties were not as high as might be expected; twenty seven men had been killed and twice that number were injured.* The damage was far too extensive for repairs to be contemplated and she was stripped of useful spares and declared a CTL a mere seven months after she had commissioned at Boston. Her hulk lingered on until long after the war, when she was broken up in Holland in 1947.

* * *

As far as U-boats were concerned, the Channel convoy routes were fairly free from the U-boat menace, thanks largely to the high success rate of the WA groups which were keeping them at bay in the western entrance to the narrow sea. The Nore Command Captains did have one success confirmed and another possible however. The positive kill was achieved by *Curzon* and *Ekins* which detected U212 whilst with a convoy south of Beachy Head on 21 July and sent it to the bottom after an action in which they shared equal credits. The other unconfirmed victory took place much later and will be recounted in due course.

Air attacks were another hazard which this group of frigates did not have to endure. Allied air supremacy was so complete that no enemy planes were ever seen in the Channel during daylight and during the hours of darkness their attacks were confined to massive minelaying forays in and around the Mulberry Harbour areas. The frigates, which spent many nights in the anchorages off Normandy waiting for return convoys to form up, frequently witnessed these attacks. *Cubitt* did have a very brief opportunity one night. One of the planes flying out very low after dropping its load amongst the massed shipping came directly towards her at little more than masthead height. The sound of its engines was loud and clear but the gunners could not see its outline

---

* I am indebted to Mike Handsford for the following information which he discovered in Admiralty files when investigating the circumstances of the death of his father who was Gunnery Officer in *Halsted,*.

First it is necessary to explain that all the Nore Command frigates carried special German speaking wireless operators when on escort or patrol duty in E-boat waters. These men, known as 'Headache operators' listened in to the frequencies used by E-boat commanders to chat to one another and relay tactical orders. Such information was of paramount importance in arranging to intercept E-boat groups or to avoid their attacks.

In *Fernie*'s report on the action to Capt(D), it is recorded that just prior to the attack on *Halsted*, the Headache operator in *Fernie* heard the senior officer of the E-boat group give orders to attack the last escort in the convoy screen, which was *Halsted*. Assuming that *Halsted* would also have heard this message and take avoiding action *Fernie*'s CO did not deem it necessary to pass on the information on TBS. Unfortunately, it appears that during the vital moments Lieutenant-Commander Westmacott in *Halsted* was actually in conversation with his Headache operator who consequently did not hear the E-boat's order to attack his ship.

Sadly, in times of war, such chance circumstances often tip the balance between life and death – and so it was for so many of *Halsted*'s crew that night.

Other Nore Command Captains were to be involved on the fringes of E-boat attacks during the many Channel convoys they escorted in following months but no others were lost and few were positively in action with the E-boats.

until it was almost upon them. The close range weapons gave it short bursts before it had zoomed over and was out of sight again. However, there was no sign of any damage. One form of air activity the crews grew to hate during these plodding Channel convoy trips was the endless stream of VI flying bombs which passed overhead on the way to targets in England. Many of them had families in the areas within range of these robot weapons and trigger fingers itched to have a go at them but this was forbidden. Several ships in company with convoys had winged some of these terror weapons and in some cases they plunged down and exploded so close to the convoy ships that the Admiralty banned this defensive action as far as escort ships were concerned.

Thus passed the summer of 1944 as far as the Nore Command frigates were concerned. They ploughed the sea lanes between the Thames and Normandy so continuously that they almost expected to see ruts in the Channel to mark their passage. In between trips there was sometimes a night or two of E-boat patrol work in the North Sea and brief exchanges of fire with the enemy boats became the only sign that there was a war on as autumn approached. Such patrols were not of the CFCF variety howver and few Nore frigates were fortunate enough to get to close grips with E-boats during this period and certainly none were sunk.

After the retreat of the E-boats to Holland, following the capture of their Channel bases, the pattern of life for the Nore Command ships changed. In the first place, although there were no longer convoys to Cherbourg they still found themselves on escort duties down the Channel and beyond. One of their responsibilities was the safe conduct of convoys from the Thames estuary to a point out in the Atlantic some ten degrees west where they would meet an incoming convoy, exchange escorts and return to Southend. *Holmes* and *Cosby* seem to have had more than their fair share of these longer convoy trips but they all did their share from time to time. *Curzon* also had a trip unique among the Nore Command Captains. The date is uncertain but she did one KMF troop convoy from Belfast to Naples with the 4th EG, possibly as a stand in for one of the Group's ships in dock.

Towards the end of the year, life began to get more exciting. The CFCF's had moved round to operate from Harwich and Nore Command ships began to be incorporated into their ranks. There is no record that *Cosby* or *Holmes* ever worked in this capacity but *Cubitt*, *Curzon*, *Dakins*, *Ekins* and *Rutherford* certainly did.

As in the case of Chapter 6, the following accounts of E-boat actions in the North Sea are only representative. Some sort of action took place somewhere on the patrol lines practically every night. Most were indecisive now that E-boat commanders seemed to avoid close action much more often than in the past but they were fierce, exciting stuff while they lasted. It is impossible to trace every one of them and in any case space forbids.

Curzon was the first of the Nore CFCF's to join action with the E-boats. She was in company with *Walpole, Torrington* and *Kittiwake* off Ostend on the night of 22–23 December, 1944, when minelaying E-boats were detected. During the close action which followed, *Curzon* opened the score for Nore Command by sinking S912 and possibly peppering two others.

Ekins joined the fray a few nights later on the Scheldt patrol line with *Thornborough*, the Colony class frigate *Caicos* and *Shearwater*, a corvette. The attacking forces were unusually strong but the defenders were unable to claim positive sinking. However, they were successful in keeping the enemy away from the convoy lanes and a number of the E-boats were badly mauled. *Ekins'* ammunition expenditure for the night – 150 rounds of 3", 1000 rounds of 20mm and 150 rounds of 2pdr – again demonstrates the intensity of fire which took place during the brief minutes when the E-boats were within range.

Dakins was an early casualty, falling victim to E-boat laid ground mines off the Belgian coast on Christmas Day. Mercifully, none of her many casualties suffered fatal wounds and the ship herself did not sink. Her hull was much damaged though and some internal machinery had broken away from the bed plates. She was towed into Antwerp but remained there *hors de combat* for the remainder of the war and is recorded as a CTL.

Curzon opened the action again in the New Year 1945. This time she was with *Cotswold* off Westkappelle on 14–15 January. Five E-boats made one of their rare penetrations of the patrol lines and were able to deliver an attack upon a convoy with long range torpedoes, claiming two hits. *Curzon* and *Cotswold* quickly closed in and gained contact and the ensuing attack was pressed home so hotly that the E-boat formation was completely scattered and driven off with several of them taking severe damage and casualties. Another recorded action involving *Curzon* took place on 16–17 January when she was again on the Scheldt patrol. Two groups of E-boats were detected near HK2 and HK4 buoys at 0127hrs. The destroyer *Cotswold* was in position to open fire immediately on one group and *Curzon* closed in at full speed on the others. By 0140hrs she had got within 3000yds and opened fire. The range later closed but the enemy soon did the usual disappearing trick behind a smoke screen and *Curzon* had to veer away as she was approaching dangerous shoal waters. The enemy were persistent enough to regroup and make another attacking attempt later on but *Curzon's* radar plot was tracking them accurately and by crafty manoeuvre she was able to get within less than a mile of them. Another brief but fierce action followed – but ended up as the last one had with the enemy retiring behind smoke.

Rutherford and *Cubitt* had little excitement during the first weeks of 1945. Their patrols were mostly to the north of the Scheldt estuary and any contacts they made were of the very long range type which rarely resulted in positive damage to the enemy. Typical of the actions at this time was the one on 29–30 January when *Cubitt* was on No1 East Coast patrol with *Caicos* and three MTB's (602, 609 and 612). At 0030hrs she was cruising leisurely at 12 knots some 9 miles from the Outer Dowsing Light when *Caicos* signalled contact with two E-boat groups. Lieutenant Gregory in *Cubitt* ordered *Caicos* to deal with the group to her north and took *Cubitt* and the MTB's towards the others. Initially *Cubitt* was some 13 miles from this group and did not make radar contact until this had reduced to about 5 miles at 0108hrs. The seas were running high enough to restrict the MTB's to less than 20 knots and the CO decided that the only hope of bringing the enemy to action was to leave the MTB's behind. Speeding on at a full 26 knots, she did actually manage to get within a mile of the E-boats but had to fire rocket flares as the gunners still could not make out the targets. This destroyed the element of surprise and the CO stamped in fury as the E-boats travelling with a speed of at least 30 knots veered away to refuse contact. The for'd 3″ gun managed to get away about 12 rounds and even the bow chaser pom pom opened up between the sporadic drenchings suffered by its crew but the range was soon opened up to 7000yds and shortly after this the E-boats were obscured behind their smoke. Both frigates set out in hopeful pursuit but had to abandon the chase as they approached a known mine barrage.

The report of this action is still on file in Admiralty records and still has the footnote that Lieutenant Gregory had attached complaining bitterly to Captain(D) about the inability of the MTB's to match the enemy's speed in rough conditions. It was a pointless comment but, like other CO's in the frigates, he was obviously determined to make the point that the Germans had designed better coastal craft than we had!

Sporadic encounters between the Nore CFCF's and E-boats continued throughout February but there is no record of sinkings. *Cubitt* went into Tilbury Docks for a few weeks where the ship repairing firm of Green and Silley Weir carried out a brief refit. She lost the bow chaser pom pom but no one really mourned its passing, especially as the two forward upper Oerlikons were removed and replaced by two single 40mm Bofors. At long last splinter shields were fitted around the 3″

guns at the same time. *Curzon* had a similar refit a little later and these two were among the very few Captains which ever had 3″ gun shields fitted.

Holmes and *Cosby* still plodded away, mainly on convoy duties and it was during one of these that Bill Wood, First Lieutenant of *Holmes* insists that she was robbed of a legitimate claim to have sunk a U-boat. She was with convoy ONA289 in the Channel on 8 March, 1945, and, just as they reached the Eastbourne area, one of the transports, *Lornaston*, suffered a violent explosion and began to sink. *Holmes* was detached to search the area and almost immediately registered what her A/S crew accepted as an almost perfect submarine contact by Asdic. Three separate depth-charge attacks were made but there were no encouraging signs of oil or wreckage. There were still some Asdic echoes however and on making a pass with echo sounding equipment working, there was a very clear trace of a submarine lying on the bottom. Since there was not much future in a submarine's attempts to escape by bottoming in these comparatively shallow waters Lieutenant Wood made the reasonable assumption that the U-boat was destroyed. However, he bitterly complains that just at that time two Fleet destroyers appeared on the scene, plastered the area with depth-charges and completely obliterated all signs of the submarine. The SO of the Escort Group was convinced by this time that *Lornaston* had struck a mine and insisted that *Holmes* abandon her mythical U-boat and rejoin the convoy and *Holmes* right to fly the Jolly Roger was denied. The mystery of this episode has never been fully explained. Official records now agree that *Lornaston* *had* been torpedoed by U275, but they also state that this U-boat met its end by striking a mine off Newhaven some two days later. Bill Wood strongly disputes this and still maintains that *Holmes* sank her on 8 March. He has had correspondence with Professor Rohwer the German U-boat historian querying the reasons for saying that U275 hit a mine but he did not get any satisfactory answers. The case is an open one but it is worth noting that post-war historians on both sides are known to have made glaring errors and there is every chance that *Holmes* should have received the credit.

Cubitt was back in operation again during March and made good use of her new Bofors in several indecisive encounters. She never sank anything with them but their siting well above breaking waves and spray and the hard hitting powers of their HE shells made them a far better counter to the E-boats than the poorly sited pom poms.

Cosby and *Holmes* were transferred out of Nore Command in April and became attached to the Devonport local flotilla. The war was as good as over but as the Allied forces had still not overrun the E-boat bases in Holland, there were still some close encounters and a final tragedy in store for the remaining frigates in the Nore.

The night of 7–8 April saw *Cubitt* and *Rutherford* with their MTB's involved in events which gave rise to headlines in the national press: CONVOY RAIDERS SUNK AT 10YDS RANGE. *Cubitt* opened the action by contacting a large group of E-boats at medium range shortly after midnight and engaged them with rapid fire. Two were severely damaged and a third took numerous hits before the group escaped out of range. Patrolling aircraft then engaged the battered group and drove them back towards the MTB's and the ensuing action was at such close quarters that there were collisions and one E-boat and one MTB sank. *Cubitt* took off casualties from one of the MTB's, which was on fire.

As witnessed from the upper deck, this night's actions did not seem to be much different from the many other brushes they had had with the enemy but seemingly the CO had conducted the battle with enough dash to earn himself a decoration. On receiving the report of the conflict Captain(D) recommended him for a DSC with a Mention in Despatches for the First Lieutenant and Engineer as representatives of the upper deck ratings and the Engine room staff. The SBA Will Patey was similarly honoured for his skilful treatment of the MTB casualties taken on board. The MO who later came over from a destroyer said he could not have done better himself.

During the following night, *Rutherford* and *Cubitt* were patrolling off Ostend when once again an aircraft first sighted E-boats and directed *Rutherford* towards them. In a lightning action which lasted a scant five minutes, at least two of the enemy were sunk and several others damaged. The remnants of the group were then engaged by *Cubitt* but the range was such that the effects of her fire could not be clearly seen before the boats were swallowed up in their own smoke screen.

Ekins had an indecisive brush with more E-boats on the night of 11–12 April but became the last of the Nore Captains' casualties four nights later on the 15th. She was on patrol in the Scheldt and there had been little action but one merchant ship was on fire. *Ekins* was sent to her assistance and shortly after this, at 2100hrs, rocked to two explosions as she passed over ground mines. ERA Lionel Morton explains:

> I was off watch at the time and was standing on the superstructure deck near the aft Oerlikon group when the two mines went off. The deck twanged under me and I was thrown bodily into the air almost to the height of the funnel top. Luckily I remained in an upright position throughout this airborne trip and by some miracle my ankles were not smashed when I landed feet first. I was dazed for some minutes but when I recovered I found that I could still walk although my knees and ankles

throbbed. I made my way below to see what damage control work I could get involved in and the first casualty I came across was my Chief ERA lying in the midships workshop with the 6″ lathe bed across his broken legs. After freeing him and handing over to a first aid party, I then went below to the aft engine room. We were still under way but things were not as they should have been. There were severe vibrations and I discovered that one of the main shaft bearings was running extremely hot. Using all the CO_2 fire extinguishers I could lay my hands on, I tried to cool the bearing by the refrigerant effect of discharging them – but it was a vain attempt and eventually I had to report to the bridge that the engine must be shut down and we idly rolled about the Scheldt as a motionless target.

The two mines had not inflicted any fatal damage. One had struck forward under the Asdic dome and the other under the forward engine room. No one had been killed but many suffered severe injuries after having been thrown around the machinery spaces like rag dolls. *Ekins* was not in a sinking condition and the paddle steamer *Royal Eagle* was able to take her in tow and got her safely back to Chatham. She had taken in much water forward but a first survey seemed to show that her damage was not too bad. Disaster followed when she was put into dry dock however. As the water was being pumped out of the dock there was a sudden rending crash and she settled down with her back broken and had to be declared a CTL – the third to be lost from the quintet which had worked up at Bermuda together *Cubitt, Curzon, Dakins, Ekins* and *Halsted*.

This was virtually the end of the war for the Nore Command Captains. After VE-Day, *Curzon* had a refit, ostensibly for service in the Far East but, as we know, none of the frigates went to the Pacific. *Cubitt* had enjoyed a few visits to ports such as Ostend and Rotterdam immediately they had been liberated and when the European war ended, she went further afield escorting merchant ships to Oslo and Brunsbüttel on the Kiel canal. By August, Harwich had ceased to be an operational base and was being prepared to receive the many destroyers that would be laid up to the Reserve Fleet now that the war was over. *Cubitt* was consequently exiled from her familiar moorings off Parkeston Quay and for some weeks she spent a life of delightful idleness tied up to the wall in Rosyth dockyard. The crew fondly imagined that the next step would be the last voyage to return the ship to America but the Admiralty had other ideas. She was amongst the unlucky ships to be allocated to Operation DEADLIGHT, which involved towing surrendered U-boats from Loch Ryan into the North Atlantic, where they were sunk by various means. This turned out to be a most tedious and thankless operation, and all were relieved when it ended by her return to the USA in March. *Cosby* had also been embroiled in DEADLIGHT after a short stay with the Devonport flotilla and she joined *Cubitt* for their last voyage on 4 March, 1946.

Holmes had escaped this colossal chore. Bill Wood had left her to take up his first command in *Cotton* but *Holmes* was still operational at Devonport in September, 1945, when Lieutenant-Commander Dudley Davenport, later Rear Admiral, took over as her CO. He records that she remained in and around Devonport with very little sea time until November when she went to Chatham to reduce crew numbers before returning to America.

Rutherford had preceded her Nore Command sisters. She had been sent to the Isle of Man after VE-Day and was earmarked for conversion into a fighter direction ship for the Pacific but VJ-Day put an end to that work and she sailed to the USA on 25 October, 1945.

Curzon was the last of the group to be sent home. Her updating refit had been completed by VJ-Day and she may have been operational for a while after this but she reached America on 27 March, 1946, shortly after *Cubitt* and *Cosby*.

TABLE OF ENEMY SHIPS SUNK BY NORE COMMAND DE's

E-Boats   No accurate record is available but a reasonable estimate would be 5 or 6 with an unknown but fairly substantial number damaged.

U-Boats   U212 by *Curzon* and *Ekins* in the English Channel 21.12.44.
U275 (probable) by *Holmes* off Eastbourne, in the English Channel 8.3.45.

SHIPS LOST BY NORE COMMAND DE's

Halsted   Torpedoed by E-boats in the English Channel 11.6.44 CTL

Dakins   Damaged by ground mine off Belgium 25.12.44 CTL

Ekins   Damaged by two ground mines in the Scheldt 21.7.44 CTL

– 8 –

DE's IN PORTSMOUTH &
DEVONPORT COMMANDS

Hotham, Hargood, Narborough, Rupert,
Waldegrave, Spragge and Rowley

The planners of Operation NEPTUNE had required so many escort vessels to be included in the support forces that even the CFCF's and Nore Command frigates did not make up sufficient numbers. The Western Approaches Command was therefore persuaded to allocate still more of its Buckley type frigates to the Channel flotillas. Their story, as related in this chapter, does not contain much in the way of intense action against the enemy; most of their time was spent in plodding convoy work to and from the eastern sector of the Normandy front but they all performed the tasks allocated to them with typical efficiency. There was a certain amount of flexibility in the secondment of these ships and, before detailing their exploits, it is as well to provide the following table to indicate their movements between the two south coast ports:

Hotham	1st DF at Portsmouth (permanent.)
Hargood	Devonport, from June to December, 1944, then Portsmouth.
Narborough	Devonport, from June to October, 1944, then Portsmouth and then 19th EG.
Rupert	Devonport, from June to October, 1944, then to the 21st EG.
Waldergrave	Devonport, from June to August, 1944, then to Portsmouth.
Spragge	Devonport, from June to August, 1944, then to Portsmouth.
Rowley	Portsmouth, from April to October, 1944, then to the 3rd EG.

Rowley and *Rupert* were both commissioned just before Christmas 1943 (on 22 and 24 December respectively) at a time when there were still manning problems at Boston and both were manned by the transfer of crews from two of the old four stackers which had been paid off and given to the RCN.

Able Seaman W. York recalls that joining *Rowley* was like moving into a palace after having suffered the discomforts of life in the primitive messdecks of the old US destroyer *Mansfield*. The men from the other four stacker (*Salisbury*) were probably even more favourably impressed because their ship had been particularly prone to defects and her last trip had been in such horrific weather that she had been rendered practically unseaworthy.

With experienced men on board, both ships were spared the full work-up routine and departed for Belfast after a week of familiarization at Casco Bay. *Rowley* departed for Britain with convoy HX273 early in January, 1944, and *Rupert* followed with *Cubitt* and *Cotton* on 21 January.

Rowley was operational almost immediately and departed to Iceland to pick up a section of ships which joined a convoy to Murmansk. Neither this nor the subsequent return convoy ran into much trouble from U-boats. These trips were probably with JW56B and RA56. *Rowley* was given no respite, even after this double trip to Russia. She was refuelled at sea and immediately sent back with a further convoy (JW57?). The destroyer *Mahratta* was lost during this latter convoy but *Rowley* had a fairly quiet trip and returned with RA57 on 2 March. Asdic conditions were atrocious, as usual, in the Arctic and the escorts were unable to make any contacts. By 10 March, *Rowley*'s only excursion into the Arctic came to an end.

While her sister *Rowley* was involved with the Russian convoys, *Rupert* operated with an existing WA group for a short time but both *Rupert* and *Rowley* were taking part in the standard Tobermory work-up during April. The ships were then allocated to Devonport and Portsmouth flotillas respectively and both took part in intensive landing operation exercises along the Devon coast. *Rowley* then joined in several convoy and E-boat patrol duties with ships of the 1st DF and she was present in an action against E-boats off Selsey Bill on 25 April in company with *La Combattante* during which one of the enemy boats was sunk and the rest driven off.

The next of the south coast Captains to be completed were *Spragge*, *Waldegrave* and *Narborough*. All were handed over to the Royal Navy during January, 1944, but were among those ferried across to Belfast by RCN crews. *Spragge* was taken over by her RN crew at Lissahally on 28 February, 1944, whilst *Waldegrave* and *Narborough* received their RN crews on 9 March. Both ships were sent to Tobermory, probably at the same time as *Rupert* and *Rowley*. The working up exercises were marred, in the case of *Spragge*, by the tragic loss of one of her experienced Leading Seamen. The accident happened as the ship was entering harbour to moor at a buoy for the night. As the whaler was being lowered, with the ship still under way, the forward falls ran away causing the boat's bows to drop, flinging its crew about helplessly. The Leading Seaman was flung out of the boat – he probably struck his head against the ship's side – and was immediately in difficulties. Without a moment's hesitation, the First Lieutenant (Lieutenant Holt) and the Chief Bosun's Mate both jumped over the side to assist him but, despite their efforts, the man drowned and they were unable even to recover his body. This was a sad start to the commission but it boosted the morale of some of the younger men to know that an officer and a senior rate made such a prompt and unselfish attempt at rescue.

With the work-up completed, all three ships were designated to join Devonport Command but they did not move down there immediately. *Spragge* spent some time at Liverpool as senior ship of the 113th EG (with *Hotham, Magpie, Hind* and *Hambledon*). However, she was clearly not destined to remain on Atlantic convoy work because she had been fitted with a pom pom bow chaser – the badge of all frigates which were to operate in E-boat waters. After her service with 113EG, she ended up moored, in company with a multitude of other ships, at Milford Haven just before D-Day awaiting orders to join in Operation Neptune.

Meanwhile *Waldegrave* had moved round to Devonport during April and took part in a number of intensive landing exercises and some A/S patrols before joining *Spragge* at Milford Haven. The last two of the south coast Captains were *Hotham* and *Hargood*. Captain Featherstone Dilke, who was then First Lieutenant of *Hotham*, recalls that it was a bitterly cold day on 8 February when his ship commissioned. The temperature was so sub-zero that the Royal Marine band, kindly lent by Commander S. W. Roskill of HMNZS *Leander*, had their instruments so badly iced up that not a peep could be coaxed out of them. Her crew therefore did not notice much difference when they reached Casco Bay on 26 February, 1944, and were not finally thawed out until reaching Bermuda on about 15 March. Five days after completing her final work-up, she joined *Riou* and *Inman* as homeward escorts for the aircraft carrier *Indomitable*, arriving at Belfast on 1 May.

Invasion exercises occupied them for the next three weeks and *Hotham* then joined the 1st DF at Portsmouth. Although not officially one of the CFCF's, she did operate with them before D-Day and began her active career in several brushes with E-boats.

Hargood had been commissioned the day before *Hotham* but lingered behind her in subsequent weeks owing to some initial engine room problems. But they could not have been serious because she resumed working-up during April and became operational in May, making the passage to the UK as an independent unit. She was subject to the usual refit in Pollock Dock after arrival at Belfast and was then allocated to Devonport Command. Her first trip was as escort to a US troop-ship which she delivered to Southampton on the day before D-Day and, after rapid refuelling, made her way back to Falmouth, which was her starting off point for the invasion.

Once the historic invasion began, all the south coast Captains were involved in one way or another. *Rupert* was at Devonport on 2 June and left there on D-Day as part of the support force for the western flank of the invasion armada. Once the landings had been made, she then began a series of convoy runs from the western end of the Channel to the Mulberry harbour and this became her non-stop duty for the next four months.

Rowley had formed part of the escort to HMS *Warspite* during her passage to take up her bombardment position off Normandy on D-Day. She then made her way across to Portsmouth to join the 1st Destroyer Flotilla (DF) ships. Her subsequent duties included the escorting of many convoys across the Channel and although she was not one of the CFCF's she did take part in anti-E-boat patrols with them upon several occasions.

Spragge had sailed from Milford Haven on D-Day escorting a convoy of 12 knot US troopships. She delivered them to UTAH Beach without untoward incident – only to watch in horror as the unfortunate troops were raked by merciless machine-gun fire as they surmounted a ridge at the rear of the beach. The USS *Wyoming* and USS *Texas* had thoroughly bombarded the landing areas but the geographical position of many pill boxes placed them out of the line of fire of low trajectory shell fire and the landings here were more costly in lives than in any other beach head.

Spragge's further employment, like that of all the other south coast Captains was to continuously escort troop and supply convoys from the central and western areas of the Channel to Normandy during the remainder of the summer of 1944. She earned no great glory but there were a number of memorable incidents.

Waldegrave had also left Milford Haven on D-Day to escort a column of US troop landing ships to the western beaches. She then joined up with the support and escort forces which were to defend the vital supply lines. She was involved in these convoy duties without very much rest throughout the four months when first Arromanches and then Cherbourg and Le Havre were the main supply centres for the land forces. Like all the south coast frigates, her service was not spectacular and she won no everlasting fame but she operated in dangerous waters where several other Captains had been lost and she performed all her duties in the highest traditions of the Service.

Hotham's part in the initial invasion was to sail from Portsmouth with units of the CFCF force at 2230 hrs on 5 June and in company with *Duff* to patrol off Pointe de Barfleur in order to prevent any of the Cherbourg E-boats passing round the peninsula to attack the assault forces. As we know, none of the E-boats put to sea that night. *Hotham* was back at Portsmouth during the afternoon of D-Day and began escort operations by taking four LST's back across the Channel to the beaches. This was largely the pattern of her existence during the following months shuttling convoys back and forth from Spithead to Normandy. Occasionally there would be a welcome break when she did the odd relief patrol with the CFCF's and the lightning swift actions with E-boats made up for the excitement which was so lacking on the routine escort trips but *Hotham* was never fated to notch up any victories.

Details of *Narborough*'s operations from D-Day onwards are very sketchy. She worked out of Devonport and without any record of positive contact with any enemy forces, one can only presume that, in common with *Waldegrave*, her occupation during the invasion summer was the monotonous routine of escorting convoys from the western end of the Channel to the landing areas.

The last mention of *Hargood* was that she had been stationed at Falmouth to stand by for invasion duties. Her part in those historic events was to be assimilated into the Western Task Force, a miscellany of British and American ships. On D-Day itself she accompanied the US assault craft to OMAHA Beach. Therefore her tasks were similar to those of all the other ships of the task force; endless convoy and general patrol duties which, as far as *Hargood* was concerned were devoid of practically all action. One of her most frigthening experiences was during the Great Storm which caused such disruption from 19–22 June. George Young recounts:

We were at anchor off UTAH Beach on the night of 21 June and I spent an anxious night on watch with the bridge officers as the force of the wind and sea caused *Hargood* to drag her anchor and be driven relentlessly towards the shore. Our boilers were flashed up and the cable party were on the foc'sle all night ready to slip the anchor if things got really rough. I guess that we dragged our anchor for about a quarter of a mile during the middle watch but fortunately we did not go aground . . . as happened to so many ships around us that night.

As autumn approached and the Allied armies had swept the Germans back towards the east, it became unnecessary to have escort forces based at Plymouth, so the frigates which had been operating from there were soon re-deployed. *Rupert* went off to join the newly formed 21st EG. Similarly *Rowley* joined the 3rd EG as we have already seen in Chapter 3. This did not change her operational area much because her new group continued to be employed on A/S patrols in the Channel but she did gain some battle honours by sharing in the sinking of a U-boat in 1945 making up for the uneventful life she had led before.

Narborough also made the move to an escort group by joining the 15th EG as substitute for the crippled *Mounsey* (as will be explained in Chapter 10) and this became the only Buckley in a group which had, until then, consisted of all Evarts type ships.

Hargood, Waldegrave and *Spragge* all went to join *Hotham* with the 1st DF at Portsmouth but this move was, in reality, only a change of scenery. They all continued to support and escort supply convoys which were now routed towards the other end of the Channel as Antwerp had been opened up as the main supply port. These four Captains had no more luck in distinguishing themselves in the eastern end of the Channel than they had when based at Devonport. It would be unfair to say that these Portsmouth frigates had a hum-drum existence during the last six months of the war. They all did their duty and endured plenty of sea time but none of them saw any further hostile action.

Spragge did come to grief on one occasion but it was one of her own side that did the damage and not the enemy. It was early in 1945 and whilst returning from a trip to land commandos at Walcheren, her group ran right through the lines of a large number of landing craft going the other way. It was rather like one of the peacetime grid iron manoeuvres but it did not quite come off. One of the landing craft was out of station and hit *Spragge* almost head on. *Spragge* had a large section of her forecastle torn open, (severely injuring PO McDonald who was asleep in his bunk.) As both Chatham and Portsmouth yards were busy at the time, *Spragge* was ordered to return to Devonport for repairs and, in order not to take in water through her gaping bows, she was forced to steam ignominiously all the way down the Channel stern first. *Waldegrave* had a grandstand view of the bombardment of Walcheren when she escorted the battleship *Warspite* on that occasion but she does not seem to have taken part in any operation of note after that. She remained operational until VE Day but was then paid off into

Reserve at Harwich and lingered on there until her return to the USA in December, 1945.

Hargood continued to operate with the Portsmouth local flotilla until VJ-Day and was then sent with other redundant frigates to while away the time at Rosyth. She may possibly have taken part in operation DEADLIGHT (see Chapter 7 page 138). She departed back to the States in April, 1946.

Hotham remained active in the Portsmouth Command right up to VE-Day and was then taken in hand for conversion into a floating power station. This work entailed the removal of all armament and the installation of the necessary electrical switchgear to enable the considerable output from her AC generators to be fed into shoreside power lines. The alterations lasted until about October, 1945, when she was recommissioned and sailed to Singapore to provide electrical power for the badly damaged dockyard there.

Ex-EA Vic Tizard confirms that *Spragge* was also disarmed and converted into a floating power station at Portsmouth but she does not appear to have been used as such. She sailed with *Hotham* for the Far East in October, 1945, and for some time was based at Hong Kong where she was used for miscellaneous peacetime roles until her complement was reduced to a steaming party and she was handed back to the USN in accordance with Lease Lend requirements at Subic Bay on 28.2.46.

Hotham was still to have a remarkable career under the White Ensign however. One of her later AB S/Ts (Able Seaman Torpedoman) Don Stevens, tells me that he served in her from May, 1946, to June, 1947, and that up to the time he left, she was still struggling on to provide the dockyard electrical supplies with the engine room staff having increasing problems over obtaining spares to keep her machinery running. Stoker PO George Wells then joined her in late 1947 and says that she was able to keep one power plant steaming continuously right up until early 1948 when the normal dockyard supplies were finally restored. *Hotham*'s long stint at Singpore then came to an end. There was apparently some difficulty in training sufficient engine room staff to run the strange turbo-electric drive but she eventually reached Portsmouth where Captain Fetherstone Dilke remembers seeing her in March, 1948, (confirming George Wells' time scale).

However, her long service was still not at an end. The Lease Lend agreement had long since run out and either the Americans were turning a blind eye to *Hotham*'s expired lease, or perhaps the Admiralty had bought her from the USN. However it happened, she remained as the longest serving Captain class frigate in the Royal Navy. The latter part of her career was as a floating test bed for the RN Engineering research team who used her to experiment with gas turbine engines. This Second World War veteran was thus possibly the forerunner of all the modern frigates and destroyers which later incorporated these sophisticated power units. Her final retirement took place in 1956 – twelve years after her handover at Boston.

So passed the last of the Captains based in the Channel ports. This particular chapter cannot end as the othes do with tables showing their losses and victories because there were none of either. The ships had performed their duty and taken part in historic events. If they saw no close action it was through no fault of theirs but their stories have been outlined here in order that this account of the Captain class should be complete.

– 9 –

DE's EMPLOYED AS
HEADQUARTERS SHIPS DURING
THE NORMANDY INVASION

Dacres, Kingsmill and Lawford

M any of the famous ships, such as *Bulolo*, which had been used as headquarters ships for (HQ(S)) Operation TORCH, the huge maritime assault in the Mediterranean in 1942, were refurbished with the latest in communications equipment and prepared for Operation NEPTUNE but the planners stipulated require-ments for many others to be provided for this final invasion of Europe. Many small ships were therefore adapted for these duties; including the Hunt class *Goathland* and *Albrighton*, the River class *Nith, Waveney, Chelmer, Exe* and *Meon*, but still more were needed and Western Approaches Command was required to give up three of their frigates for this purpose.

Two of those selected, *Kingsmill* and *Lawford*, were designated for these conversions right from the date of their handover to the RN but later on there was an afterthought and *Dacres*, which had already been operating in the Atlantic for some time, was added to the list. *Lawford* had commissioned at Boston on 3 November, 1943, and *Kingsmill* followed three days later on the 6th. Neither of them did the complete work-up programme in the Western Atlantic since it was known that both would be going into dockyards for extensive modifications on arrival in Britain. So after a short shakedown at Casco Bay, both sailed for home on 6 December, 1943. This arrangement probably suited their original crews very well, with the prospect of Christmas leave at home, but it turned out to be an unwise decision. Untrained crews should not have been allowed to cross the Atlantic without the Bermuda work-up.

The first part of the crossing was in the teeth of gales of such fearsome intensity that the ships had virtually to heave to for a couple of days with bows into the wind to ride out the storm without actually rolling right over. Then, having recovered from this shattering experience, hearts began to pound and adrenalin flowed as the two ships' companies heard the insistent clanging of the electronic action alarms calling them to A/S action stations.

Lawford had picked up a very definite radar echo during the dog watches of 10 December and the excited bridge lookouts were soon confirming the sighting of a U-boat on the surface. The boat was several miles away but both gunnery officers soon had the 3″ gun crews firing away with great enthusiasm but little effect. With more experience, the CO's would probably have held fire in the hope that the U-boat had not seen them. In the event, the only result of the gunfire was to cause the U-boat to dive hastily. The Asdic operators in both ships made fleeting contacts throughout the night of 10–11 December and several depth charge attacks were made but all to no avail. Some of the attacks were delayed by problems with the handling gear in the DC magazines and affairs on *Lawford*'s quarterdeck in particular degenerated into a hopeless shambles. She ended up in the ridiculous situation of having firm contact with the U-boat at 500ft but with only one depth charge on the upper deck. In sheer desperation, her CO decided upon a Hedgehog bomb attack. These weapons were remarkably accurate against targets at lesser depths but at 500 feet the sinking time was so long that such an attempt was virtually hopeless. Even that desperate attempt had to be abandoned for just as the last moment, before discharging the bombs, *Kingsmill* was sighting crossing *Lawford*'s bows no more than 250yds ahead, the attack was hastily aborted and Asdic contact was lost. During the forenoon, the depth-charge supply problem was improved and both ships continued to search but by noon the Admiralty had wisely signalled them to abandon the chase and proceed home. Both CO's made much of the failure of the magazine handling equipment in their subsequent reports but, in all truth, this had not been the major cause of the debacle. There *were* faults in the gear which were due to be remedied during the alterations and additions work during the Pollock Dock refits but other Captains had had similar early encounters with U-boats which had not ended up so disastrously. It does not require much perspicacity to divine that the major problem had been the complete lack of training of the officers and men in these two ships.

However, the ships did get home safely for Christmas and were immediately sent to Cammell Laird's yard at Liverpool where most of the crews were paid off and work began to convert the ships for headquarters duties. The alterations were considerable; the aft 3″ gun was completely removed and the superstructure extended to provide accommodation for the extra Staff officers who would be carried; two deck houses were also built to contain the vast amount of radio equipment to be installed and a small main mast was added to support the many extra aerials. Extra Oerlikons were also mounted, increasing the total to no less than 16, and a number of British radar sets were fitted (Types 242, 253, 271, and 391).

Dacres, the third Captain to be modified, had not been earmarked for the purpose from her earliest days, like Lawford and Kingsmill. The decision to modify her seems to have been a hasty one, taken at the last moment and announced at very short notice. Commissioned on 31 August, 1943, much earlier than the other two, she had gone through all the normal trials and working-up routines at Casco Bay and Bermuda. After arriving in Belfast, she had been incorporated into the B4EG with Highlander, Helmsdale, Winchelsea, Foley and Bayntun and had operated with them on a number of Atlantic escort duties. Her last trip with that Group was with a convoy sailing from St John's on 27 November. On arrival at Belfast, two of her three watches had been sent on leave, a certain indication that up to that moment there had been no plans to convert her into a headquarters ship. Whilst the men were away on leave, the sudden decision was made, however. A signal was received giving Dacres forty-eight hours notice for sailing to Dundee.

Panic arrangements were made to borrow men from the base ship Caroline to make up numbers for a steaming crew and the personal kit of the men on leave was packed up and landed unceremoniously on the jetty. Dacres then sailed round the north of Scotland to the small civilian shipyard at Dundee. This yard had sufficient facilities to carry out the modification work, which was similar to that of the other two ships, but there was cold comfort there for the few men allocated to stand by during the refit.

*   *   *

Lawford and Kingsmill had been completed at about the same time as Dacres and the subsequent events in their histories were as follows.

Lieutenant Maurice Forte was destined to be First Lieutenant of Lawford and stood by her from the early days of her refit. He recalls that during the subsequent sea trials, which were conducted somewhere in the mouth of the Mersey, two merchant ships collided in thick fog and caught fire. Lawford approached to give assistance and her motor boat's crew did magnificent rescue work, going right into a huge patch of burning oil to pick up a number of the merchant seamen. Following this, the ship went across to Belfast and to Tobermory for the standard escort ship work-up programme. She then moved down to Portsmouth, which became her base during invasion training with various assault craft along the south coast. The staff at Portsmouth had become familiar with the Buckley frigates of the 1st DF but *Lawford* was the first diesel ship they had seen. They were much intrigued by the fact that she could start engines and proceed to sea at a moment's notice, instead of having to wait to raise steam as conventional ships did. For a time, they took unfair advantage by sending her to sea on all manner of trivial duty destroyer tasks. Eventually her CO managed to get the message across that she did not really belong to Portsmouth Command but to the high powered staff who were planning the forthcoming invasion. Intensive training exercises kept them busy right through April and May and culminated in a full scale dress rehearsal with live ammunition in Studland Bay. *Lawford* then remained at anchor off Cowes to await her historic duty.

Kingsmill had meanwhile been through a similar process after leaving Liverpool. And when her additional W/T Staff arrived they were much dismayed at the terrible overcrowding in her messdecks. The ship already had her normal crew of about 180 but with the various parties that came on board as part of the invasion staff, this number escalated to some 240 men. Living conditions now became almost impossible, as there were less than 200 bunks on board. The situation was alleviated when the ship was based at Weymouth however. Most of the radio training was done ashore and the Wireless ratings were billeted in hotels in Devonshire Place. Later on, when the ship was based on HMS *Squid* at Southampton, there were similar arrangements. However, during exercises at sea and in the actual invasion operation, life was only tolerable because the ship was at continuous three watches and a third of her company was always on duty. There had to be a great deal of good natured sharing of the overcrowded spaces – and a number of men had to share bunks with others, according to the duty rosters. By the end of May all exercises were complete and *Kingsmill* joined *Lawford* to wait for the fateful day when they would be carrying out their practised tasks for real.

* * *

Dacres' refit at Dundee was completed on 19 March. After she had been recommissioned with a new crew, some acceptance trials were carried out in the Firth of Tay. Her working-up period took place at Invergordon before she moved down to Portsmouth. There she took part in all the same training with assault craft as the other headquarters ships to prepare for the great day.

In the following accounts of each ship's part in Operation NEP-

TUNE, we will take them in order of seniority and treat *Lawford* first. She was senior because she carried Captain Pugsley, who was designated to take over command of all the patrol activities off Normandy once a foothold had been made ashore and the headquarters ships had fulfilled their purpose.

Lawford sailed from Cowes at 2100hrs on 5 June bound for J1 sector of GOLD Beach and led a column of ten cross-Channel ferries carrying Canadian assault troops. She arrived off Corseulles-sur-mer at first light on D-Day and had a grandstand view of the RAF carpet bombing of the shore defences, watching in awe as this was followed up by the battleship bombardment and salvoes of rockets from the specially adapted landing craft. By afternoon 140,000 troops were ashore in J1 sector and Captain Pugsley then assumed the role of Officer-in-Charge of defence of the anchorage and of the CFCF patrols which operated further out to ward off E-boats.

All went well with *Lawford* during the first two days of the landings but disaster struck early on D+2. At 0400hrs there were reports that MGB's were hotly engaging E-boats to seawards and Captain Pugsley took *Lawford* out to join the action. Before they had gone very far, however, there were signals that the coastal forces had driven the enemy away and *Lawford* turned round to resume her anchorge at 0500hrs. What happened after that is best told in Lieutenant Forte's verbatim account:

The cable party were preparing to anchor and I was watching them from the bridge. With the ship still swinging slowly to port, the sudden very loud and very close roar of aircraft engines burst upon us from the starboard quarter. This was instantaneously followed by the loudest bang I ever heard and I saw a huge shower of red sparks rise from abaft the funnel. It appears that a twin engined bomber had glided in from seaward with his engines switched off and had aimed at the largest vessel he could see in the first light of dawn. As we were the only ship moving, his attention was drawn to us and, switching on his engines at full throttle at the last moment, he dropped two 500lb bombs right into our main motor room. The explosion blew out the bottom of the ship as well as blowing the lids off all the Oerlikon ready use ammo lockers and fully loaded 20mm magazines were hurled skywards from whence they descended in a lethal shower – even a tin hat is small protection against such missiles! *Lawford* lost all way and began listing to starboard. Lieutenant-Commander Morris sent me to investigate the damage and my subsequent report was that the internal explosions had perforated the upper deck amidships and that the ship was breaking in half – and that the alarming list to starboard indicated that our days were numbered in minutes only. I then went down to investigate the possibility of launching our motor boat as we had a number of upper deck casualties who would be unable to swim. The list was now so pronounced that the USN type motor boat was only a few feet above the water. The PO of the messdecks appeared with a knife and I ordered him to cut the falls allowing the boat to drop into the water. I then noticed the body of a sailor hanging over our compressed air siren horn at the top of the funnel. I sent a PO up the ladder to identify him and ascertain if he was still alive. Sad to say he was one of our best Leading Seamen and was indeed dead. We left him in this rather bizarre resting place as our time was getting very short indeed. Lieutenant-Commander Morris gave the order to abandon ship and those of us on the starboard side literally walked into the water which was above our waists as we stood on the deck. To everyone's surprise the usually temperamental motor boat engine started at first pull and the wounded were taken into her. It was exactly ten minutes from the time that the bombs struck that *Lawford* became untenable and she sank to the bottom with her bows and stern sticking out of the water (and were used for some days as a navigational mark for craft heading for the beach.) Boats from nearby minesweepers helped with the rescue and I took many of the injured in our boat to HMS *Gorgon*.

The survivors on *Gorgon* totalled 7 officers and 145 ratings and the assistance they received was as always unselfish and generous. The CO and another 65 men had been picked up by another minesweeper, so the final casualty figure was 26 – mostly engine room ratings, of course. So ended the short career of *Lawford* and the inevitable question follows. How was she caught napping in spite of her much vaunted radar? And were the radar operators in *all* the ships at the anchorage fast asleep? The simple answer must be that, as in the case of modern cruise missiles, the aircraft came in at low altitude under the radar beam. If modern radar can be foxed in this way, how much more so the comparatively primitive sets of 1944?

Kingsmill invasion tasks were very similar to *Lawford*'s. She sailed from Portsmouth on the evening of 5 June and was on station with G2 Group off GOLD Beach. Her CO was not content merely to witness the battering of the West Wall, he wanted to actually take part and made earnest requests to FOBAA for permission to bombard with the 3″ guns but, for obvious reasons, this was brusquely refused. She had no allocated targets, her fire power was insignificant and in any case the additional shock and noise of her guns firing would have increased the difficulties under which her radio staff were working. They were already being hampered by the regular crash of the 120mm guns of the Dutch gunboat *Flores* which was anchored close by. With this and the general bedlam of the big ship bombardments, it must have taken a great deal of determined effort to concentrate on sending and receiving the hundreds of signals which passed back and forth between the Staff and the beach parties.

Kingsmill continued these duties off the beachhead until the end of June when FOBAA set up his headquarters on shore. She then became the headquarters ship for the CFCF forces. It had been intended that Captain Pugsley would control these patrols from *Lawford* but after her early loss he and his staff had had a nomadic existence for some time and took up residence in several of the CFCF frigates in turn. When *Kingsmill* was released from headquarters ship duties, there were therefore sighs of relief all round as the CFCF Staff took her over as the permanent control ship.

Lacking the speed of the turbo frigates, *Kingsmill* was unable to take part in the many extremely close range encounters with the E-boats but she was by no means passive in her role of Captain of Patrols. As her prime duty was the protection of ships in the anchorage, she rarely went out on the distant patrol areas but there was action enough around the defensive Trout Line, particularly when the German Neger manned torpedoes and Lentil explosive motor boats were brought into action. Telegraphist George Lester remembers many exciting nights working directly with the CF control officer in *Kingsmill's* operations room. She was also in company with *Quorn* on 2–3 August when the latter was sunk by a Lentil. She later earned the distinction of being the only one of the Captains to have shot down an enemy aircraft. A Ju88 had made a pass over the anchorage and flew well within range of *Kingsmill's* impressive battery of Oerlikons. The gunners gleefully plastered it and had the satisfaction of seeing it burst into flames and crash into the sea. Just as it was about to hit the water, the Canadian ship *Alberni* also opened fire on it and there was great indignation in *Kingsmill* when FOBAA's signal later gave the Canadians an equal credit for the plane's destruction!

As the E-boat flotillas retreated to the east after the Allied advance along the Channel coast, the CFCF's moved to the Nore Command but there is no record that *Kingsmill* was associated with them beyond August, 1944. She was recalled to perform headquarters ship duties again in the autumn, however, and helped to control the subsidiary landings at Walcheren in order to secure the Scheldt estuary, so that Antwerp could be developed as the Allied supply port. The hospital ship which was standing by for that operation was sunk by the Germans and *Kingsmill* then had another important role. Over 300 casualties were brought on board and her MO, plus a surgeon from *Warspite* who joined them, treated this large number of wounded men as best they could in *Kingsmill*'s crowded spaces. The ship was already crammed with the extra staff personnel and it must have been an extremely difficult time for the ship's company with all the messdeck space taken up by the casualties.

The Walcheren operation ended on 8 November and there is little evidence of *Kingsmill*'s movement after this. She probably remained in her headquarters ship configuration and was taken in hand to be prepared for Pacific service in 1945. However, as we have already seen this work ended with the Japanese surrender. *Kingsmill* then became one of the earliest of the Evarts to be returned to the USA in August, 1945.

Dacres was the last of the headquarters ship trio but she had an unfortunate start to her active role in this capacity. Whilst at Portsmouth, just before D-Day, her forward motor room was mysteriously flooded. The circumstances are vague but they were suspicious enough to warrant a full scale police inquiry. D-Day arrived before this investigation had reached any firm conclusion but even though her power was reduced by fifty per cent her CO was determined that she would perform her allotted duty. He was heard to say that *Dacres* would reach her billet off Normandy, even if she had to be towed there but, of course, there was no need for that. Even with one engine out of action, she could still maintain 16 knots and this was quite enough to keep up with the assault ships. Her station was with S3 Group off SWORD Beach and she did indeed reach this position without any problems early on D-Day as scheduled – having been involved in the excitement of an unproductive attack on a suspected U-boat on the way across.

Her duties during and immediately after the landings were similar to those of the other two and there was nothing of particular note about her ship's company's experiences during these eventful days. Some remedial work must have been carried out by the engineers during this period but their efforts would not have been wholly successful. When the landings had been well established and the staff officers moved ashore, *Dacres* joined with *Kingsmill* in patrol duties around the Normandy anchorages. Her tasks off Normandy were concluded during August and, after only five months of her second commission, she was paid off again at Portsmouth, having salvaged an abandoned Liberty ship on her way across Channel, and was put into dockyard hands. One purpose of this refit was no doubt to complete the overhaul of her flooded motor room but during its course she was restored to her normal Evarts class configuration with all the extras added for her headquarters ship role removed! Early in the New Year, she was back with the Western Approaches escort groups at Belfast and, for a brief and uneventful period, she operated with 10EG and 15EG in April, 1945.

Dacres lingered on under the White Ensign longer than most of the Evarts and did not return to the USA until 26 January, 1946.

This concludes the brief chapter on the three HQ(S) Captains. None of them were involved in spectacular individual actions but their role in the invasion had been of vital importance . . . and of all the DE's which earned NORMANDY Battle Honours *Lawford, Kingsmill* and *Dacres* were probably the most deserving.

THE 15th ESCORT GROUP

Inglis, Lawson, Loring, Louis, Moorsom,
Mounsey and *Narborough* (*Dacres* briefly).

Prior to April, 1944, each of the DE escort groups had been made up from three Evarts and three Buckleys but owing to the large number of Buckleys co-opted into the Channel and Nore Commands in preparation for the invasion, there was a preponderance of Evarts left to be allocated. Six of them were formed into the 15th Escort Group. From its very inception this group was fated to become one of the hardest worked of them all, as the diesel-powered Captains had much greater endurance at sea. Six to eight weeks was to become the norm for the 15th EG's operations and they rarely had much time in harbour between them.

Only three of the Group had been commissioned by their RN crews at Boston in the normal manner. The first of these was *Louis*, the future Group Leader, which was completed and handed over on 18 November, 1943. She suffered no delays in her basic training programmes and set out for the UK with convoy HX275 from Argentia on 18 January, 1944.

Lawson was commissioned just a week later on 25 November. She should have kept pace with her sister ship *Louis* during the early days but fell considerably behind by virtue of some serious mechanical failures. First, as she was about to leave Norfolk Virginia for her first convoy trip, there was consternation when she did not move from the jetty when the engines were started. It transpired that an 'A' bracket supporting the propeller shaft had suffered a weld failure and, once loosened, had sheared all the bolts on the adjacent shaft couplings. The result of this was that a section of the shaft actually fell off, leaving no connection between engine and propeller. However, the ensuing delay was not very serious. Divers soon recovered the missing parts and it did not take long to replace them, re-weld the support strut and check shaft alignment. *Lawson* had, however, missed her original convoy rendezvous and was sent to join another one off Bermuda.

Further weld problems arose shortly after they began the Atlantic crossing. Seas were running high and the hull stresses were severe enough to shear a number of welded junctions in longitudinal joists under the upper deck. The engineer officer soon established that these were vital to the ships strength. No less than seven breaks had occurred and if there were many more it was possible that the ship would break her back. Emergency strengthening was carried out by stretching all available steel hawsers along the upper deck between bollards fore and aft. Then, by means of Spanish Windlasses, these hawsers were tightened like bow strings. The principle was that these would help support the ship against the hogging strain when the crest of a wave amidships left each end of the ship unsupported. This may seem to have been a crude remedy but apparently it worked!

Many of the ship's company prayed for the first time in many years that night and there was certainly no need to remind them to wear their lifebelts during the remainder of this hazardous voyage. Providentially, everything held together and there were no more weld failures but few men have ever been more grateful to make landfall than the men of *Lawson* when Bermuda was at last in sight!

The dockyard welders made short work of repairing the fractured joints and the Constructor's department carried out a very thorough survey to ensure that there were no more hidden failures. They examined every inch of *Lawson*'s vital stringers, ribs and cross beams minutely but no other faults were found. She was pronounced fully seaworthy and eventually got away to join a homebound convoy to the UK.

Those weld failures were seen by many of the old school in *Lawson* as justification of their worst fears about the weakness of all-welded ship construction but such extensive failures were an exception. Other Captains had minor weld failures but none as bad as this. One can only imagine that the inspection procedure in the construction gang which produced *Lawson* must have been less thorough than that applied to the other British DE's.

Her mechanical problems were still not over, however. On reaching Belfast, she was due for routine maintenance on her engines and suffered a disastrous failure of one of the big end bearings when the engines were first run up again. The maintainers (ship staff or dockyard?) had assembled the bearing the wrong way up, masking the oil ways providing essential lubrication. The bearing naturally became hot, so hot in fact that there was a deafening explosion and the motor room filled with smoke as the crank case blew open. Once again, the damage was not all that serious but did delay *Lawson*'s progress towards operational status. Life seems to have gone smoothly for *Lawson* after this and she is reported to have been ready to join the 15th EG early in April, 1944.

Mounsey was the last of the conventionally commissioned 15EG ships having taken on her RN crew at Boston on Christmas Eve, 1943. Nothing out of the ordinary comes to light in the accounts of her early days on the other side of the Atlantic. Her trials passed off smoothly in a matter of ten days and there could have been no snags at Casco Bay or Bermuda because she was ready to be incorporated into 15EG with *Lawson* in early April 1944.

Loring, Moorsom and *Inglis* reached completion during the awkward period when the manpower pipeline to Boston had temporarily dried up. (27 November, 12 December and 30 December, 1943, respectively). The first two had pseudo commissioning ceremonies and were then taken to join the laid up ships at Halifax to await promised RCN ferry crews. These became available in time to have a few weeks familiarization and sail for the UK on 14 February, 1944. *Inglis* was also ferried by Canadians but these men had joined her at Boston and she was ready for passage to Belfast about a week before the other two.

All three ships were joined by their RN crews at Lissahally on about 25 February, 1944. Some of the Canadian engine room staff remained in the ship to give some basic instruction on running the diesel electric plant but this did not last very long and the three ships were soon suffering the nerve wracking experience of the WA working up programme at Tobermory. Those who have gone through this unique form of torture will know exactly what a gruelling time they had. Others should read Richard Baker's famous book '*The Terror of Tobermory*'. This routine was followed by extensive gunnery training against towed targets. This training work progressed throughout March, 1944, and the first record of the new 15th EG coming into being is a Pink List of 2 April which lists, *Louis, Lawson, Inglis, Moorsom* and *Mounsey* as being allocated to this group. *Louis* became Group Leader and the Senior Officer was Commander J. P. Majendie.

Loring is not shown as a group member at this early date; Admiralty records show her as being unallocated at Holy Loch at that time and a later entry puts her as refitting in the Clyde during June, so the assumption is that Pollock Dock were too busy to take her on for the customary modifications prior to becoming operational. Like several other frigates, she was sent to a Clyde shipyard for this work to be done and consequently fell behind her group-mates.

The first Group operation was thus undertaken as an incomplete unit; *Lawson* did not take part, and *Loring* was unallocated, but the remaining ships left Belfast on 3 April as close escorts to a convoy to Newfoundland. Few U-boats were operational in the Atlantic at this time and those who were at sea for the first time were able to find their sea legs under fairly peaceful circumstances. One of the advantages of these close escort trips (as opposed to support group duties) was that they very often entailed a stopover at the convoy base at Argentia before the return voyage. This was the case with 15EG's first trip and although *Louis'* ship's company had fond memories of good living in the USA, the other crews were quite unprepared for the luxuries in store in this USN administered convoy base. The bleakness of the landscape as they entered Placentia Bay was not very encouraging; it gave the impression of being no more than a colder version of Scapa Flow but, once ashore, all comparison with that barren place became a nonsense. After sampling steaks, turkey and ice cream, visiting the well stocked PX and the usual extensive recreational facilities, there was a general consensus that this escort duty was not going to be so bad if it entailed a taste of US luxury from time to time. But hopes for future visits never came to fruition. That was the last time that ships of 15thEG ever visited that USN base.

The Group was back at Belfast in early June after an uneventful return convoy. *Loring* was still undergoing her modification refit but all the other five ships were allocated to take part in Operation NEPTUNE and joined most other WA frigates at anchor in Moelfre Bay to await orders. Their role was to become part of the screening force for the western flank of the invasion armada and they sailed on the eve of D-Day to take up position with the assault forces gathered at the ports in the western end of the Channel. They escorted the landing craft to the US landing areas and for the next ten days they continuously patrolled the convoy lanes against the expected attacks from the U-boats which, as we know, did not turn up at this stage. By 14 June the 15th EG was back at Belfast awaiting a new assignment.

Their next operation was to join the A/S patrols which were set up to keep watch against U-boats from the French Atlantic coast ports. Their patrol area was from the Bay of Biscay, round Ushant and up Channel as far as the Channel Islands. Several groups had notched up victories in these areas by this time and the 15th EG A/S teams were eager to join the ranks of successful U-boat hunters but they had no luck in that direction. Their only contacts with the enemy were sporadic bombardments from shore batteries on the Channel Islands whenever they ventured within range of these large calibre guns. It was a messdeck rumour that the frigates were often sent as bait for the shore batteries, merely to test out whether the German garrison was still manning them but this is an unlikely theory. It was known that U-boats passing through the area often kept close inshore under the cover of those guns and the A/S patrols accepted the possibility of bombardment as a calculated risk. None of them were ever hit. The German gunners seemed to be quite expert at finding the range but (perhaps through lack of practice) they did not seem to be able to calculate the necessary deflections to hit moving targets.

This particular patrol stint ended on 4 August when the Group made a brief refuelling call at Devonport and at once sailed south again to pound a patrol line further south in the Bay of Biscay. Frank Woodley the PO HSD in *Louis* records that he began to suspect that there was something basically wrong with the Group's tactics at this stage. They had been on almost continuous patrol for two months in waters where U-boats were known to be operating quite regularly yet they had not made a single attack that could be claimed to have been even a probable success. Readers may recall that in Chapter 1 it was mentioned that PO Woodley was horrified to find how inexperienced his junior operators were during the ship's first work-up at Casco Bay but that had been all of eight months ago. By this time they should all have become at least reasonably expert at the art of detecting submarine echoes but their lack of success was casting doubts on their ability.

There were contacts enough, it is true, and many of them in the shallower areas they had patrolled in the Channel were no doubt spurious but out in the deep ocean there were no rocks, wrecks or tide rips to give them false alarms. Yet they still had no success. Time and again there were good solid contacts and the A/S teams were confident that their attacks were made with text book precision but they still failed to produce any evidence that would persuade the Admiralty committee that a U-boat had been sunk.

After making a close analysis of the plots of unsuccessful attacks, Frank and his A/S officer reached the conclusion that part of the failure in *Louis* might be attributable to the Coxwain. During the final stage of an attack, the bridge officer gave up the con to the Asdic cabinet crew who passed on helm orders to the Coxwain. Correct course was vital for success and Frank suspected that *Louis*'s wheel was being handled too gently during this stage and went into many huddles with the Coxwain to discuss A/S tactics. The results were no better than before however and at the end of the day there simply was no answer to the question of why *Louis* and all the other ships of the 15th EG were destined to have such a poor record against U-boats. The five ships called at Devonport briefly for refuelling on 18 August and it was here that *Loring* at last caught up with them and made up the full complement of the group for their next operation. This was another patrol in the Biscay area but this time there were great expectations of breaking their jinx. The Allied breakout from the Normandy perimeter was not only driving the E-boats eastwards out of the Channel but was also forcing the U-boats hastily to evacuate their safe havens along the French Atlantic coast. German records show that there were seventeen or eighteen U-boats in various non-operational states in these Atlantic ports and as they were hastily made seaworthy and sent by circuitous routes to bases in Norway, it was hoped that there would be excellent chances to pick a number of them off.

Hopes ran high in *Lawson* when they actually sighted a U-boat on the surface during the first few days of the new patrol but the hunt deteriorated into a twenty-four hour cat and mouse game with contacts being made and lost a number of times. Their final attack was deemed to be successful as there were no signs of asdic contact after it but without the definite evidence required by the Admiralty to confirm destruction, they were only awarded probable honours. This cautious verdict was justified after the war when German records failed to show any U-boat lost in this area at the time in question.

Then on 24 August the Group Leader notched up the first victory. *Louis* made a perfect contact some 80 miles south of Ushant and with the Coxwain at the wheel and Frank Woodley in charge in the Asdic cabinet, they made a text book attack run which quickly sent U445 to the bottom without a single survivor. This success raised the flagging morale within the group for a while. A/S teams in the other ships became determined to emulate their Group Leader's prowess during the final two weeks of the patrol but, despite the fact that there were U-boats about in their operational zone, they were all disappointed. When the group returned to Belfast in mid-September it was still only *Louis* that proudly flew the Jolly Roger.

This six week foray into the Bay of Biscay was to be their last experience in reasonably temperate climes for some considerable time. U-boats equipped with the Schnorkel gear were bringing submarine warfare right into British coastal waters and were particularly active around the Scottish and Irish coasts where convoys funnelled into the ports of Liverpool and the Clyde. Several DE groups were therefore deployed in these inhospitable waters and the 15th EG was detailed to join them for their next operation.

At around this time there was a change in group constitution. *Moorsom* left on 30 September to become a member of a new group (the 17th EG) and her place was taken by the Buckley class *Narborough* which until this time had been operating in the Channel, as noted in Chapter 8. It is not very clear why this substitution took place. The usual three Buckley/three Evarts constitution of other Captain class groups was at least balanced but to have one Buckley amongst five Evarts seems incongruous. It may be that the intention was to provide a faster ship as Group Leader but if this was the case the idea was never implemented. A list of CO seniorities of WA Command issued by Max Horton in early 1945 shows Commander Majendie still leading the 15th EG in *Louis* even at this late stage.

* * *

As autumn deteriorated into winter, life became dreary, monotonous, miserable and generally uncomfortable during 15EG's patrols in an area noted for vile weather. The Evarts class were poorly designed in one respect. The Buckley's had uninterrupted access from forward to aft entirely under cover inside the superstructure but, for some strange reason, the Evarts had a break in the continuity of the superstructure in the region of the after Oerlikon group. This resulted in the aft and forward messdecks being completely isolated in heavy weather when it became too dangerous to walk along the upper deck. In British destroyers with the same problems, the situation was ameliorated by the fact that even the small Hunt class had a galley aft as well as forward. The Evarts had no such luxury and, in consequence, the after messdecks were cut off from all sources of cooked meals whenever upper deck traffic was forbidden due to storm conditions. This added to the general miseries of life at sea at such times. Phil Webb (an LTO (Leading Torpedo Operator) in *Lawson*) writes in this vein:

Frequently in rough weather we were forbidden to go forward. This restricted my meanderings to the after messdeck where I lived, the tiny shelter on the quarter deck which was my cruising station to maintain communication with the bridge or my action station on the port depth charge throwers. This indicates how very parochial life became. We hardly knew which ships we were in company with and in line abreast during typical A/S patrols we hardly ever even saw the next ship in line. our world shrank into such restricted confines that we lost all knowledge of things outside it. The watch routine of four on, four off, was punishing enough but when the four off coincided with action alarms or daywork duties it became truly physically exhausting. Our vital priorities became the daily rum ration, sleep and food in that order. Coupled with the other hardships, there was always the terrible smell in the messdecks with fifty men crowded together, often unwashed; this was not because of laziness or general negligence of simple hygiene but because fresh water was always at a premium in the Evarts during long trips when usually all domestic water supplies were locked off except for two fifteen minute periods each day. Condensation ran down the bulkheads but was hardly noticed because there were a few inches of sea water swilling around the deck. Such was our existence for many days on end and it is no wonder that we lost all track of the operations we were engaged upon. The highlights of our lives were not money, food or whatever but merely the anticipation of having an entire night in blissful oblivion in one's bunk during the twenty-four or forty-eight hour stopovers at Belfast at the end of each trip.

There is little else to say about 15EG's existence during this period. There were frequent alarms and great expenditure of depth charges but never the satisfaction of a successful action to make it all seem worthwhile. The same punishing routine became the norm during this six week period but towards the end of October, there were rumours that the Group was to be released from the A/S patrol drudgery at the end of the current patrol. This rumour did in fact turn out to be true, but when the nature of their next duty became known there was little to be cheerful about. Convoy JW61 to Murmansk was due to leave Loch Ewe on 20 October and the 15th EG was one of the groups allocated as escorts. Powerful protection was provided for this convoy; in addition to the humble escorts (EG's 8, 15, 20 and 21) there was the cruiser *Dido*, three escort carriers *Vindex, Nairana* and *Tracker*, and the six 'O' class destroyers of the 17th DF. These Russian convoys were no longer the deadly affairs of earlier days. After the disaster of PQ17 and consequent extensive use of air cover, few of the later convoys suffered many losses. Nevertheless, they were, of course, feared because of the horrendous weather and arctic cold that had to be endured. The duration of the trip was looked upon by the 15th EG as merely a short hop. Most convoys to Murmansk took only about seven to nine days on passage whereas the 15th EG had been accustomed to operations measured in weeks rather than in days. Nevertheless, they found the voyage no sinecure. As humble frigates they were frequently called upon as tenders to the escort carriers, a job which entails much dashing about and changes of course as well as the constant requirement to maintain an efficient Asdic watch.

Many U-boats were deployed in the path of convoy JW61 to the north of Norway and a number of them made contact after six days free of any alarms. The carrier-borne aircraft and the many escorts fought such a successful defensive battle that none of the U-boats penetrated the screen to make torpedo attacks on the convoy ships. They fired a large number of acoustic T5's at the escorts in an attempt to break gaps in the defence lines but none found a target. 15EG's Asdic teams tried hard to improve the group score during this trip to Russia but the water temperature layer problems in these northern latitudes defeated all their efforts. Not a single U-boat was sunk and, as usual, the escorting ships had to be content that it was victory enough to deliver all the merchant ships intact in the Kola Inlet on 28 October.

The 15th EG had three whole days to recover from their first taste of arctic convoy work. This was an unusually long lay off for them but, apart from the fact that they could sleep soundly in their bunks in harbour, this spell in the northern territories of their Russian allies was not much appreciated. In common with all other ex-Captains men, those of 15EG firmly voted that runs ashore in Polyarnoe were amongst the most dismal they had experienced. There was no question of them being entertained in gratitude by the Russians. For the most part they were treated in a manner which varied between indifference and scarcely veiled hostility. None of the men had expected a heroes welcome, but having just risked their lives to bring a vital convoy to Russia it would have been appreciated if there had been some friendly recognition. In the few cases where the locals did seem ready for fraternisation they were firmly sent on their way by brutal armed guards. It was thus almost a welcome relief when the time came for the return convoy to form up.

Having watched the convoy arrive, the U-boats were keeping close watch for the next home bound one. RA61 sailed on 1 November and by that evening it became obvious that there was a reception party lined up to meet them. The first and only victim was *Mounsey* which was severely damaged by a prematurely exploding T5 at 1930 hrs. This hit her between frames 108 and 123. Above the waterline in this section was the aft messdeck and below this were oil tanks. Two of the latter happened to be empty at the time and this fact possibly cushioned the explosion and prevented more serious damage. Ten men were killed. Four of the side plates were buckled, two oil tanks were flooded and the upper deck was bowed upwards in the vicinity, but *Mounsey* was able to limp back into Polyarnoe under her own power. She was taken in hand for temporary repairs by the Russians but it was a most uncomfortable period. Being in dry dock with the ship's power shut down is always a miserable experience at the best of times but in the frigid arctic climate with little sympathetic assistance from their Russian hosts, *Mounsey*'s crew spent most of their time trying to keep the frost out of their bones. A Pink list entry has *Mounsey* listed as being back at Belfast for completion of repairs in Pollock Dock before Christmas.

Meanwhile, the remainder of 15EG had made the return trip with convoy RA61 which was a carbon copy of the outward run. Numerous U-boat attacks were all repulsed without losses on either side and the Group was back at Belfast by mid-November. For some reason, they appear to have had a longer than usual lay off in harbour before their next trip to sea but before mid-December they were operational again, patrolling in the Atlantic off Scotland. This trip lasted until the end of January, 1945. There is some evidence that during that period *Dacres* operated with them to make up for *Mounsey*'s absence. As we saw in Chapter 9, after being restored to her normal state after service as a headquarters ship, she seems to have worked with both 15EG and EG17 for a time. Several frigate groups had attacked and sunk U-boats in the offshore waters where they now worked but 15EG were unable to improve their score. Their patrol extended from the Kyle of Lochalsh to the Faeroes in the north but, despite numerous hopeful attacks, they still had no successes. They spent the worst of the winter in these inhospitable waters and it was not until mid-February that they had a respite. By the end of the month *Mounsey* had rejoined them with her honourable wounds healed and the Group was then sent south to finish the war operating on A/S patrols in the Channel approaches, with Devonport as their base. There were quite a few Schnorkel fitted U-boats operating in this area at this late stage of the war but 15EG did not encounter any. Right up until VE-Day, *Louis* remained the only member to have hoisted the Jolly Roger.

The Group had certainly put in more than its share of sea time. *Lawson*'s CO said that the ship had covered 100,000 miles during its first year. If this was true, it was a phenomenal achievement (the equivalent of sailing at 12knots, day and night, without a break for the whole year!).

One of the more pleasant aspects of their existence in the Channel during the last months of the war was the equable weather and moderate seas they enjoyed as a most welcome change from the perpetual heavy weather around Cape Wrath and the Pentland Firth! They had some reasonable runs ashore at places such as Le Havre, Cherbourg, Devonport and Portsmouth. They also experienced some unreal situations such as carrying out a U-boat attack so close to the Cornish coast that they could clearly see the faces of holiday makers in a train steaming along the coastal railway . . . but as always, the attack was abortive.

The Group were fortunate enough to be in Belfast when VE-Day came along and the crews took part in the triumphant official Victory Parade through the city but their group identity began to crumble even before the Pacific war came to an end.

Louis, Mounsey, Lawson and *Inglis* were laid up in Reserve Fleet at Hull in early June with *Loring, Moorsom* and *Dacres* suffering the same fate at Hartlepools. The newcomer, *Narborough*, did remain in commission for a while, returning to operate for some months in the Plymouth Command carrying out odd duty destroyer tasks but the rest remained as dead ships until steaming crews could be raised to take them back to America.

Moorsom was the first to go on 25 October, 1945, followed by *Dacres* on 26 January, 1946, *Mounsey* on 25 February, 1946, whilst *Inglis, Lawson* and *Louis* made that last voyage on 20 March, 1946. *Loring* lingered on at Hartlepools for much longer. She was used as an accommodation ship for the care and maintenance staff of the Reserve Fleet and became the last of the Evarts to be handed back on 7 January, 1947.

TABLE OF U-BOAT SINKINGS BY THE 15th ESCORT GROUP

Date	U-boat No.	Ships Involved.
24.8.44	U445	*Louis*

SHIPS LOST FROM THE 15th ESCORT GROUP

None. *Mounsey* severely damaged off Murmansk 2.11.44

– II –

THE 21st ESCORT GROUP

Byron, Conn, Deane, Fitzroy, Redmill, Rupert

T he last chapter dealt with the only escort group to be entirely composed of Evarts class ships. This chapter is about the other unconventional group, which had Buckley class ships only as members during its short existence. It was one of the last escort groups to be formed during the war and after its inauguration in October, 1944, there were only a scant seven months left before the war in Europe came to an end. None of its ships had lacked experience before joining 21EG however; they were all among the first of the Buckleys to be completed and all had worked in the North Sea and Channel with Nore Command before becoming an escort group.

All six ships were completed at a time when production at the Hingham yard had begun to get into top gear and the commissioning dates of the first five all fell within six weeks of one another: *Fitzroy* on 16 October, 1943, *Byron* on the 30, *Conn* on the 31, *Deane* on 26 November, and *Redmill* on 30 November. *Rupert* tailed along later on 24 December.

Fitzroy, being so far ahead of the others, should have been the first to reach Belfast but she had been much delayed at Casco Bay by being appointed as the Base Training Officer's ship at that inhospitable place and she remained there on that duty from November, 1943, to 7 January, 1944, when she was relieved by *Riou*. Her crew had watched enviously as all her juniors had passed through their week at Casco and disappeared to the warm sunshine of Bermuda and thence to Britain. By rights, *Fitzroy* should have reached Belfast before Christmas but with this early hold up, it was March before she got there.

Byron and *Conn* kept pace with one another during the early trials and training period and, with no problems to delay progress, they both sailed homewards as escorts to convoy HX275 towards the end of

January, 1944, and both were in Pollock Dock for the usual refit during February.

Deane and *Redmill* also worked together. They completed trials, cursed the blue nose weather at Casco and suffered the usual battering by hurricanes in the Bermuda triangle before becoming operational in February, 1944.

Rupert's early days have already been mentioned in Chapter 8, since her early operational days were with the local flotilla at Devonport. Three of 21EG's ships (*Conn, Deane,* and *Redmill*) are shown as being members of the 11th EG in an Admiralty Pink List entry of 28 February together with *Cranstoun, Dakins* and *Halsted* but that Group seems to have been disbanded almost immediately. They may have been involved in one convoy escort operation during its short existence but by early April, 1944, all six had been transferred on temporary loan to the Nore Command and moved round to Sheerness where they were joined by *Byron* which had had a brief connection with B1EG at Belfast (including service as an escort to a Russian convoy JW57) and *Fitzroy*.

Their employment during the next six months was identical with that of the permanent Nore Command Captains dealt with in Chapter 9 and there is little to add here. These ships on loan made a total of fourteen extra frigates to operate in the North Sea where previously there had been only the 16th and 21st Flotillas at Harwich and Sheerness. With such a wealth of new blood, the Captain (D)'s of the Nore cheerfully reduced the work load on their ships, veterans of many E-boat and air attacks, and shared their duties among the fresh crews of the frigates. Most of those duties were now fairly tame and mundane convoy trips up and down the East Coast and occasionally from the Thames estuary down Channel and part way across the Atlantic. There were also night E-boat patrols across the North Sea towards Holland but, until the invasion got under way, the enemy coastal craft were keeping a fairly low profile along the East Coast. It is often said that British matelots are never happy unless they have something to complain about and there were certainly enough grumbles in the Nore frigates at this time. Signalmen and Telegraphists in several of the ships have kept records which show how little sea time the Nore destroyers put in compared with the Captains but, as has been mentioned before, the destroyers had certainly earned a rest and the inexperienced crews of the frigates needed a period of hard work before they were called upon to provide essential support for the coming invasion.

When Operation NEPTUNE actually began there were no longer grounds for complaint. The harbours of Sheerness and Harwich were virtually emptied as all ships of Nore Command played some part in the historic events following 6 June. None of the future 21st EG ships distinguished themselves during this busy period but they all had excitement enough during these epic days.

Redmill, however, did have a unique experience on D-Day. After leaving Harwich, she became escort to the monitor HMS *Roberts* and, after accompanying her to the bombardment position, remained to act as A/S screen. A number of other Captains are mentioned in these pages as having escorted bombarding ships to the beach heads without being allowed to take part by actually firing on the enemy held coast. For some reason, *Redmill* was the exception. As she circled the monitor to protect it from U-boat attack she was allowed to open fire with her 3″ guns every time she was between *Roberts* and the coast. It cannot be imagined that her 13 lb projectiles did much more than knock a few chips off Hitler's West Wall but it did much for the morale of *Redmill*'s gunners to be actually taking aggressive action against the enemy on this momentous day and her whole ship's company felt pride in taking an active part in the assault, however small, instead of being in a support role, as were so many of the Captains.

As all the ships dealt with in this chapter had similar experiences while briefly serving with the Nore Command it would be repetitive to include their individual accounts. *Deane* can be taken as a representative of their corporate experiences and of which a brief résumé is given in these further reminiscences by ERA AJ Brown.

The pattern of life during our time in the Channel and North Sea covered the whole spectrum from comedy to excitement and tragedy. One of the comic incidents occurred when we were passing through the Straits of Dover with a convoy before D-Day. We passed close to a tug which was obviously having great trouble trying to handle one of the unwieldy concrete landing barges in the face of strong currents and cross winds. Our Skipper generously asked (over the loud hailer) whether there was anything he could do to assist and was most indignant at the tug master's rude reply: 'Yes, if you can sink the bloody thing, if not then you might as well bugger off', he said – and we did. We often wondered whether he did manage to get the concrete monster to turn right into the Channel or whether he gave up and took it back into the Thames.

Convoy runs to and from the landing area became the monotonous pattern of our existence after D-Day. The only dangerous incident I can recall is when a V1 flying bomb, passing over our convoy one night, was hit by the escort's AA fire and crashed right under the bows of one of the biggest merchant ships close astern of us. Her bows were somewhat crumpled and the shock of the explosion bent one of our prop shafts, so that we had to drop out of the escort and had a couple of days in dock at Chatham out of the incident. No one ever fired at V1's after that. One of our most tragic experiences happened off Cherbourg. Having lost vacuum, due to some blockage in the condenser cooling system intake, we used the usual ploy of blasting out with steam. This cleared the obstruction but we were quite shattered to discover that the offending object had been the body of one of our own soldiers. Further mutilated in death by our steam blast it was not a pretty sight and was an object of great pity. I completely lost track of how many convoys we took down the Channel. As each one passed without us seeing too much violent action, we felt that we were not doing very much towards the war effort. Many of the ship's company were pleased when our stint of duty with Nore Command came to an end in the autumn and we went back to hunting U-boats with the WA Command

* * *

The return to Belfast was made in October, 1944, when the Allied advance had reduced the need for Channel escorts. *Conn*, *Deane*, *Fitzroy* and *Redmill* were already earmarked for the newly formed 21st Escort Group and to make up its numbers *Rupert* joined from the Devonport Command. *Conn* became Group Leader under the command of Lieutenant-Commander Raymond Hart DSC*, an officer who had already gained a great reputation as an escort commander and had had shares in the destruction of no less than eleven U-boats before taking over 21EG. The Group insignia was, somewhat predictably, a gold key on a light blue ground and, with this proud emblem painted on their funnels, the new group were given a short time to work up tactics together before becoming fully operational in the Westerm Approaches Command. The shakedown did not last very long and their first mission began with a trip through the Minches to Scapa Flow to become attached to Home Fleet units.

They sailed from Scapa on 21 October in company with *Vindex* and two other escort carriers and were soon told, as they had already guessed, that they were indeed bound for arctic waters. Convoy JW61 had left Loch Ewe the previous day and the 21st EG was scheduled to meet it and proceed to Murmansk. We have already read about this convoy in other chapters, so it is unnecessary to repeat that it was a successful run. No ships were lost and no U-boats sunk, from the many which tried to attack. The convoy and escorts battled on against the weather and, as we know, reached Murmansk on 28 October. We also know that this visit was a pretty miserable affair with no fraternization with the Russians so that all were relieved to leave these northern climes after just four days. Apart from the damage to *Mounsey* (described in Chapter 10) in the Kola Inlet, the return convoy was as uneventful as the outward trip, except that the weather was possibly worse. 21EG was back in Belfast again by 9 November. *Byron* was the only member of the Group not to complete this operation. On the return voyage, her CO, Lieutenant-Commander Southcombe, was stricken with acute appendicitis. Gallant attempts were made to get the ship's motor boat across to a Fleet destroyer to collect an MO to carry out an emergency operation but the seas were very rough and, just as the doctor had got into the boat, it was swamped by a huge wave. All further attempts were abandoned. *Byron* was then released from the escort and sent back at full speed to the UK to get her CO to hospital. He was later relieved in *Byron* by Lieutenant J Burfield RN.

Redmill had taken a hard beating from heavy seas during the home run and had a short period in dock to repair her underwater fittings. Nevertheless, she did not miss any group operations since the next trip to sea was not until 14 December, when the Group was sent to augment the escort of an incoming Atlantic convoy on its way into the English Channel. Tragedy struck on the night of 16 December, when the destroyer *Tanatside* mistook *Byron* for a surfaced U-Boat in the darkness and set course to ram. *Byron* switched on riding lights and took avoiding action but hit *Tanatside's* stern killing one of her depth charge party. Damage was slight but the accident earned *Byron* a spell in dry dock at Glasgow. The Group was to hand over to another escort group off Portland. Just as the handover had taken place, and the 21st EG had moved off, two of the transports were sunk in quick succession. Turning back to assist the Channel escort group to hunt for the attacker, 21EG spent many hours diligently searching the area but no U-boat was ever contacted. After this unsuccessful hunt, the Group put into Devonport to refuel and replenish stores. This completed, they left immediately to rendezvous with an incoming convoy at longitude 10 degrees west and ran into the father and mother of all gales. All the ships were battered to some extent but *Deane* came off worst. Not only had heavy seas carried away many of her upper deck fittings but some depth charges had broken loose on the quarterdeck and careered around like miniature steam rollers creating much damage. The results of this drubbing were serious enough to put *Deane* into dock at Devonport for a spell when the Group returned with the inward convoy. She was the only one of them which escaped being at sea on Christmas Day. With the storm ravages repaired, *Deane* set out to rejoin EG21 again and within two hours of sailing her A/S crew were jubilant to pick up a very definite submarine contact. With great confidence, they delivered a text book Hedgehog attack and there was an explosion as the bombs hit something. There were rousing cheers a moment later when a submarine hastily broke surface but these cheers soon turned into groans of dismay as they recognized the submarine as one of ours! Shaken and indignant, the CO of the submarine lost no time in making a blistering signal to his Flag Officer and *Deane* was unceremoniously ordered back to Plymouth for a Board of Inquiry. Her CO was found blameless however. The Board accepted that he had been given no warning of submarines exercising in the area and the surface escort which should have been in attendance, to warn off approaching vessels, was not on station. After this further delay, *Deane* really did manage to rejoin the remainder of 21EG which was now engaged in A/S sweeps in the Channel entrance. Nothing of great import had happened to her group mates while she had been held up at Devonport except that *Redmill* had been fired on by shore batteries in the Channel Islands.

In the New Year, 21EG had a change of operational area. Several U-boats had been operating in St Georges Channel and the Irish Sea during the latter part of January, 1945, and a massive search (Operation CE) was set up by several Belfast escort groups. 21EG was included and was operating off Liverpool when two ships of an incoming convoy (believed to be HX322) were torpedoed within sight of them. This attack, right under the noses of six frigates plus the convoy escorts, was a typical instance of the daring exploits of German U-boat commanders in our inshore waters during this late stage of the war.

Lieutenant-Commander Hart, with his impressive record of previous U-boat skills must have been despairing of ever increasing his score with 21EG. The ships went right through the CE operation without any success and then continued to work in the waters between the north of Ireland and the Scottish Isles where their ill luck continued, despite numerous contacts and great expenditure of depth charges.

Redmill had one respite from these patrols during late January. She was sent as escort to a large floating dock on its way to Gibraltar and thence to India. She only accompanied it as far as Gibraltar, but her crew welcomed the chance to enjoy a visit to this matelots' paradise of many bars and duty free merchandise. They were soon back to the usual routine though and rejoined the group on 9 February just in time to share in its great moment of glory.

Convoy RU156, escorted by 25CEG, had been attacked and lost one ship off the Hebrides on 16 March. On the 21st, HMCS *New Glasgow* got revenge by ramming U-1003 off N Ireland. There was evidence that this boat had not been alone, however, and it was believed that other U-boats in company with her had escaped northwards. 21EG was called upon to make extensive search through the Minches and all their previous ill luck changed with a vengeance. It transpired that no less than three U-boats had sought sanctuary in these narrow waters and, in a well concerted group operation, the 21st EG located and sank each of them in turn.

First victory went to *Conn, Deane* and *Rupert*. They ran down U965 midway between The Butte of Lewis and Cape Wrath on 27 March, sharing the honours for its destruction. Later that same day, the Group's second division had a similar success when *Fitzroy, Redmill* and *Byron* made a positive contact between Eriskay and Skye and sent U722 to the bottom in a combined attack.

After this double victory, with all the ships having had shares in the action, it seemed to be nothing less than wishful thinking that any more U-boats could be lurking in the Minches. However, Lieutenant-Commander Hart kept the Group resolutely on the hunt, minutely investigating every nook and cranny in this 100 mile long channel. Keyed up by success, and with renewed confidence in their prowess, the Asdic crews were determined that if there were any more U-boats then they would certainly find them. Nothing succeeds like success and their double victory had put a very keen edge on 21EG's deadly blade.

Three more days passed without contact and a little of the keenness began to fade but on 30 March the Asdic operators in *Rupert* were at last rewarded by another most definite contact. This was in an inshore position hardly 10 miles north-west of Enard Bay. Calling in *Conn* and *Deane* to assist, *Rupert* steered the 1st Division to a second kill and shared honours for destroying U1021.

The triumphant return to Belfast after this hat trick was an experience that none of the crews of the 21st EG ships will ever forget. All flew makeshift Jolly Rogers, run up from sheets and bits of bunting, and the men in all the ships in harbour lined the rails to cheer them in. Admiral Bevan was there on the jetty to greet them in person. There was a national press release about the triple victory in mid-April but this had been delayed in order to announce yet another 21st EG victory – which will be described in due course.

Groups were not often given a very long break between operations and, after a few days to replenish and refuel the 21st EG were back at sea on another patrol. This time it was in the area to the south-west of Ireland. The monumental beer celebrations during their few runs ashore in Belfast to celebrate their victories had not taken the keen edge off their previous efficiency and on 8 April, they located a fourth U-boat victim 50 miles south-west of the Fastnet Rock. This time it was *Fitzroy* and *Byron* which shared equal credit for sinking U1001 and the group's tally of successes went up to four within twelve days, a most creditable result for a group which had only been in existence for about six months. They had come well up in the league table of the Belfast groups. Only 3EG were ahead of them, with six after much longer as an operational group and the Asdic operators in 21EG were keen to challenge this score if they could. Luck was not with them however. They were back at Belfast and were to have only one more patrol before the European war ended. This took them round the north-west of Ireland but instead of the hoped for last minute victory, the war ended on a sad note for them. *Redmill* was torpedoed off Sligo Bay on 27 April. Twenty four of her crew were killed and many wounded. The ship itself was sorely damaged and was towed back to Belfast as a CTL.

Thus ended 21EG's wartime career but not their sea time. Like so many other Captains, they had no long VE-Day celebrations. The group was split up and distributed around the British coast to receive the surrender of the many U-boats still at sea. Quite a few gave them up to 21EG ships. *Byron* collected three including U1009 which surrendered on 10 May.

One of *Deane*'s captures was accompanied by events which were condemned as most unseamanlike by senior officers. ERA AJ Brown was in the boarding party sent across to take charge of the prize and recalls:

The yacht *Philante* (almost top-heavy with newsreel cameramen and senior officers) was standing by to record this surrender for posterity. We crowded into the boat armed to the teeth with pistols, rifles and sub-machine guns and all went according to plan until we got alongside the U-boat. We suddenly realised that it was not going to be at all easy to clamber out of the boat on to the Sub's casing. The sea was choppy and the boat bobbed up and down alarmingly. We were much encumbered by our arsenal of weapons and, after several of the lads had made undignified (and unsuccessful) attempts to get on board, we were somewhat flummoxed. Then someone, with true matelot's resourcefulness, solved the problem. We calmly handed up our guns to the bemused Germans and climbed aboard with ease. Nonchalantly taking our guns back from the enemy, we went about the normal procedure of taking them prisoner. This unmilitary behaviour did not seem at all out of place to us but the top brass in *Philante* were LIVID!! We were all given a hell of a dressing down when we eventually got back on board but no disciplinary action was taken. I have seen this episode on cinema newsreels on several occasions and the reel of film has also been included in the well-known TV series *War at Sea* – but you will note that the censor has very definitely cut out the bit showing us handing our guns up to the Germans!!

The surrendered U-boats were slowly mustered in serried ranks in Loch Ryan and Loch Eriboll whilst the Allies squabbled over whether they should be shared out or scuttled. The ships of 21EG spent much time as shepherds and guard dogs for this deadly assemblage but they were back at Belfast before VJ-Day and, with a mixture of rejoicing and regret, the Group was disbanded and the individual ships went their several ways.

Fitzroy had been chosen to be refitted as a fighter direction ship for the Far East and some work was actually progressed but when Japan surrendered she was hurriedly put into reserve at Hartlepools to await her time to return to the USA – which she did on 5 January, 1946.

Conn was exiled to the Rosyth Flotilla and remained there for some time with very little employment, although she did take part in the Norwegian mail service, visiting Oslo and other ports. She sailed for America on 26 November, 1945.

Rupert also went to the Rosyth flotilla and had the misfortune to become involved in the long, boring Operation DEADLIGHT – during which the U-boats were towed out and sunk in the Atlantic. This kept her occupied until January, 1946. She was released for her final trans-Atlantic voyage on 20 March.

Byron, like *Conn*, had an interesting round trip of all the Norwegian ports, delivering mail to the British occupation troops. She was then sent to Dundee where she operated as target towing ship for the Fleet Air Arm base (HMS *Condor*) at Arbroath. After a short spell of this work, she was sent south to Portsmouth, where her crew was reduced for the trip back to America on 24 November, 1945.

Deane also had a run to Norway after the war. She took a peacetime convoy of merchant ships to Christiansands and was then employed on a miscellany of tasks including acting as guardship when the King and Queen flew to Northern Ireland – and escorting the fishing fleet through minefields outside of Milford Haven. She was at sea on VJ-Day as tender to a submarine on diving trials off Northern Ireland but had her own fireworks celebration on return to Rothesay. She ended her useful life as tender to the U-boats in Loch Ryan. When the last of these had been towed out and sunk, she went in to Glasgow to land some of her British equipment and departed to Philadelphia on 4 March, 1946.

TABLE OF U-BOAT SINKINGS BY THE 21st ESCORT GROUP

Date	U-boat No.	Ships Involved.
27.3.45	U965	*Conn, Rupert, Deane*
27.3.45	U722	*Fitzroy, Redmill, Byron*
30.3.45	U1021	*Conn, Rupert, Deane*
8.4.45	U1001	*Fitzroy, Byron*

SHIPS LOST FROM THE 21st ESCORT GROUP

Redmill   Torpedoed off Sligo Bay 27.4.45 (CTL)

– 12 –

SERVICE IN MIXED
ESCORT GROUPS

*Bayntun, Braithwaite, Bullen, Burges, Balfour,
Cotton, Cranstoun, Foley, Gardiner, Goodall,
Hoste, Manners, Inman, Stockham.*

The allocation of the Captains to Western Atlantic escort groups began in what seems to have been a logical manner, creating groups consisting entirely of ships in the Captain class. This admirable system did not, however, become a fixed rule; all the ships listed above were put into groups which contained a mixture of escort types, ranging from old Fleet destroyers to new construction frigates and Flower class corvettes. Several of these ships have been met with in previous chapters because they began their service as members of purely Captain class groups. Others have not been mentioned before, as their whole careers were with mixed groups. To adopt a systematic approach, this chapter will deal, as far as is practicable, with the ships in order of the seniority of their commissioning dates. This quite properly puts *Bayntun* at the head of the list and her story is coupled with two other ships of lesser seniority but which served in groups with her.

THE B4 ESCORT GROUP AND 10th ESCORT GROUP

Bayntun, Braithwaite and Foley

She was Hull No. DE1, an Evarts class and the very first of all the Captains to be completed. She was handed over to the RN as *Bayntun* on 13 February, 1943. Her construction had begun way back in March, 1942, but as she was a prototype, building time had been much the same as for conventional ships and she did not commission until mid-February, 1943. The trials period which later took no more than a week in most cases was much protracted by virtue of the ship being First of Class and many senior officers (both RN and USN) were much interested in monitoring her progress. Consequently she did not reach Bermuda until April, having attained notoriety for landing a 3″ shell in a Boston cemetery (as related in Chapter 1). The work-up at Bermuda was remarkable only for the fact that, like most of her successors, *Bayntun* experienced a battering from a hurricane force storm which so upset her Arma gyro that she became the first to be utterly lost at sea, until her W/T staff made a radio fix.

Even after arriving in the UK, *Bayntun* was still delayed by the onus of being the first of the Captains. Her First of Class trials in the Clyde were lengthy and it was autumn before she was released as operational and joined the B4EG.

Foley was much further down the seniority list. Her completion date was 16 September, 1943, and after the usual trials and work-up programme, she made passage to the UK via the Azores in company with *Gould* and *Essington*. This was to prove a memorable passage. The excitement began when *Foley* and *Gould* were caught up in the 40th EG's battle with U-boats around convoy MKS30/SL139 off the Azores. Called to assist the convoy's escorts, *Foley* joined in an Asdic search with the Frigate *Crane*. Between them they located and hung on to contact with U538 for a long cat and mouse chase which ended in the U-boat's destruction and an equal share of credit for *Crane* and *Foley*, which earned the latter much kudos as the first of the Captains to fly the Jolly Roger, even before becoming fully operational with an escort group. (Her CO, Lieutenant-Commander Mansfield, earned a DSC and her SD rating, Ordinary Seaman Green, a DSM).

Following this morale boosting success, *Foley* was taken in hand for the usual Pollock Dock refit and joined *Bayntun* with B4EG in January, 1944. B4EG was employed on convoy work to and from Gibraltar and neither *Bayntun* nor *Foley* distinguished themselves during that time.

Dacres was associated with the group for a short time before being converted into a headquarters assault ship for Normandy but the permanent group members were the destroyers *Helmsdale* and *Highlander* plus the corvettes *Asphodel* and *Clover*. They were, of course, involved in a number of U-boat actions in defence of the convoys and air attacks were also common on this route but none of them achieved any positive success during their time with this group.

Bayntun had an unfortunate experience during November, 1944, when one of her engine rooms was flooded whilst she was in Pollock Dock. The exact circumstances of this event are not clear. There were suspicions of Irish Republican involvement but, whatever the cause, the flooding was of such serious proportions that at one time there was talk of *Bayntun* being sent back to Boston for expert attention. Although this did not happen, her original crew were paid off. By late December, she was ready for trials again.

This requirement for a new crew coincided with a snap decision to send *Dacres* to Dundee for headquarters ship conversion. Two thirds of *Dacre's* crew were on leave at the time and she sailed without them. When these men returned from leave, they were bemused to find their ship gone and their kit piled on the jetty. Still dazed, they were transferred to *Bayntun* to recommission her and take her out for sea trials. One advantage of this move was that this crew, being no novices, did not need to go through another work-up period. She rejoined B4EG in the new year and continued with their regular Gibraltar convoy runs and almost immediately gained a success, sharing honours with the Canadian ship *Camrose* for sinking U757 on 8 January, 1944, while supporting a convoy south-west of Ireland.

Asphodel was torpedoed and lost during convoy MKS41/SL139 out of Gibraltar on 9 March. *Bayntun* and *Clover* began a search for the attacking U-boat at 0154 hrs and conducted two creep attacks during the morning watch. They claimed a kill but the claim was downgraded to credit for inflicting slight damage when the Admiralty experts studied the report. This action was typical of many which took place during B4EG's Gibraltar convoy runs between January and August, 1944, but they suffered no further losses and gained no more victories in that period. The Group was disbanded in September and some of its members (*Helmsdale*, *Bayntun* and *Foley*) joined the newly formed 10EG with *Loch Eck* and *Loch Dunvegan*. A third Captain, *Braithwaite*, was transferred from her association with 3EG and became the sixth member of 10EG.

This new group began operations in October, 1944, and during the autumn and winter joined frigate groups engaged upon support roles off Northern Ireland and the Scottish coast but 10EG had no success during its first four months of existence. The only slight casualty was *Foley* which first of all had a period in dock at Devonport to repair the Asdic dome badly crumpled by heavy weather and on 16 February, 1945, she was docked again, having dropped a shallow pattern of depth-charges off Northern Ireland whilst proceeding at too slow a speed. The explosions had shattered both her rudders and as she was only steerable by engines she had made a most awkward journey through the Irish Sea and up Channel to Portsmouth, where her repairs took place between 19 and 28 February. These defects resulted in *Foley* missing out on 10EG's great moment of glory when they sank three U-boats in the short space of three weeks. They had been supporting EN and WN convoys off the north-west coast of Scotland and had their first victory on 3 February when *Braithwaite, Bayntun* and *Loch Eck* attacked U1279 north of the Orkneys and gained equal credits for its destruction. They celebrated this victory in the bleak surroundings of Scapa Flow on 9 February and then resumed patrol in the same area as before. Just eleven days after the first kill, the Group detected another U-boat in almost exactly the same place on 14 February. This time it was *Bayntun, Loch Eck* and *Loch Dunvegan* which shared the honours for confirmed destruction of U989. Seemingly encouraged by this second success within a small area, the Group continued to operate there on the remote chance of making a hat trick and, amazingly enough, a third U-boat *did* appear. This proved to be U1278. It was rapidly despatched by *Bayntun* and *Loch Eck*.

This triple victory proved to be the Group's swan song, however. They continued to work in the same northern regions for another month but failed to add to their score. For some reason 10EG seems to have been disbanded even before VE-Day came along. An Admiralty Pink List places *Braithwaite, Bayntun* and *Foley* at Portsmouth in late April, 1945, with the notation 'Non-operational'.

Braithwaite moved to Southampton and paid off after VE-Day, being intended for modification into a fighter direction ship for the Far East. Some work had been progressed by VJ-Day but it was never completed and she was sent into the Reserve Fleet with many other Captains at Hartlepools. There she remained until her return to the USA on 17 December, 1945.

Foley and *Bayntun* continued in commission during May and June, 1945, and escorted a number of peacetime convoys to various Norwegian ports, Oslo, Stavanger, Bergen and Christiansands. As soon as the Pacific war came to an end, both ships were put into reserve at Harwich and were among the first of the Evarts to be taken back to the USA on 22 August, 1945.

THE 17th ESCORT GROUP.

Burges, Cranstoun, Stockham and *Moorsom.*

Burges was one of the very first Evarts to commission in June, 1943, and her early operations were mentioned in previous chapters when she was serving with the 3rd and 4th EG's. She had been taken into dock with engine trouble on 12 June, 1944. When her troubles had been resolved, she returned as operational with the newly formed 17thEG in October.

Moorsom is another of the Evarts which has been dealt with earlier, in Chapter 10, which describes her association with the 15th EG from which she was detached to join the 17th.

Stockham and *Cranstoun* should also have had mention in previous chapters since they served with the Devonport and Nore Commands respectively for the Normandy invasion operations. However, since they were to be included here it has been left until now to trace their early movements.

The Buckley class *Stockham* was commissioned on 28 December, 1943, and was one of the several ships to be ferried to the UK under the arrangements made with the RCN, making the crossing to Lissahally on 1 February, 1944, and being taken over by her RN crew about a fortnight later. She had no early operational experience with any of the WA escort groups since, immediately after her work-up at Tobermory, she was despatched to operate with the Devonport Command. In common with the other ships which worked in the Channel, her employment was to carry out support duties with the Western Task force and she put in much hard work escorting landing craft and supply ships to the Normandy beaches from D-Day onwards. She left Devonport and joined the 17th EG in the autumn.

Cranstoun was also a Buckley class frigate and had been commissioned in the normal manner at Boston on 13 November, 1943. Her progress towards operational status was slightly delayed by propeller damage and a collision with a USN destroyer but after the Bermuda work-up, beginning on 8 January, 1944, she was at Norfolk Virginia on 6 February, ready for her passage to Britain. She is reported as being at Belfast on 28 February, 1944. Her first operation as an unallocated unit was as escort as far as Gibraltar to two aircraft carriers taking planes to Malta. Immediately after this she was seconded to the Nore Command and was at Sheerness in April, taking her place with the Captains of the Nore Command. During the few weeks before D-Day she carried out East Coast convoy work and E-boat patrol work. She then had four hard months in support of the convoys sailing from the Thames to the Normandy beaches.

Cranstoun was then allocated to serve in 17EG with *Loch Lomond*, *Loch Killin* and the US-built Colony class *Ascension*. Their base of operations was the Clyde. To begin with, their working area was off the north-west coast of Scotland, where they provided support to any threatened convoys throughout the winter of 1944–45 but the only success which rewarded them was the sinking of U322 off the Shetlands on 25 November, 1944. *Cranstoun* played a major part in this attack but got none of the credit, which was shared equally between *Ascension* and a Norwegian aircraft. During December, 1944, she was separated from the Group to form part of the escort to SS *Rimutaka* which was taking the Duke and Duchess of Gloucester to Australia but only went as far as Gibraltar. On her return, she joined the 1st EG patrolling off Cherbourg over Christmas and was with them when *Affleck* and *Capel* were torpedoed.

She then rejoined 17EG and their sphere of operations moved to the Channel during 1945. It was in this zone that *Burges* and *Cranstoun* shared honours with *Loch Killin* for the destruction of U1063 west of Lands End on 16 April. (*NOTE: The two DE's received no official credit but the action report clearly states that they both took part in the DC attack and subsequent gun action. However, the Group Leader claimed all credit*).

Stockham and *Moorsom* finished the war as replacements in the depleted 1st EG and there is no further record that the Group had any more successes.

Cranstoun went into Reserve at Harwich in mid-May, 1945, and remained there until she was taken back to the USA on 3 December.

Stockham was scheduled for conversion into a floating power station after VE-Day and went to Portsmouth for this work to be carried out. In the event, it was never started and she was absorbed into the local flotilla to carry out maid of all work tasks for several months after the war had finished. She returned to the USA on 15 January, 1946.

Burges and *Moorsom* did not linger long after 1EG was finally disbanded and by August both were in reserve fleets (at Harwich and Rosyth respectively). *Moorsom* sailed for New York on 25 October, 1945, but *Burges* did not make her return voyage until 27 February, 1946.

B2 AND B3 ESCORT GROUPS

Gardiner

Although she was commissioned comparatively early, on 30 September, 1943, and was available when frigate groups were being formed at Belfast, *Gardiner* never did have a permanent association with any of her sister ships and spent almost the entire war with mixed groups. She had passed through all the initial routines at Casco and Bermuda and reached Belfast in early December, 1943. Next official mention of her is her allocation to the 5th EG in January, 1944 but she never did become an operational member of that group. Some serious defect developed at around this time and she was refitting in Tilbury Dock from 7 January to 9 February, 1944. On completion, she was sent to join B2EG, operating from Liverpool.

This group escorted both Atlantic and Gibraltar convoys and *Gardiner* was involved in a number of skirmishes with U-boats without ever achieving positive victories. One of her actions took place in mid-Atlantic some 500 miles north of the Azores whilst escorting convoy SC155 on 24 March. Her HFDF operators obtained clear indications that at least one U-boat was shadowing the convoy and a Liberator from 59 Squadron RAF was sent to investigate. This aircraft actually sighted and mounted an unsuccessful attack on a surfaced U-boat on the indicated bearing but then lost contact. *Gardiner* homed in on its last known position and soon picked up clear asdic echoes. Ten separate attacks were made and her A/S team claimed that the last was definitely successful. However, they failed to convince the Admiralty adjudicators. It was the same story during the next six months – much arduous close escort convoy work with many alarms and attacks but no success. By September, *Gardiner* was transferred to another mixed group (B3) with *Flint Castle, Exe* and some Flower class corvettes. The operations with them were the same mixture as before, with long boring convoy trips to and from St John's during February, 1945. Their poor luck continued right until the end of the war and *Gardiner* was never destined to hit the headlines. She retired into oblivion in the reserve fleet at Hull as soon as the European war ended, lingering there to await a steaming crew and eventually going back to the USA on 12 February, 1946.

B6 AND B2 ESCORT GROUPS.

Manners

This Evarts class DE had the shortest career of all amongst the Captains which served in mixed groups. She commissioned in the normal manner at Boston on 17 December, 1943, and had no problems while progressing through her trials and working-up programmes. She reached Belfast in March, 1944, and a Pink List shows her refitting at Liverpool from 2 April until 22 June. This protracted period in dockyard hands meant that she was one of the very few Captains which did not take part in any of the D-Day operations and she is still listed as being unallocated to any group at the end of June. She had a brief association with the 4th EG (possibly as a relief for one of the regular group members) and is reported in a Pink List as being in Naples with them in July but there is no other confirmation of this (and Pink Lists are *not* infallible!). She had a short period with B6EG and then transferred to B2EG in October as a replacement for *Gardiner* which had moved to B3EG.

The remainder of the year saw *Manners* constantly on the Liverpool-Newfoundland convoy runs. She was tragically involved in a collision with the Norwegian manned corvette *Rose* on the western side of the Atlantic on 26 October, 1944, in thick fog during one of her convoy escort trips. *Manners* suffered no great damage, but *Rose* sank and there were many casualties. She gained no honour or glory until the very last day of her operational life. Several U-boats had penetrated to operate in the Irish Sea in January, 1945. During passage northwards in the Irish Sea, *Manners* was sighted by one of these about 30 miles south-west of the Isle of Man on the 26th. The U-boat loosed a T5 which struck *Manners*. Some ten minutes later, a second torpedo struck, blowing off the entire stern section. Although severely damaged, she remained afloat and her crew behaved in exemplary fashion tending the casualties and carrying out damage control. Her Asdics remained in contact with the U-boat and forced it to lie on the bottom. (The German CO was, of course, ignorant of the extent of damage to which *Manners* had been subjected and dared not surface to have a look). As we have already seen elsewhere, ships of 4EG and 5EG rushed to the scene and finished off the U-boat. Happily, this did not do *Manners* out of her rightful share of the credits. Although her damage was such that she was declared a CTL, she is still on record as having shares in the sinking of U1172.

18th ESCORT GROUP

Hoste, Balfour

The 18th Escort Group was another mixed one which was formed rather late during the war, in October, 1944. The first of its members was the very experienced *Balfour* which had already had a successful career with the 1st EG and came to the new group with the prestige of having shared in two U-boat kills with that latter group. As her early days have already been chronicled in Chapter 5, there is no need to make further mention of them here.

Hoste had no such distinguished pre-career. She had been ready for handover at Boston on 1 December, 1943, but no crew had been available and, after one of the pseudo commissionings, with a borrowed ship's company, she became one of the laid up ships at Halifax, not reaching the UK (with a RCN crew) until 27 February, 1944. Her RN crew joined her at Lissahally in March and, following the WA frigate work-up at Tobermory, she is listed as unallocated on 17 April.

She remained in this indeterminate category until June and her employment was no doubt as a supernumerary working with various escort groups without ever becoming a permanent member of any of them. She is shown (in Pink Lists) to be refitting in Pollock Dock on two occasions from 30 June to 8 July and again from 4 August to 4 September, 1944. The first of these refits was no doubt a regular maintenance period and, in all probability, the second was a delayed modification refit to bring her into line with WA standards.

Following this long period with no group affiliation, *Hoste* was allocated to the Clyde based 18EG in September. This included *Towy* and the US-built *Zanzibar* and most of this Group's work was as close escorts to Atlantic convoys. However, they also did their share of the patrols off Northern Ireland and Scotland since *Hoste* is reported at Scapa on 2 October, 1944. Neither of the Captains had any victories against U-boats whilst serving with this Group and after working with it for six months, they both moved on to *Balfour*'s original group, 1EG, in February, 1945, as replacements for *Affleck* and *Capel*, which had both been torpedoed on Boxing Day, 1944.

The final days of these two ships have been dealt with at the end of Chapter 4 but, for the record, *Hoste* was returned to the USA in August, 1945, and *Balfour* followed on 25 October, 1945.

B1 ESCORT GROUP

Inman

The arrival of *Inman*'s crew at Boston in early December coincided with the beginning of the acute manpower problems. Two of her predecessors had both had mock commissionings and there was urgent need to get them out of Charlestown Navy Yard to make room for other ships, so before taking over their own ship, *Inman*'s ship's company had the task of ferrying both *Loring* and *Moorsom* to Halifax to remain laid up there until crews could be found.

Inman then commissioned on 13 January, 1944. Trials presented no problems and she was at Casco by 13 February but her Bermuda work-up was subject to some delay. Many members of her crew had been in contact with a scarlatina outbreak and the medical authorities decreed that they must all be landed and accommodated in a derelict hospital for a quarantine period. It was therefore April before she had become an operational unit. She left Norfolk Virginia on 11 April as one of the escorts to the aircraft carrier *Illustrious* which was returning home after repairs in the States. The steaming orders were to press on at 18 knots which was near maximum for an Evarts at the best of times and when the weather deteriorated, so that seas were even breaking over *Illustrious*, life in the struggling frigate became a nightmare. To complicate matters, a fire broke out in one of her motor rooms and the shut down of an engine considerably reduced her speed so that it was as much as she could do to struggle on at 12 knots. She was therefore relieved of her escort duties and left to her own devices. Life became more bearable after this and the lame duck struggled on her own to reach the Azores on 29 April. There her engineers cleared up some of the damage resulting from the fire and she then carried on to Belfast, where the Pollock Dock experts completed the repair work.

After this refit, *Inman* worked out of Belfast as an unallocated unit for some time (May to August) and was another of the few Captains which took no part in the D-Day operations. She had made a contribution towards the preparations for that event however by spending several uncomfortable weeks wallowing about in the Bay of Biscay as one of the weather observation ships gathering meteorological data for the planners of Operation NEPTUNE.

Towards the end of August, she achieved group status by becoming the only Captain in the B1 Escort Group. The remainder of this unit were corvettes and, in common with other close escort groups, their fate was to plod wearily back and forth from the UK to Newfoundland with endless convoys. Few U-boats were operating in the broad reaches of the Atlantic at this time and the group saw little in the way of action. *Inman* had a couple of breaks from this monotonous grind by acting as escort to Fleet units carrying out carrierborne aircraft strikes on Norway but these too were largely uneventful. Her short active career was less distinguished than that of many of her sister ships in the more dashing support groups – but that was the lot of so many escort vessels during late 1944–45. They put in long months of weary plodding convoy work, suffering conditions and privations such as cannot even be imagined by those who did not share them; the fact that glory and success eluded them was not their fault. At the very least, their story is one of endurance and courage in the very best traditions of the Royal Navy.

When the European war had ended, the B1EG was disbanded and *Inman* was eventually put into reserve fleet at Hull in company with *Gardiner*. It was not until March, 1946, that a steaming crew was available to take her back to the land of her origin.

ESCORT GROUPS B2, B6 AND 19th

Bullen, Cotton, Goodall.

Cotton was one of the many Buckleys completed in November 1943 and hoisted the White Ensign at Boston on the 8th of that month. There were a number of initial problems during her trials period but these were all overcome and during December, 1943 and January, 1944, she was passing through Casco and Bermuda in company with *Cubitt*. The two ships left Argentia for the UK on 31 January and reached Belfast on 8 February. *Cotton* had some mechanical problems however and lingered on in Pollock Dock until 24 April.

Her first allocation in June was to the B2EG (*Hesperus, Vesper* and *Mourne* and some corvettes) and she continued to work with them until the end of August. Most of their operations were close escorts to Gibraltar and across the Atlantic, but none of the ships had any success against U-boats during the time *Cotton* was in the Group. There was a reshuffle in August, 1944, which resulted in *Manners* taking *Cotton's* place while she moved on to the 22nd EG but this brought little change to either her employment or her fortunes and there was another change when she joined the newly formed 19th EG in December 1944.

Bullen and *Goodall* had kept pace with one another ever since their early days at Boston, where they had commissioned within two weeks of one another, *Goodall* on the 11th and *Bullen* on 25 October, 1943. There was nothing out of the ordinary about either ship's early days. They had been at Bermuda together but *Goodall* completed before *Bullen*, joining convoy HX273 for passage to the UK on 3 January, 1944. *Bullen* followed on with HX274 a short time after.

After their Pollock Dock treatment, both ships began operational life with the B6EG and their first foray was to escort convoy ON228 to St John's on 17 March.

The outward leg was without notable incident but during the return convoy, a radar echo was picked up at 2221 on 5 April. Paul Mallett, who was *Goodall's* South African Gunnery Officer, recorded in his journal:

> *Goodall* closed up at action stations at 2221 but seven minutes later the echo faded and the Asdic crew reported hydrophone effect noises. The last radar range had been 6,500 yds and a 30/30 A/S sweep was started. Initially there were some faint Asdic contacts but by 2235 even these were lost. We continued the search unsuccessfully but the U-boat was still about and made its presence known by torpedoing one of our tankers at midnight – and escaped unscathed.

Next morning, *Goodall* was given the unpleasant task of sinking the stricken tanker and Paul Mallett, who had always doubted the 3″ guns, had his first confirmation of their uselessness. Some thirty-six rounds of armour-piercing shell were fired and at least twenty-five of them were hits – but they merely bounced off the tanker's plates. Eventually, they had to sink the ship by shallow set depth-charges.

The group was back at Liverpool by 13 April and both *Bullen* and *Goodall* were then detached from B6EG and became independent units until August. They made two trips before D-Day. The first was to Iceland as escorts to SS *Cameronia* on 28 April, followed by close escort duty to a convoy to 30 degrees west on 22 May. They arrived at Belfast just before D-Day and, according to Paul Mallett, were lumbered with hundredweights of signals and orders. Few had any doubts about their contents!

Goodall and *Bullen* sailed in company with *Duncan* to Milford Haven on 5 June and then made rendezvous with the battleship *Nelson*, escorting her to her bombardment station off Normandy on the fateful 6 June. They were not allowed to linger to watch the fireworks though, and were back at Liverpool by the 7th. The two were then sent on a sixteen day A/S sweep in company with *Bulldog* and others from 10–16 June. The area was from Bloody Foreland and Slyne Head to a point 15 degrees west. However, *Bullen* and *Goodall* were relieved of this uneventful slog by being sent to escort SS *Highland Princess* to Iceland. A run ashore there was much appreciated – with reservations. Paul remembers that it was pleasant enough to enjoy a hotel meal and eye up the local girls but this is as far as it went, as the Icelanders looked upon the British and Americans as little better than invaders at this time.

July brought the two ships the task of acting as tenders to the escort carrier *Vindex* during A/S patrols off Tiree and through the Minches. There was an alarm as a trawler was torpedoed in the vicinity but although both *Bullen* and *Goodall* made contacts and dropped a large proportion of their DC outfit during the subsequent merry-go-round search off Rockall, there were no signs of any success and the carrier's aircraft patrols were similarly out of luck.

It was back to the Iceland run again on 26 July, this time as escorts to SS *Otranto*. This was followed by a convoy run to Gibraltar from 10 August to 7 September. It happened to be the last operation the two ships did as independent units and was notable only for the extremely heavy weather encountered (which caused a minor panic in *Goodall*, as Hedgehog bombs broke loose and careered around in the magazine) and for a firm Asdic contact off Lundy Island on the way back, which failed to result in a successful attack.

When they arrived back at Belfast, *Goodall* had experimental anti-cavitation devices fitted around both her screws (as a hoped for defence against T5's) and then, together with *Bullen*, joined the newly formed 19th EG.

The destroyer *Hesperus* was the Senior Officer's ship and other members were *Loch Insh*, *Antigua* and *Anguilla*. The training programme for the new Group included a gunnery exercise in which a target was towed between two columns of ships simulating a surface U-boat infiltrated into a convoy. During the course of this the unreliable 3″ guns earned *Goodall* a severe black mark. *Hesperus* was towing ship and just as she was on *Goodall*'s beam, one of the latter's guns fired a 3″ shell which whistled dangerously over the SO ship's quarterdeck. When Paul Mallett and his OA (also a South African) hurriedly investigated, it was discovered that the gun's crew had been loading in readiness for their turn to open fire and one of the tight fitting plungers in the firing mechanism had stuck, making the gun fire the moment the breech closed. The incident had very fortunately passed off without any casualties but *Goodall*'s gunnery department were not at all popular with the Group Leader after that!

HFDF calibrations took place in the Clyde by 16 November and the new Group began operations by carrying out a number of support and escort duties around the North of Scotland, off Loch Ewe, Dunnett Head, Butte of Lewis and the Shiant Isles. After a few days respite at Belfast, the Group returned to the same patrol area on 6 December and suffered their first tragic loss. They were sweeping, in line abreast, off Cape Wrath with *Bullen* closest inshore and the rest at 2000 yard intervals. Paul Mallett had just gone off morning watch when he heard a distant explosion. On returning to the bridge, to the sound of action alarms, he saw that *Bullen* had been torpedoed amidships and already seemed to be breaking in half. *Goodall* closed in dropping Carley floats and lowered her whaler with a two man crew but the SO in *Hesperus* brusquely ordered her to begin operation OBSERVANT, a square search on an increasing perimeter. Reluctantly, *Goodall*'s CO obeyed.

During the first leg of the search, *Hesperus* picked up a contact and turned hard to starboard to home in on it. Tragically, her wash swamped *Goodall*'s whaler. Its two man crew, and some survivors who had already been picked up, were all lost.

Goodall also made rapid contact but it turned out to be a very long chase. *Loch Insh* joined her and during the next thirty-six hours both ships made a number of attacks – *Goodall* dropping seven full patterns of charges and *Loch Insh* firing four Squid salvoes. They claimed a kill but they had insufficient evidence to convince the Admiralty adjudicators and were not given any credit for the sinking. This turned out to be an unfair decision however. Post-war German records proved that they *had* sunk a U-boat (U297) and Roskill's official list gives equal credit to *Goodall* and *Loch Insh*.

Bullen's losses were heavy because early rescue operations had to be abandoned so hastily. Fifty-five of her crew were killed or had succumbed to exhaustion before they were picked up.

* * *

It was at this point that *Cotton* joined the 19th EC (as *Bullen's* replacement) and she remained with them for the remainder of the war. Their next operation was further south. U-boats had become active in the Channel and the Group became based at Devonport as from Xmas Eve. They spent a month covering convoys off the Cornish coast. Some of the patrol trips were as far afield as the Channel Islands (home of Paul Mallett's forbears) but there were no more enemy contacts during this time. By 28 January the Group was back at Liverpool where Paul left the ship, being relieved to enjoy a long overdue spell of leave in South Africa.

His notes record that up to that time *Goodall* had sailed 50,000 miles in the previous nine months of her operational life.

During this spell at Liverpool both *Goodall* and *Cotton* had shields fitted to their 3" guns and a great deal of insulation was added in the messdecks. Both ships were operational at Belfast by 14 February and carried out some further support operations until they were moved up to Scapa Flow to begin their last fateful task as escorts to the minelayer *Apollo* during convoy JW66 to Murmansk.

The outward run was achieved with no losses and towards the end of April the escorts put to sea again to cover the home-bound convoy RA66. There was much evidence that a large number of U-boats were set in ambush for this convoy. *Alnwyck Castle* was narrowly missed by a torpedo and Russian aircraft sighted several U-boats, which they attacked (unsuccessfully). 19EG were carrying out a sweep in advance of the convoy and on 29 April *Loch Insh* had a notable victory, sinking U307 by gunfire after blowing her to the surface with a Squid salvo. Then, very soon after this, *Goodall* was rent by a terrific explosion; a torpedo had hit her forward magazine and her entire bows were blown off. *Farnham Castle* and *Honeysuckle* were nearby and closed in to drop rafts and *Honeysuckle's* CO bravely took his ship right alongside *Goodall's* remains to take off survivors. Things were going well until oil flooding out of *Goodall's* tanks caught fire and surrounded her wreck with a sea of flame. *Honeysuckle* braved the flames and her First Lieutenant heroically went over to the burning ship to try to rescue any casualties. However, the heat became so fierce that rescue attempts had to be abandoned and *Honeysuckle* backed away with her own paint-work ablaze.

After *Goodall*'s loss, the remainder of 19EG carried out A/S sweeps through the night. Between them they contacted and sank U286 – with credits shared between *Cotton, Anguilla* and *Loch Shin*.

The Group was disbanded shortly after the war in Europe ended and it now remains but to record the last days of *Cotton* before she returned to USA. At first she was earmarked to be modified to serve as a radar picket ship for Far East service and some work towards this actually started at Liverpool. During that refit, Bill Wood (ex First Lieutenant of *Holmes*) was appointed as her First Lieutenant with Dudley Davenport as CO. When VJ Day came along, all conversion work ceased and there was another reshuffle. Dudley Davenport left the ship and Bill Wood took over as CO. She remained at Liverpool for some weeks while some of her dismantled bits and pieces were bolted back in place and she finally set out for her last journey to the USA in mid October, arriving there on 5 November, 1945.

TABLE OF U BOAT SINKINGS BY DE's SERVING IN MIXED ESCORT GROUPS

Date	U-boat No.	Ships Involved.
21.11.43	U538	*Foley (Crane)*
8.1.44	U757	*Bayntun (Camrose)*
6.12.44	U297	*Goodall (Loch Insh)*
26.1.45	U1172	*Manners* (others (but see note on Page 113))
3.2.45	U1279	*Bayntun, Braithwaite (Loch Eck)*
14.2.45	U989	*Bayntun, Braithwaite (Loch Eck, Loch Dunvegan)*
17.2.45	U1278	*Bayntun (Loch Eck)*
16.4.45	U1063	*Burges, Cranstoun (Loch Killin)*
29.4.45	U286	*Cotton, (Loch Shin, Anguilla)*

DE's LOST WHILE SERVING WITH MIXED GROUPS

Manners	Torpedoed in the Irish Sea 26.1.45.(CTL)
Bullen	Torpedoed and sunk off Cape Wrath 16.12.44.
Goodall	Torpedoed and sunk in the Kola Inlet 29.4.45.

BIBLIOGRAPHY

Anon, *Afloat and Ashore with the 4th EG* (unpublished)
   A collected work of contributions from members of the 4th EG produced as a 'paying off' momento.
Chavasse, Commander E., *Business in Great Waters* (unpublished)
   An autobiographical account of the Author's service at sea in the Second World War including his time as SO of the 4th EG.
   Note: Both these unpublished works are in the library of the Imperial War Museum.
Elliott, Peter, *Escort Vessels of WW2* (McDonald and Jaynes, 1974)
Elliott, Peter *American Destroyer Escorts of WW2* (Allmark, 1976)
   These books contain details and many photographs of the Captains.
Gibson, the Rev. Sir D. Bt, *Battles of the Irish Sea* (Maritime Books, Liskeard, 1994)
   The Author was A/S Officer in HMS *Manners*
Lenton & Colledge, *Warships of WW2* (Ian Allen, 1980)
   Contains details and many photographs of the Captains
Macintyre, Captain D., *U-Boat Killer* (Weidenfeld & Nicolson, 1956)
   An autobiography which includes the Author's memoirs of his time as SO of the 5th EG.
Poolman, K., *Escort Carrier VINDEX* (Secker and Warburg, 1993)
   Contains details of the 5th EG's operations in company with the carrier.
Rohwer & Hummelchen, *Chronology of the War at Sea* (Greenhill Books, 1992)
   A monumental work describing every action at sea by all belligerent navies. Although it contains some errors and incorrect dates, it mentions most of the actions involving the Captains.
Ross, Al, *The Destroyer Escort ENGLAND* (Conway Maritime Press, 1985)
   Contains detailed drawings of every part of a Buckley Class DE.

– APPENDIX A –

THE ROLL OF THE CAPTAIN CLASS FRIGATES

Ships are shown in alphabetical order with their DE Hull No. (based on order of construction), RN Pendant No. (prefixed K for frigates), Class (Buckley or Evarts), origin of their name, and the names of their CO's and the Escort Groups in which they served.

AFFLECK
DE71; K462; Buckley.
Named after Admiral E Affleck of *Bedford* during the American War of Independence.
Commanding Officers: Lt K Pilditch on commissioning, then Cdr C Gwinner (SO of 1stEG)
Served only with 1st EG.

AYLMER
DE72; K463; Evarts.
Named after Admiral Aylmer (at Barfleur)
Commanding Officers: Lt Cdr ADP Campbell RN 2.43
Cdr BW Taylor (SO of 5thEG)
Lt Cdr WL Smith RNR 2.45
Served only with 5th EG

BALFOUR
DE 73; K464; Evarts.
Named after Capt. Balfour of *Conqueror* at battle of The Saints.
Commanding Officers: Lt Cdr CDB Coventry on commissioning.
Cdr Gwinner took over as SO EG1 after loss of AFFLECK
Served with 1st and 18 EG's

BAYNTUN
DE1; K310; Evarts.
Named after Capt H Bayntun of *Leviathan* at Trafalgar.
Commanding Officers: Lt Cdr JH Wright RNR 9.43
Served with B4 and 10th EG's

BAZELEY   DE2; K311; Evarts.
Named after Capt Bazeley of *Bombay* at Algiers.
Commanding Officers: Lt Cdr JV Brock RCNVR 2.43
Lt Cdr JW Cooper RNR 5.44
Served only with 4th EG

BENTINCK   DE52; K314; Buckley.
Named after Capt J Bentinck of *Niger* in Seven Years
War.
Commanding Officers: Cdr EH Chavasse RN (SO of
4thEG)
Cdr R Garwood RN.
Served only with 4th EG.

BENTLEY   DE74; K465; Buckley.
Named after Sir J Bentley of *Warspite* 1759.
Commanding Officers: Lt Cdr PC Hopkins RN 8.43
Lt Cdr E May RN 5.44
Lt FL Boyer RN 12.44
Served only with 1st EG

BERRY   DE3; K312; Evarts.
Named after Sir E Berry of *Agamemnon* at Trafalgar.
Commanding Officer: Lieutenant Commander CS Pirie
RNVR.
Served only with 3rd EG.

BENTINCK   DE75; K466; Buckley.
Named after Sir R Bickerton of *Terrible* at Ushant.
Commanding Officers – Lt EM Thorpe RN 10.43
Cdr. D McIntyre RN (SO of 5th EG)
Served only with 5th EG.

BLACKWOOD   DE4; K313; Evarts.
Named after Capt H Blackwood of *Euryalus* at Trafalgar.
Commanding Officers – Cdr E Chavasse (SO of 4th EG)
10.43
Lt Cdr LT Sly RNR 1.44
Served with 4th and 3rd EG's.

BLIGH   DE76; K467; Buckley.
Named after Capt W Bligh of *Director* at Camperdown.
Commanding Officers: Lt Cdr RE Blyth RNVR 8.43
Lt Cdr JW Cooper RNR.
Served only with 5th EG.

BRAITHWAITE   DE77; K468; Buckley.
Named after Capt S Braithwaite of *Kingston* 1727
Commanding Officers: Lt Cdr E McKay RNR 11.43
Lt Cdr PJ Stoner RN 7.44.
Served with 3rd and 10th EG's.

BULLEN	DE78; K470; Buckley.
	Named after Capt C Bullen of *Britannia* at Trafalgar.
	Commanding Officer: Lt Cdr AH Parrish RN
	Served with B6 and 19th EG's

BURGES	DE12; K347; Evarts.
	Named after Capt R Burges of *Ardent* at Camperdown.
	Commanding Officers: Lt Cdr H Hill RNR 4.43
	Lt C Cornelius RN 10.44
	Served with 3rd, 4th & 17th EG's.

BYARD	DE55; K315; Buckley.
	Named after Sir T Byard of *Bedford* at Camperdown.
	Commanding Officers: Lt Cdr LH Phillips RN 2.43
	Lt Cdr K Ferris RNVR 1.44
	Lt JI Jones RN 6.44
	Served only with 4th EG.

BYRON	DE79; K508; Buckley.
	Named after Admiral J Byron of *Fame* during the 7 Years War.
	Commanding Officers: Lt KCL Southcombe RN 10.43
	Lt J Burfield RN 2.45
	Served in Nore Command and 21st EG.

CALDER	DE58; K349; Buckley.
	Named after Admiral Calder Captain of the Fleet at Trafalgar.
	Commanding Officers: Lt Cdr AD White RNR 3.43
	Lt Cdr E. Playne RNVR 2.45
	Served only with 4th EG

CAPEL	DE266; K470; Evarts.
	Named after Capt T Capel of *Phoebe* at Trafalgar.
	Commanding Officers: Lt Cdr P McIver RNVR 8.43
	Lt B Heslop RN 11.43
	Served only with 1st EG.

COOKE	DE267; K471; Evarts.
	Named after Capt J Cooke of *Bellerophon* at Trafalgar
	Commanding Officers: Lt Cdr Hill RNR 8.43
	Lt ND Cornwall RN 11.44
	Served only with 3rd EG

CONN	DE80; K508; Buckley.
	Named after Capt. J Conn of *Dreadnought* at Trafalgar.
	Commanding Officers: Lt CD Williams RN 10.43
	Lt Cdr R Hart (SO of 21st EG)9.44
	Served in Nore Command and 21st EG

COSBY	DE94; K559; Buckley.
	Named after Capt P Cosby of *Robust* 1781.
	Commanding Officers: Lt Cdr RS Connell RN 12.43
	Lt L Pepperell RN 8.44
	Served in Nore and Devonport Commands.

COTTON	DE81; K510; Buckley.
	Named after Sir J Cotton of *Majestic* at the Glorious 1st June.
	Commanding Officer: Lt Cdr IW Belroe RN
	Served with B2 and 19th EGs

CRANSTOUN	DE82; K511; Buckley.
	Named after Lord Cranstoun of *Formidable* at the Battle of the Saints.
	Commanding Officers: Lt (later Lt Cdr) EW Rainey RN
	Served in Nore Command and 19th EG

CUBITT	DE83; K512; Buckley.
	Named after Capt J Cubitt of 2nd *Mary Rose* 1661.
	Commanding Officer: Lt GDD Gregory RN
	Served only in Nore Command.

CURZON	DE84; K513; Buckley.
	Named after Capt H Curzon of *Pallas* . . . or Capt E Curzon of *Asia* at Navarino. There is official uncertainty about this.
	Commanding Officers: Lt Cdr A Diggens RN 11.43
	Lt D Walters RN 2.45
	Served only in Nore Command.

DACRES	DE268; K472; Evarts.
	Named after Capt J Dacres of *Barfleur* at Cape St Vincent.
	Commanding Officers: Lt Cdr LP Bourke RNZNVR 8.43
	Lt Cdr GC Juliens RNZNVR 9.44
	Lt KI Hamilton RN 1.44
	Served as HQ ship (in Normandy) and with B4 and 15th EG's.

DAKINS	DE85; K550; Buckley.
	Named after Capt Dakins of *Advice* during the Dutch Wars.
	Commanding Officers: Lt RS Blacker RN 11.43
	Lt Cdr F Brock RCNVR 11.44
	Lt MGH Arbuthnot RNVR 2.45
	Served only in Nore Command.

DEANE	DE86; K551; Buckley.
	Named after Capt J Deane of *Lowestoft* 1760
	Commanding Officers: Lt VA Hickson RN 11.43
	Lt EL Cooke RN 2.45
	Served in Nore Command and 21st EG.

DOMETT	DE269; K473; Evarts.
	Named after Sir W Domett of *Royal George* at the Glorious 1st June.
	Commanding Officers: Lt Cdr D Mansfield RN 7.43
	Lt Cdr S Gordon RNVR 8.43
	Served only with 3rd EG.

DRURY	DE46; K316; Evarts. (originally Cockburn)
	Named after Capt T Drury of *Alfred* (West Indies 1795)
	Commanding Officer: Lt Cdr NJ Parker RN
	Served only with 4th EG.

DUFF	DE64; K352; Buckley.
	Named after Capt G Duff of *Mars* at Trafalgar.
	Commanding Officers: Cdr IJ Tyson RNR 9.43
	Lt Cdr F Brock RCNVR 11.43
	Lt AA Harry RNVR 8.44
	Served as a CFCF at Portsmouth and with the Nore.

DUCKWORTH	DE61; K351; Buckley.
	Named after Capt J Duckworth of *Orion* at the Glorious 1st June.
	Commanding Officers: Cdr CP Mills (SO of 3rd EG)
	Lt D Jermain RN 3.45
	Served only with 3rd EG.

EKINS	DE87; K552; Buckley.
	Named after Sir C Ekins of *Superb* at Algiers 1815.
	Commanding Officers: Lt G Bonner-Davies RN 11.43
	Lt A Tandevin RNVR 10.44
	Served only in Nore Command.

ESSINGTON	DE67; K353; Buckley.
	Named after Capt W Essington of *Triumph* at Camperdown.
	Commanding Officer: Lt Cdr W Lampard RNVR
	Served only with 3rd EG.

FITZROY	DE88; K553; Buckley.
	Named after Vice-Admiral Fitzroy of *Beagle* (Darwin expedition)
	Commanding Officers: Lt J Duggan RN 10.43
	Lt Cdr PJ Miller RNVR 4.44
	Lt Cdr OG Stewart RCNVR 2.45.
	Served in Nore Command and 21st EG.

FOLEY	DE270; K474; Evarts.
	Named after Capt T Foley of *Brittania* at Cape St Vincent.
	Commanding Officers: Lt Cdr C Bird RNVR
	Lt Cdr D Mansfield RNR.
	Served with B4 EG and 10th EG.

GARDINER	DE274; K478; Evarts.
	Named after Capt A Gardiner of *Foudroyant* 1758.
	Commanding Officer: Lt Cdr WG Bolton RNR
	Served with EG's B2 and B3.

GARLIES	DE27; K475; Evarts.
	Named after Lord Garlies of *Lively* at Cape St Vincent.
	Commanding Officers: Lt R Caple RN 8.43
	Lt Cdr LM Stamp RNVR 10.44
	Served only with 1st EG.
GOODALL	DE274; K479; Evarts.
	Named after Capt S Goodall of *Defiance* at Ushant
	Commanding Officer: Lt Cdr J Fulton RNVR
	Served with B6 and 19th EG's.
GOODSON	DE276; K480; Evarts.
	Named after Capt W Goodson of *Entrance* 1653.
	Commanding Officer: Lt Cdr J Cooper RNR
	Served only with 5th EG.
GORE	DE277; K487; Evarts.
	Named after Sir J Gore of *Triton* 1796/1801
	Commanding Officer: Lt J Reeves-Brown RN
	Served only with 1st EG.
GOULD	DE272; K476; Evarts.
	Named after Capt D Gould of *Audacious* at Battle of Nile.
	Commanding Officer: Lt DW Ungoed RN.
	Served only with 5th EG.
GRINDALL	DE273; K477; Evarts.
	Named after Capt R Grindall of PRINCE at Trafalgar.
	Commanding Officers: Cdr W Cole RNR 9.43
	Lt Cdr Turquand-Young RNVR 11.44
	Served with B7 EG.
HALSTED	DE91; K556; Buckley.
	Named after Capt L Halsted of *Namur* 1805.
	Commanding Officer: Lt Cdr J Westmacott RN 2.44
	Served only in Nore Command.
HARGOOD	DE573; K583; Buckley.
	Named after Capt W Hargood of *Bellisle* at Trafalgar.
	Commanding Officer: Cdr P McIver RNR
	Served in Devonport and Portsmouth Commands.
HOLMES	DE572; K581; Buckley.
	Named after Sir R Holmes of the Dutch Wars.
	Commanding Officers: Lt DL Davenport RN 1.44
	Lt DAG Dumas RN 3.44
	Lt Cdr P Boyle RNVR 12.44
	Served only with Nore Command.

HOSTE

DE521; K566; Evarts.
Named after Sir W Hoste, frigate captain of 1811.
Commanding Officer: Lt JH Hoare RN
Served with 18th and 1st EG's.

HOTHAM

DE574; K583; Buckley.
Named after Capt W Hotham of *Adamant* at
Camperdown.
Commanding Officer: Lt Cdr S Ayles RNR
Served in Portsmouth Command, then as power supply
ship at Singapore 1945–48
then as an experimental ship for gas turbine units until 1957.

INGLIS

DE525; K570; Evarts.
Named after Capt J Inglis of *Belliqueux* at Camperdown.
Commanding Officers: Lt RS Beveridge RN 12.43
Lt Cdr A Cobbold RNVR 9.44
Served only with 15th EG.

INMAN

DE526; K571; Evarts.
Named after Capt H Inman of *Desirée* at Copenhagen.
Commanding Officers: Lt Cdr PG Evans RNVR 1.44
Lt Cdr H Petrie RNR 2.45
Served only with B1 EG.

KEATS

DE278; K482; Evarts class.
Named after Sir R Keats of *Superb* 1801–7.
Commanding Officer: Lt Cdr NE Israel RNR
Served only with 5th EG.

KEMPTHORNE

DE279; K483; Evarts.
Named after Sir J Kempthorne of 2nd *Mary Rose* 1669
Commanding Officers: Lt Cdr A Brown RNR 10.43
Lt HJ Wilson RN 12.44
Served only with 5th EG.

KINGSMILL

DE280; K484; Evarts.
Named after Sir R Kingsmill of *Vigilant* at Ushant.
Commanding Officer: Lt GH Cook RN
Served as HQ ship in Normandy and as CFCF Command
ship.

LAWFORD

DE516; K514; Evarts.
Named after Capt J Lawford of *Polyphemus* at
Copenhagen.
Commanding Officer: Lt Cdr MC Morris RN
Served only as HQ ship in Normandy.

LAWSON

DE518; K516; Evarts.
Named after Sir J Lawson of *Fairfax* during 1st Dutch War.
Commanding Officer: Lt JP Somerville RN.
Served only with 15th EG.

LORING	DE520; K565; Evarts. Named after Sir J Loring of *Niobe* 1805–13. Commanding Officers: Lt AJ Sangster RN 11.43 Lt J Ogilvy RN 12.43 Served only with 15th EG.
LOUIS	DE517; K515; Evarts. Named after Sir T Louis of *Minotaur* at the Battle of the Nile. Commanding Officer: Cdr JP Majendie RN (SO of the 15th EG.) Served only with 15th EG.
MANNERS	DE523; K568; Evarts. Named after Lord R Manners of *Resolution* at the Battle of the Saints. Commanding Officer: Lt D Germaine RN Served with B6 and B2 EG's.
MOORSOM	DE522; K567; Evarts. Named after Sir R Moorsom of *Revenge* at Trafalgar. Commanding Officer: Lt AC Martyne RNVR 5.44 Served with 15th and 17th EG's.
MOUNSEY	DE524; K569; Evarts. Named after Capt W Mounsey of *Bon Citoyen* 1809. Commanding Officers: Lt FAJ Andrew RN 12.44 Lt FL Boyer RN 2.45. Served only with 15th EG.
NARBOROUGH	DE569; K578; Buckley. Named after Sir J Narborough (Dutch Wars). Commanding Officer: Lt Cdr W Muttram RN Served in Devonport Command and 15th EG
PASLEY	DE519; K564; Evarts (originally named *Lindsay*) Named after Admiral Sir T Pasley of *Bellerophon* (the Glorious 1st June) Commanding Officers: Lt PRG Mitchell RN 11.43 Lt Cdr JH Wright RNR 2.45 Served only with 4th EG.
REDMILL	DE89; K554; Buckley. Named after Capt R Redmill of *Polyphemus* at Trafalgar. Commanding Officer: Lt JRA Denne RN Served in Nore Command and 21st EG.
RETALICK	DE90; K555; Buckley. Named after Capt J Retalick of *Defiance* at Copenhagen. Commanding Officers: Lt Cdr JS Brownrigg RN 12.43 Lt Cdr AA Gotelee RN 2.45 Served as CFCF in Portsmouth and Nore Commands.

RIOU

DE92; K557; Buckley.
Named after Capt H Riou of *Amazon* at Copenhagen.
Commanding Officers: Cdr C Campbell RN (BTO Casco
Bay)
Lt FL Boyer RN 3.44
Lt Cdr IR Griffiths RN 11.44
Served as CFCF in Portsmouth and Nore Commands.

ROWLEY

DE95; K560; Buckley class.
Named after Sir J Rowley of *Montague* at Quiberon Bay.
Commanding Officer: Lt Cdr FJG Jones RNR
Served in Devonport and Portsmouth Commands.

RUPERT

DE96; K561; Buckley.
Named after Prince Rupert (English Civil War)
Commanding Officer: Lt PCS Black RN
Served in Devonport Command and 21st EG.

RUTHERFORD

DE93; K558; Buckley
Named after Capt J Rutherford of *Swiftsure* at Trafalgar.
Commanding Officers: Lt JG Brooker RN 12.43
Lt RS Beveridge RN 1.45
Lt B Pengelly RN 2.45
Served only in Nore Command.

SEYMOUR

DE98; K563; Buckley.
Named after Lord H Seymour of *Leviathan* at the Glorious
1st June.
Commanding Officer: Lt Cdr P King RNVR
Served as CFCF in Portsmouth and Nore Commands.

SPRAGGE

DE563; K572; Buckley.
Named after Admiral E Spragge (Dutch Wars)
Commanding Officers: Lt Cdr Grant RNR
Lt Muir RN 12.44
Served in Devonport and Portsmouth Commands.

STAYNER

DE564; K573; Buckley.
Named after Sir R Stayner (1st Dutch War)
Commanding Officer: Lt AV Turner RNVR
Served in Portsmouth and Nore Commands.

STOCKHAM

DE97; K562; Buckley.
Named after Capt J Stockham of *Thunderer* at Trafalgar.
Commanding Officers: Lt Cdr BC Hamilton RNR 12.43
Lt Cdr JV Brock RCNVR 1.44
Served in Devonport Command, 17th and 1st EG's.

THORNBOROUGH

DE565; K574; Buckley.
Named after Sir E Thornborough of *Robust* 1795.
Commanding Officer: Lt CG Brown RN
Served in Portsmouth and Nore Commands.

TORRINGTON	DE568; K577; Buckley.
	Named after Admiral G Torrington at Cape Pessaro 1718.
	Commanding Officer: Lt CF Parker RN
	Served in Portsmouth and Nore Commands.

TROLLOPE   DE566; K575; Buckley class.
                Named after Admiral Sir H Trollope of *Russell* at
                Camperdown.
                Commanding Officer: Lt Cdr H Westmacott RN
                Served only in Portsmouth Command.

TYLER   DE567; K576; Buckley.
                Named after Sir C Tyler of *Tonnant* at Trafalgar.
                Commanding Officer: Lt CH Rankin RN
                Served in 5th EG.

WHITAKER   DE571; K580; Buckley.
                Named after Sir E Whitaker of *Dorsetshire* 1704.
                Commanding Officer: Lt GDW Edwards RN
                Served in Devonport and Portsmouth Commands

WALDEGRAVE   DE570; K579; Buckley.
                Named after Adm W Waldegrave of *Courageux* 1793.
                Commanding Officer: Lt May RN
                Served in Devonport and Portsmouth Commands.

NOTES

Listed Commanding Officers

CO's changed frequently and the notations above are probably incomplete. I am grateful to John Brady (who served in *Whitaker* and whose hobby is tracing the careers of Naval Officers) for most of the entries. The dates do not necessarily indicate the date of assuming command but rather that the officer concerned was in command at the date shown.

The Naming of Captain Class Ships

It is believed that the original intention was to name all ships in the Class after the Captains of ships of the Royal Navy in Nelson's time but, in the event, it became necessary to include some names of distinguished Admirals and Captains of much earlier periods in the history of the Royal Navy.

Of the seventy-eight Captains, sixty-six were the first ships to bear the names allocated. Of the remaining twelve:

Lawford, Louis, Manners, Moorsom, Mounsey, Narborough, Pasley and *Seymour* were names first used for destroyers in the First World War.

Rupert was the 5th of the name since 1666.

Torrington was the 4th of the name since 1654, although the 1st was named after the town of Torrington, not Viscount Torrington as the others were.

Holmes was the 2nd of the name which was first used in 1671.

Fitzroy was the 2nd of the name, first used for a survey ship in 1919.

British Destroyer Escorts Originally Launched as Ships of the United States Navy
It was not always known when the hulls were launched which ships were to be allocated to the Royal Navy. In consequence, whilst those that had been definitely allocated to Britain were not named at the time of launch, others, which had initially been allocated to the United States Navy, were given American names on launching. These were later changed to British names at their commissioning ceremonies. By Classes, these were:

EVARTS

Capel (USS *Wintle*); *Cooke* (USS *Dempsey*); *Dacres* (USS *Duffy*); *Domett* (USS *Eisner*); *Foley* (USS *Gillette*); *Garlies* (USS *Fleming*); *Gould* (USS *Lovering*); *Grindall* (USS *Sanders*); *Gore* (USS *Herzog*); *Gardiner* (USS *O'Toole*); *Goodall* (USS *Reybold*); Goodson (USS *George*); *Keats* (USS *Tisdale*); *Kempthorne* (USS *Trumpeter*).

BUCKLEY

Aylmer (USS *Harmon*); *Affleck* (USS *Oswald*); *Bentinck* (USS *Bull*); *Byard* (USS *Donaldson*); *Calder* (USS *Formoe*); *Duckworth* (USS *Gary*); *Duff* (USS *Lamons*); *Balfour* (USS *McAnn*); *Bentley* (USS *Ebert*); *Bickerton* (USS *Eisele*); *Bligh*(USS *Liddle*); *Braithwaite* (USS *Straub*).

INDEX